THE XIT RANCH OF TEXAS

And the Early Days of the Llano Estacado

THE
XIT RANCH
OF TEXAS

And the Early Days of the Llano Estacado

J. EVETTS HALEY

UNIVERSITY OF OKLAHOMA PRESS

Norman

BY J. EVETTS HALEY

Charles Goodnight: Cowman and Plainsman
(Boston, 1936; Norman, 1949)
George W. Littlefield, Texan (Norman, 1943)
Charles Schreiner General Merchandise,
The Story of a Country Store (Austin, 1944)
Jeff Milton: A Good Man with a Gun (Norman, 1948)
Life on the Texas Range (Austin, 1952)
Fort Concho and the Texas Frontier (San Angelo, Texas, 1952)
The XIT Ranch of Texas and the Early Days of the Llano Estacado
(Chicago, 1929; new edition, Norman, 1953)

Library of Congress Catalog Card Number: 53–8818

To my cowhorses

And especially to those superb in any man's roundup—

To Keno, Dusty, Red Wing, Baldy, Tio,
and Strawberry—

To them and many noble others that faithfully shared
my roughest trails, longest hours, and hardest ranges
with unflagging love
and zest for our life and work together

Back of the Story

TWENTY-FIVE YEARS have passed since I made my first inquiry into the history of the XIT Ranch of Texas—the most extensive Western range ever placed under one barbed-wire fence. At that time some of the principals and many of the cowboys who had a hand in its vast development and its vivid life were still here.

Now most of them have loped over the divide to what, we trust, may be greener pastures. For if long and courageous battle with the sometimes ruthless and always frugal elements of this land—a struggle by rugged men supported by little beyond hope and faith—is worthy of any reward, then they at last deserve a little grass.

To the memory of their own adventures in and with unbridled nature I have since then personally added another quarter-century of experience in the intriguing calling of my own people —years that have stiffened my joints a lot and should have seasoned my judgment a little. But neither dessicated time nor trying circumstance has dimmed the imaginative splendor of this bold enterprise burnt in the hides of hundreds of thousands of Texas cattle under the symbol of the XIT—the enterprise that built the capitol of Texas and conceived the useful end for three million acres granted in payment on her remote and arid borders beyond the frowning caprock of the *Llano Estacado*.

The descendants of the men who dreamed up this venture, and who had the fortitude, the reserves, and the credit to push it through, were originally responsible for this story. The pioneer Farwell family, of Chicago, with proper pride, brought it out as a privately issued memorial to their people, their associates, and their cowboys. It has been out of circulation for a long time.

The complete records of the ranch were given to the Panhandle-Plains Historical Society, of Canyon, Texas, by the Capitol Reservation Lands, of Chicago, in perpetuation of the Western tradition. However, the men who rode its expansive ranges in Texas and related its story to me are gone. Likewise the prejudices and passions inherent in its size, its vigorous policies, and its dynamic operation seem to be past. But the original judgments as to its historical nature, significance, and importance are unchanged. It was an outfit worthy of the West.

This new edition is the first publication of the story for the general public who find the chronicles of the great range days interesting. It makes no pretense of telling the whole story. The ramifications of this enterprise on the plains of Texas will encourage inquiry so long as men struggle hopefully with the eternal problems of the soil, or find heroism in free and mighty effort against great odds, or tragedy in individual defeat and failure.

For the challenge and the exactions of this rigorous land, where God is more manifest in His elemental wrath than in His benedictions, are unchanged. Each generation of its cowmen feels their impact and adds a chapter to the story. But nature still dictates the plot and largely determines the outcome. Hence it may be that this account of the first cowmen who, by virtue of their individual efforts alone, took these sere plains for their herds, may be worthy of retelling.

I am grateful to the broad-gauged gentlemen of the Capitol Reservation enterprises, to widely scattered readers of Western history, to a few ardent lovers of books, of horses, and of freedom, and to the generous interest of the personnel of the University of Oklahoma Press for this volume.

J. Evetts Haley

JH Ranch, Canyon, Texas
July 14, 1953

Contents

xi

List of Illustrations

List of Illustrations

Aberdeen-Angus bulls
Cowboys riding in to Tascosa
Sheriff Tobe Robinson
The bull pasture at Escarbada
James H. East

XIT chuck wagon and chip wagon *between pages* 210 *and* 211
Roundup on the Rito Blanco
Goodnight, Stephens, Boyce, and John V. Farwell
The Escarbada outfit
Windmill on the lower Rito Blanco
Corralling a herd on the XIT
James D. Hamlin
The valley of the Canadian

Maps

THE XIT RANCH OF TEXAS
And the Early Days of the Llano Estacado

CHAPTER I

Early Explorations

DURING THE middle eighties the XIT Ranch was established. It was the largest ranch in the cow country of the Old West, and probably the largest fenced range in the world. Its barbed wire enclosed over 3,050,000 acres of land in the Panhandle of Texas, patented by the state to a Chicago firm in exchange for the capitol at Austin. From 100 to 150 cowboys, with combined remudas of more than 1,000 cow ponies, "rode herd" upon approximately 150,000 cattle that wore the XIT brand. This story is concerned with the development of this pastoral enterprise and its relation to the history of Texas.

The XIT brand was conceived by an old Texas trail driver named Ab Blocker, who placed it upon the first cow. She was not an animal of high pedigree, but a Longhorn from South Texas. Her color, gauntness, and perversity were historic. Nearly two centuries before, with the initial Spanish expedition into the province for the purpose of founding a settlement in 1690, there came a similar Mexican cow. She walked streaming from the waters of the Río Grande, cropped the first grass on the northern shore, switched her tail at a persistent fly, and felt at home. Long of horn and leg, variegated in color, and belligerent of disposition, she was prophetic of the millions and millions of others to fatten upon the grasses of the border state.

As she pushed north and east with the expedition of Governor Alonzo de Leon and Father Massanet, the tallow thickened over her ribs, a little bit, and she became smooth and glossy.

She sprang of hardy and wily stock. As she fled to the nearest pool or mud hole to escape the attentions of the heel fly, as she fought off the wolves by night and outran the thieving Indians by day, she built up a spirit of independence and of resourcefulness that made her a companion of the wilderness and a fighter of the frontier.

By the time the East Texas missions were abandoned in 1693, this Longhorn had broken the ties that bound her to her native range, and when the soldiers and missionaries returned to Mexico, she stayed in Texas. The Mexican cows matched wits with the wilderness, met claw and fang with horns and cow-sense, and when the Spaniards came again, twenty-three years later, Longhorn cattle grazed the East Texas grasslands. Since that first memorable day Texas has never been without cattle. For more than two centuries livestock has formed one of its chief sources of wealth. Wherever "Texas" is heard, steers are thought of, and the head of the Longhorn is as emblematic of Texas as is the lone star. Texas and cows are almost synonymous.

In 1836, nearly a century and a half after this first expedition into Texas, the Anglo-American pioneers wrested the state from Mexico and pushed the last soldier of the southern republic from her borders. There remained, fortunately for the Texans, a phase of life and an industry suited to the frontier— an industry essentially Spanish in origin and methods. Ten years later the Congressional struggles were ended, and Texas entered the Union with the important provision that she retain all her public lands. Texas then possessed vast millions of acres unmeasured by surveyor's chain and prairie lands untrod by white men's feet. Her first bid to international attention was made through land. As the most effective utilization of the soil by a limited population lay in the frontier pursuit of grazing, it was natural that among her first claims to economic consideration were herds of Longhorn steers trailed to other states.

A scattered and meager population lived in East and South Texas, occupying but a small portion of the state. Texas had more land than people, and there was much truth in the time-worn saying that she was land poor. However, in large measure, it was upon that so-called poverty that her public school system was built, that her state university was founded, that her generous homestead policy was adopted, that large ranches secured their holdings, and that the state capitol was built.

The Texas State House was built in exchange for three million acres of land set aside by an act of the Texas Legislature in 1879. The tract lay along the western border of the Panhandle. At that time scarce a score of people were upon it. Not a plowshare had broken the sod, and not a wire fence had enclosed an acre of its grass. These three million acres were converted into the XIT Ranch pending the arrival of the farming settler. The history of this ranch is a story of cows, horses, and cowmen. Further, it is the story of the pioneer farming settler in the Panhandle-Plains country of Texas, a story of the struggle of men with the soil.

Very little was known of the Panhandle by the legislators "down in the skillet" when this land was set aside. Therefore they congratulated themselves upon rare business judgment when they traded three million acres of "arid" land for a great building, and their sectional partisanship still smouldering in the heart of Texas may be seen from their pride in driving such a hard trade with a "bunch of Yankees."

The satisfaction felt by the legislators is understandable, because the earliest descriptions of the country, filtering back to the settlements from uncertain sources, marked the region as arid land—a part of "the Great American Desert." In the absence of accurate information, legend supplied the deficiency, and this popular myth clung with pertinacity. So persistent was the belief in aridity that in the *Census Reports* of 1880 a man of some vision, who was said to have "carefully explored the Panhandle and adjacent Texas," reported that "not more than 7,000,000 acres of the Llano Estacado within the state of Texas can be regarded as an absolute desert. . . ." [1] Even among the

[1] *United States Census Reports,* 1880, III, 967.

ebullient natives, unfortunate seasons since have sometimes revived his original impression.

But the men who contracted to build the capitol were more optimistic than the man who reported for the Census. A state commissioner surveyed the lands, rejecting those portions he felt unfit for either farming or grazing purposes, and published his report. It was accurate and truthful. The fact that the land was accepted without being seen bespeaks the confidence of the contractors in the report, even though such was not indicative of sound business policy.

The tremendous influx of English, Scotch, and Eastern capital into the West was just beginning, and the wild and furious scramble of syndicates after cattle and land may have made them a little less cautious. In reality, they looked to a day nearly fifty years ahead, though hardly aware it was that far distant, when the land-hungry settlers who lived by the plow should stampede across the plains of Texas and cause the XIT lands to enhance in value many fold. In part it seems that the action of the Texas Legislature was dictated by that foe of sound administrative policy—expediency. The action of the other party to the contract was in part impelled by a vision of settlement. But the results have been mutually beneficial.

Though settlement of this region did not begin until the middle seventies, some little knowledge of the area had been gained from explorers. Undoubtedly the first white man to look across the Staked Plains and marvel at its vast expanse was a Spaniard. Just twenty years after Hernán Cortez captured the city of Mexico and shattered the kingdom of the Montezumas, another conqueror in armor pushed far to the north, into New Mexico, to disturb the aborigines. His name was Francisco Vásquez de Coronado and he was searching for the "Seven Cities of Cibola," which were supposed to be "situated on a great height. Their doors were studded with turquoises, as if feathers from the wings of the blue sky had dropped and clung there. Within those jeweled cities were whole streets of goldsmiths, so great was the store of shining metal to be worked." It was a gilded prospect, but beyond these cities lay others of even greater splendor. Disillusioned in New Mexico, Coronado's spirit flamed forth again as he heard of another El Dorado called Gran Quivira, a wonderful city across the plains to the east.

The chief of that country took his afternoon nap under a tall spreading tree decorated with an infinitude of little golden bells on which gentle zephyrs played his lullaby. Even the common folk there had their ordinary dishes made of "wrought plate"; and the pitchers and bowls were of solid gold.

Coronado impatiently awaited the arrival of the spring of 1541, when he set out for this essentially treeless but belegended land. By June he was in western Texas, crossing the future Capitol Reservation. Just where he went from here is a matter of some confusion, but the most competent students now agree that he reached the Palo Duro Canyon and headed northward, toward Kansas. But one thing sure is the fact that he found no spot anywhere among its scattered Indian villages or even in the fantasies of its mirages, where ". . . sparkling sails floated like petals on the clear surface of an immeasurable stream. No lordly chief drowsed to the murmur of innumerable bells. The water pitchers on the low entrances of their grass thatched huts were not golden." Yet Coronado, with that fire that consumed his kind, pushed on in hopeful but fruitless quest. His guide, induced by the Pecos Indians to lead the Spaniards out upon the plains, lose them, and allow them to perish of thirst, was suspected and put to death. And so Coronado returned to New Mexico with no more gold than that which glinted from his own armor.[2]

About 1593 an unauthorized Spanish expedition into New Mexico under Bonilla and Humana crossed to the buffalo country of the Panhandle.[3] But after Coronado's explorations the Texas plains were rarely disturbed by white men for nearly

[2] G. P. Hammond, "The Founding of New Mexico," *New Mexico Historical Review,* January, 1926, pp. 45–47, and Herbert E. Bolton, *Texas in the Middle Eighteenth Century.*

[3] Hammond, "The Founding of New Mexico," *New Mexico Historical Review,* January, 1926, p. 52.

three hundred years. Only a few explorers penetrated the region. Don Juan de Oñate, as every other *conquistador* of New Spain, heard of the marvels of Gran Quivira, and in June, 1601, set out from Galisteo, New Mexico, to find this city for himself. He reached the Canadian and followed it eastward nearly to Antelope Hills. His men caught fish from the Canadian, killed buffalo upon the plains, and gathered wild plums and grapes in the valleys. Oñate turned northward, evidently reached the Arkansas River, found an Indian town of over five thousand inhabitants, but not a street crowded with goldsmiths. From the vicinity of Wichita, Kansas, Oñate and his men backtrailed to San Gabriel.[4] History presents no explorers comparable to the *conquistadores* of New Spain; even legend reveals no more zealous searchers after treasure.

Finally peace with the Comanches made feasible the opening of a route connecting San Antonio, Texas, with Santa Fé, New Mexico. In 1786, Pedro Vial, a Frenchman, was commissioned by the governor of Texas to explore a route. Vial came north, passing east of the plains to the Red River, somewhere near Ringgold. He turned up the stream, crossed to the Canadian, pushed through what came to be known as the Alamocitos country of the XIT Ranch, and reached Santa Fé in May, 1787. A few months later José Mares crossed the Panhandle by a more southerly route upon a like exploration.[5] But three centuries passed from the time of Coronado before much was known of this country. Then a few explorers from the United States began to trace the river courses.

The Red River of Louisiana claimed the attention of several early exploring parties. In 1806 Captain Richard Sparks, in the service of the United States, attempted to ascend the river to its source. He was stopped far short of his goal by a detachment of Spanish cavalry. Lieutenant Zebulon M. Pike ascended the Arkansas River the same year with instructions to cross to the source of the Red and follow down the stream. He first mistook

[4] *Ibid.*, October, 1926, pp. 474–77.
[5] Bolton, *Texas in the Middle Eighteenth Century*, 128–130.

the Arkansas and then the Río Grande for the Red. He never reached Texas from the west, as the Mexicans cut short his explorations by placing him under arrest. Then came Major Stephen H. Long, in 1820, bent upon the third effort to discover the source of the stream.[6] He came south from the Arkansas and followed down the Canadian until near its mouth before he discovered his mistake. During 1823 John H. Fonda crossed the Panhandle on his way to Santa Fé from Fort Towson, Indian Territory. He is reputed to have traveled up Red River to its source before turning north to the Canadian.[7]

The ill-fated Texan–Santa Fé Expedition, which represented the only attempt of the young republic to share in the profits of the caravan trade with the New Mexican settlements, wandering aimlessly through the breaks and across the plains of the Panhandle, probably came to the source of the river in 1841, but left no accurate topographical data.[8] In 1852 Captain R. B. Marcy crossed the Panhandle from east to west, explored the Palo Duro Canyon, and claimed the distinction of being the first thoroughly to explore Red River to its source.[9] Before this noteworthy exploration the "commerce of the prairies" had made a contribution to topographical knowledge.

The Santa Fé Trail, stretching from Independence, Missouri, to Santa Fé, New Mexico, had become an institution of the Southwest. Essentially a highway of commerce, it came into prominence in the decade following 1820 and continued to be an important thoroughfare for many years. Along its rutted course cling memories colorful and romantic, drab and tragic. One branch of this trail looped to the south and crossed the Panhandle, but the Comanche hazard was always too great to make it an enticing gamble, and it was used but little.

Among those to travel the southern route was Josiah Gregg,[10] who in 1831 as a physical weakling and convalescent

[6] Edwin James, *Account of S. H. Long's Expedition* (vols. XIV–XVII of R. G. Thwaites, *Early Western Travels*), XVI, 85.

[7] Cardinal Goodwin, *The Trans-Mississippi West*, 68–69.

[8] See H. Bailey Carroll, *Texan–Santa Fé Expedition*.

[9] R. B. Marcy, *Exploration of the Red River of Louisiana*, 29–57.

[10] Josiah Gregg is the foremost historian of the Santa Fé trade. He ob-

set out from Independence seeking health more than profit.[11] He soon recovered his health, became intrigued with the romance of the trade, the freedom of prairie life, and the spirit of the trail, and actively engaged in the business for several years. In 1839 the French were blockading Mexico. Gregg saw great profit in supplying shut-in Chihuahua with needed goods. He resolved to make an early start and go by way of Santa Fé. In the region farther south an earlier spring meant earlier grass. Therefore, Gregg shipped $25,000 worth of goods up the Arkansas River to Van Buren, five miles below Fort Smith. Here the earlier season enabled him to embark ahead of the Independence caravans. The outcome of the venture is not of particular interest to this story, but his observations and experiences as he crossed the Panhandle are.

The last outpost was Camp Holmes, in Indian Territory, where Auguste Pierre Chouteau had built a fort to trade with the Plains Indians. From this point the course across the Panhandle was unbroken and unknown. Gregg wrote:

We had to depend entirely upon our knowledge of the geographical position of the country for which we were steering and the indications of a compass and sextant. This was emphatically a pioneer trip, such a one as had, perhaps, never before been undertaken—to convey heavily laden wagons through a country almost wholly untrod by civilized men, and of which we, at least, knew nothing.

At Chouteau's fort he met and talked with a Comanche chief, Tabba-Quena, or the Big Eagle. The Indian informed Gregg "that the route up the Canadian presented no obstacles according to *his* mode of traveling." Since the Indian traveled wherever a saddle horse could pass, this was small comfort to a man

served that the "virtual commencement" of the trade may be dated from 1822, when the trek was being made with pack trains. Two years later a venturous party, with twenty-three four-wheeled carts and two of two wheels began the wagon traffic. Several years later more "adventurers with large capital" began entering the trade, and it swelled to importance. Josiah Gregg, *Commerce of the Prairies* (vols. XIX, XX of Thwaites, *Early Western Travels*), XIX, 180–81.

[11] *Ibid.*, 193.

with heavy wagons. Big Eagle drew a map which Gregg declared "a far more accurate delineation of all the rivers of the plains, the road from Missouri to Santa Fé, and the different Mexican settlements, than is to be found in any of the engraved maps of those regions." [12]

The caravan traveled in accordance with the practice of the trail. While crossing the Indian country, the wagons moved in double file, so that they could be "corralled" more quickly in case of an attack and all stock turned inside the enclosure.[13] Gregg stopped to smoke the pipe of peace with a war party of Comanches who were on their way to fight the Pawnees; again to trade blankets, looking-glasses, flints, tobacco, beads, and other trinkets, for mules. Generally the traders avoided any barter with the Indians through fear of their duplicity. But Gregg passed through the Panhandle without serious mishap and followed up the Canadian into New Mexico.[14]

In 1841, two years after Gregg's trail-blazing trip from Fort Smith, the Texan–Santa Fé Expedition crossed the Panhandle. Its uncertain course was a trail of woe. It moved out from the Texas settlements to a bugle call, with men in high spirits responding to the charm of camp life, sped on their journey with the well-wishes of President Lamar of the Republic. Weeks later, lost among the canyons and breaks along the eastern edge of the plains, provisions gone, game scarce, and water uncertain, the party was in a sorry plight.

Prairie dogs killed for food proved "exceedingly sweet, tender, and juicy," and the wild horse furnished excellent meat. But both became scarce and starvation faced the party. Hackberries were picked from the trees, and a wretched but hopeful life was eked out upon tortoises, snakes, and "every living and creeping thing" which might be seized upon for food. Occasionally a skunk, peculiarly and most effectively protected from almost every animal of prey, "would reward someone more fortunate than the rest." A few of the men were killed by Indians, articles of trade were burned by a prairie fire, and the entire

[12] *Ibid.,* 100–10.   [13] *Ibid.,* 110.   [14] *Ibid.,* 125–31.

force was arrested by Governor Armijo and sent to Mexico City and to prison. Thus the venture turned out the most abject tragedy of the long list of tragedies of the Santa Fé trade.[15]

Some years later another party crossed the Panhandle following Gregg's trace along the Canadian. Captain R. B. Marcy piloted a party of emigrants from Fort Smith to Santa Fé in 1849. But for the birth of twin boys, perhaps the first white children native to the Panhandle, the trip was uneventful.[16] Except for such explorations as these, the Panhandle was the undisputed and uncoveted home of the Plains Indians, happy mortals in their nomadic life and tribal wars.

Most feared of these tribes were the Kiowas and Comanches, who gave much trouble along the Santa Fé Trail. Gregg was not molested as he passed through Texas in 1839, but an engagement, illustrative of the dangers of the trail, occurred in the western Panhandle in the winter of 1832 and 1833. A party of twelve traders had wound up their business in Santa Fé at a late date, and, fearing to venture by the northern and more frequented way, chose the Texas branch of the trail and followed down the Canadian. They must have had a successful season, for they possessed $10,000 in specie, loaded upon pack animals. Anticipation of the happiness of reaching home evidently lent spurs to weary muscles as the pack animals were urged across the grama-covered slopes bordering the river and were driven splashing through its dancing eddies. But grim tragedy trailed behind. Fond hearts "back in the States" vainly listened for the beat of horses' hoofs and the creak of saddle leather, heralds of a trader's return.

The men were versed in Indian treachery, and when they met a party of Comanches and Kiowas, preparations for defense were hastily made. Observing this, the Indians stopped at a distance and professed friendship. Then a few advanced to the traders, one or two more joined them, and others came in like

15 G. W. Kendall, *The Narrative of the Texan–Santa Fé Expedition,* I, 195, 199, 201, 206, 253.
16 R. B. Marcy, "Report of . . . ," *Ex. Doc. No. 64,* 31 Cong., 1 sess., 169–84.

manner until the traders were surrounded. The traders pushed forward, hoping that the Indians would drop behind and leave them. But the Indians turned their ponies and rode alongside.

The first hostile move came when two mules veered from the course and the trader who reined off to drive them back was shot and killed. A general fire opened; the traders jumped from their horses, threw off the pack-saddles for protection, and began banking dirt around them. All the while an active fire was maintained on both sides, and another of the traders was killed. The horses and mules were soon shot down, making escape in this way impossible, and the siege continued for thirty-six hours. Sufficient food could be obtained from the dead pack animals lying about, but there was danger of dying of thirst. A bold break was resolved upon.

The owners of the train allowed each man to take as much of the specie as he could carry. The remainder, all but a few hundred dollars, was buried, and the men made their escape. Upon running short of provisions and with no ammunition for game, the men lived upon roots and tender bark of trees. Dissension arose over the right course to follow, and the ten separated into two parties of five each. One of these, after untold suffering, reached the Creek settlements upon the Arkansas and was treated kindly. The other did not fare so well. Three of the five were abandoned to an unministered end, among them a Mr. Schenck who had been wounded in the thigh, a man of "talent and excellent family connections." [17] But a stern frontier made no distinction in its exactions. Cultured and uncultured followed the same trails, fought the same fights, and died similar deaths.

At that early day the Indians rode the plains, hunting where game grazed most abundantly. This land was theirs. Here they made their last stand, and fought savagely. The most powerful tribes frequenting the upper Red River country were the Kiowas and Comanches.[18] Known as "the Arabs of the deserts of North

[17] Gregg, *Commerce of the Prairies*, XX, 133–36.
[18] Marcy, *Exploration of the Red River*, 94.

America," the Comanches were addicted to a transient life. They hunted as far north as the 38th parallel, and to the south they raided the ranches and settlements of northern Mexico.[19]

Captain Marcy observed the Comanche with interest, a man "free as the boundless plains over which he roams, as he neither knows nor wants any luxuries beyond what he finds in the buffalo or the deer around him. These serve him with food, clothing, and a covering for his lodge, and he sighs not for the titles and distinction that occupy the thoughts and engage the energies of civilized man. His only ambition consists in being able to cope successfully with his enemy in war, and in managing his steed with unfailing adroitness." [20]

The Comanches all but lived astride a horse. From the plunder of a Santa Fé caravan they might sweep south to depredate upon the frontier of Texas, or farther still, to strike terror into the hearts of the Mexicans and drive away their horses and mules. A well-worn trail stretched from the upper plains of the Arkansas through the Panhandle and West Texas into Mexico. It was tramped deep and hard by the scurry of thousands of hoofs of great herds of horses, stolen in Mexico and driven north for trade. The trail intersected the valley of Red River, skirted the Llano Estacado on the east, crossed the Brazos, and connected "the extreme western permanent watering-places." From the Brazos it bore south and southwest, crossing the headwaters of the Colorado, touching at Sulphur Springs, north and west of Big Spring, to the next water at the Mustang Springs and across a long stretch of unwatered country to the Horsehead Crossing on the Pecos.[21]

Captain John Pope, while exploring a prospective route for the first Pacific railway, crossed the South Plains in 1854 and met a party of Kiowas at Mustang Springs. Some thousand head of horses driven by the fifty members of the band indicated the success of their raid into Mexico.[22]

---

[19] John Pope, "Report to War Department," 1854, p. 14.
[20] *Exploration of the Red River,* 95.
[21] Pope, "Report to War Department," 1854, pp. 16, 78.
[22] *Ibid.,* 16, 72.

The Comanches were even more efficient thieves than the Kiowas. "They are perhaps as arrant freebooters as can be found upon the face of the earth," Marcy wrote, "and they regard stealing from strangers as perfectly legitimate and honorable, and that man who had been most successful in this is the most highly honored by his tribe; indeed a young man who has not made one or more of these expeditions into Mexico is held in but little repute." An old chief of the Northern Comanches called Os-sa-keep, fond father of four sons, "as fine young men as could be found," took much comfort from the fact that these hopefuls could steal more horses than any other young men in the tribe.[23] Paternal pride pleasantly sped his later years as his sons grew up, virtuosos among the thieves.

Generations of Mexican ranchmen suffered from these Indian ravages. The Comanches rode into the settlements of the northern states in broad day, and almost unopposed drove off stock and carried away many captives. Strangely enough, after the captives had tasted the lotus of nomadic prairie life for a time, they rarely wished to return to their homes. The Indians were "objects of the extremest terror to the Mexicans; and it is related that a single Comanche even at mid-day, dashed at speed into the city of Durango, and by his mere presence caused the hasty closing of the stores and public places of the city, and the rapid retreat of a population of thirty thousand souls to their barred houses. He remained an hour roaming through the deserted streets, and was only captured by being lassoed from the window of a house as he was riding triumphantly but carelessly from the suburbs." [24]

These Indians wintered in the valleys of the upper Colorado, Brazos, and Red rivers. In the summer season, the greater part of the tribe migrated north to hunt the buffalo and mustang upon the plains of the upper Arkansas.[25] Major Long, who met a party of Kaskaskia Indians in the Panhandle in 1820, wrote

[23] Marcy, *Exploration of the Red River*, 97.
[24] Pope, "Report to War Department," 1854, pp. 14, 15.
[25] *Ibid.*, 15–16.

that they showed "great dexterity in throwing the rope, taking in this way" many wild horses.[26] They crossed long stretches of dry country, carrying water in flabby canteens made of undressed buffalo stomachs.[27] Modern nurseries were unknown, nor had baby buggies reached the plains, but children too young to sit upon a horse were lashed to the saddle by their legs, and rode along "in entire unconcern." [28]

But their days of plains life were numbered. Placed upon the reservations of Indian Territory in the early seventies, they broke forth again to their prairie hunting grounds, to be corralled at least by the troops of R. S. Mackenzie, Nelson A. Miles, and others in 1874. Thereafter, except for a few more outbreaks in different parts of the country, the last raids were done. The fine physical specimen degenerated, the exquisite folklore conjured by the rich imaginations of centuries died with silent tongues, the horseman became a pedestrian, the buffalo lance fell to rust, and the finely tempered mustang of the buffalo chase became a plow horse. "Boasted progress" decreed these changes.

Yet the explorers of the early days never imagined the plains as a home for many thousands. Major Long did "not hesitate" to give the opinion that the northern Panhandle was "almost wholly unfit for cultivation, and of course uninhabitable by a people depending upon agriculture." Edwin James, who accompanied Long, had "little apprehension of giving too unfavorable an account of this . . . country." To him it was an "unfit residence for any but a Nomad population. The traveller who shall at any time have traversed its desolate sands, will, we think, join us in the wish that this region may forever remain the unmolested haunt of the native hunter, the bison and the jackall." [29]

Gregg wrote in similar vein that the plains were too dry for agriculture, and "seem only fitted for the haunts of the mustang, the buffalo, the antelope, and their migratory lord, the

[26] James, *Account of Long's Expedition*, XVI, 119.
[27] *Ibid.*, 104–105.   [28] *Ibid.*
[29] James, *Account of Long's Expedition*, XIV, 20–21.

prairie Indian." [30] Marcy's original impressions were not much better. He too had little more hope for the "inhospitable" plains and felt sure they were destined to remain the home of the savage, "possessing as they do, so few attractions to civilized man."

Prophecy, like pioneering, can likewise be hazardous. These early explorers would never have made land-promotion agents or chamber of commerce secretaries. But, as Reuben Gold Thwaites wrote, "such a verdict was not welcomed by an expansive people, eager to enter into and possess a land which imagination pictures as suitable for the seat of an empire." The farming frontier, however, marched with too eager tread, and there was much harm done by optimistically flying into the face of nature's limitations.

Eager settlers, with no knowledge of dry-land farming, rushed into the west from regions of abundant rainfall. The hundreds of abandoned claims of the middle nineties, marked by dugouts and tumbling sod shacks, expressed a graphic story. These reverses lead one to doubt whether the conservatism of the early explorers "was not wiser than the confidence of the more ardent expansionists." [31]

However, it was a land where a man could starve to death in the best of health. Marcy was impressed with the healthfulness of the country, and Gregg saw more when he uttered, almost prophetically, that "this unequalled pasturage [of] the great western prairies affords a sufficiency to graze cattle for the supply of the United States." [32]

When the Indian could no longer range at will and when the Anglo-American hunter was slaughtering the last of the buffalo, the day of which Gregg wrote had come. The shivering seas of grass then invited the hot-hearted man on "the hurricane deck" of the Spanish pony.

[30] *Commerce of the Prairies,* XX, 248; also pp. 111–12.
[31] Thwaites, *Early Western Travels,* XIV, 20–21.
[32] *Commerce of the Prairies,* XX, 248.

CHAPTER II

Traces of Spanish Life
Upon the Plains

B EFORE THE coming of the cowboy, before the buffalo hunters straggled in, and even before the earliest Anglo-American explorers came, the Panhandle of Texas was known to the
Spaniard and the Mexican. To the plains, Spanish buffalo hunters or *ciboleros* came annually from the little New Mexican
villages shut off from the rest of the world, and hunted, not with
high-powered rifles, but with betasseled lances and fleet ponies.
Thus they put up their winter's meat, and at times brought
hard-baked loaves of bread and other articles to trade to the
Indians.[1] But the more extensive trading was the work of the
Indian traders—the *Comancheros*.

It is a part of our history that vigor is dependent on beef.
Men who push trails into the wilderness, who live rigorous outdoor lives, must have meat. When early expeditions into New
Mexico heard of the buffalo plains where "humpbacked cows"
grazed in uncounted thousands, they went to hunt them. The
New Mexican Indians told Coronado of the buffalo, and brought
him a picture of one sketched upon a piece of hide. Alvarado and
twenty men were sent to the plains to hunt them.[2] Later Coro-

[1] Gregg, *Commerce of the Prairies*, XIX, 239–40.
[2] Hammond, "The Founding of New Mexico," *New Mexico Historical Review*, January, 1926, p. 45.

nado crossed the buffalo country and gave to literature one of the earliest descriptions of these animals.

Espejo found the buffalo range attracting him, and in September of 1598, Oñate sent his officer Zaldivar, with sixty men, to the Canadian country near the western border of the Panhandle. The buffalo were sluggish in appearance, and the Spaniards expected to capture some. They built a corral of logs, with wings long enough, they estimated, to hold ten thousand head. Then they rode out to drive the herds in. The historian of the party described what happened.

The cattle started very nicely towards the corral, but soon they turned back in a stampede towards the men, and, rushing through them in a mass, it was impossible to stop them. . . . For several days they tried a thousand ways of shutting them in or of surrounding them, but in no manner was it possible to do so. This was not due to fear, for they are remarkably savage and ferocious, so much so they killed three of our horses and badly wounded forty.

Then Zaldivar decided to capture some calves. But the calves too are notorious fighters. A number were caught, "but they became so enraged that out of the many which were being brought, some dragged by ropes and others upon the horses, not one got a league toward the camp, for they all died within about an hour." Failing in this attempt to take the animals alive, the party killed some and carried the meat back to Oñate and his men.[3] Thus ended the first attempt to round up buffalo on the plains of Texas, and thus, in 1598, did buffalo hunting begin with the early settlers of New Mexico.

In time the Spanish-speaking people from the valleys of the Pecos and Río Grande came to hunt over a wide range. A hunter's trail led to Buffalo Springs (later one of the headquarters of the XIT Ranch), thence to Agua Fria, and on into the country to the east. It was known to some of the pioneers as "the old buffalo trail."[4] The country about Buffalo Springs was a great

[3] *Ibid.*, 445–46.
[4] Olive K. Dixon, *Life of Billy Dixon,* 139.

hunting ground, fairly "alive with buffaloes and mustangs."
Many Indian campfires of buffalo chips reflected their glow in
the deep holes of water there. Broken flints and arrows upon the
near-by hills suggest ancient Indian struggles, the traditions of
which are kept alive by the remnants of the Plains tribes.

John Skelley, an old-time buffalo hunter, says that there
were several Anglo-American hunters camped at Buffalo
Springs in 1878. "A long time ago," he said, "I talked to old
Mexicans who told me that they hunted buffaloes at the Springs
when they were boys. They said that expeditions of both Mexicans and Navajos came here from the settlements on the Río
Grande, in New Mexico, to procure their winter's meat." [5]

Probably the first hunters' trail which was used extensively
crossed from the Pecos settlements to the Canadian, and followed down the stream into Texas. This cart road was established as early as 1839,[6] but had probably been used years before that time. By another trail the hunters came to a point
about two hundred miles south of Buffalo Springs, known as
Las Casas Amarillas, or the Yellow Houses. This trail appears
to have led across by the site of Fort Sumner, and by Portales
Lake.[7] If sufficient game was not found, the hunters pushed on to
the breaks of the plains. They were seen as far east as the Blanco
Canyon in 1877.[8]

The Mexicans sometimes hunted alone, but usually they went
in parties. As early as 1831, while on the Santa Fé Trail, Josiah
Gregg met a hunter north of the site of Clayton, New Mexico,
and left us his best description:

His picturesque costume [Gregg wrote] and peculiarity of de-
portment . . . soon showed him to be a Mexican *cibolero* or buffalo
hunter. These hardy devotees of the chase usually wear leather
trousers and jackets, and flat straw hats; while, swung upon the
shoulder of each hangs his *carcage* or quiver of bow and arrows.
The long handle of their lance being set in a case, and suspended by
the side with a strap from the pommel of the saddle, leaves the

[5] *Ibid.*, 138–39.   [6] Gregg, *Commerce of the Prairies*, XX, 136.
[7] John R. Cook, *The Border and the Buffalo*, 220.   [8] *Ibid.*, 246.

point waving high over the head, with a tassel of gay parti-colored stuffs dangling from the tip of the scabbard. Their fusil, if they happen to have one, is suspended in like manner at the other side, with a stopper in the muzzle fantastically tasselled.[9]

The lance, a steel blade about fourteen inches long, was fastened to a staff seven or eight feet in length. At times the hunters used the bow and arrow, but more often the lance, with which they quickly killed enough buffalo to supply their needs.[10]

Hunting parties often consisted of from fifteen to twenty-five men; women were never taken on the hunts. Sometimes the meat was loaded upon burros and pack mules, but usually upon *carretas*, the cumbersome Mexican carts, drawn by slow but dependable oxen. A party of fifteen or twenty men might have from four to ten wagons, each drawn by two to four yoke of oxen. The party would have from ten to fifteen lance horses, often of race stock, very fleet,[11] corn-fed, trained and hardened to their work. The "meat hunts" were held in the fall by the border Mexicans, but sometimes those of the interior participated. Usually some elderly man was in charge of the hunt, which lasted from six weeks to three months.[12]

These hunters saved all the meat. Gregg observed in 1831 that the Mexicans "find no difficulty in curing the meat even in mid-summer, by slicing it thin and spreading or suspending it in the sun; or, if in haste, it is slightly barbecued. During the curing operation they often follow the Indian practice of beating or kneading the slices with their feet, which they contend contributes to its preservation." The Santa Fé traders dried, or jerked, meat in much the same way. They strung lines on either side of their wagons, draped the strips of meat over these, and left them to dry until ready to pack away.[13] After the meat was thoroughly jerked, it would keep indefinitely.

[9] *Commerce of the Prairies*, XIX, 235.
[10] Cook, *The Border and the Buffalo*, 54; Gregg, *Commerce of the Prairies*, XIX, 240.
[11] Charles Goodnight to J. Evetts Haley, April 8, 1927.
[12] Cook, *The Border and the Buffalo*, 54.
[13] Gregg, *Commerce of the Prairies*, XIX, 240.

In 1874 John R. Cook, a member of an Anglo-American hunting party, upon the invitation of Antonio Romero, joined a party of *ciboleros* at Glorieta. They left Romero's ranch in October, came by Bernal Springs, and thence to Fort Bascom. There they met another party from Galisteo, New Mexico. They proceeded eastward to the Staked Plains and found the first buffalo north of the Canadian at Blue Water, or, as the Mexicans called it, *Agua Azul*. Getting the wind on the buffalo, the hunters raced out at full speed from behind a knoll, their horses excited and eager, the hunters leaning forward in their saddles, lances ready for action. The buffalo were lying down, less than two hundred yards away, and the riders were among the animals before they could break into a dead run. Each Mexican rode close beside a buffalo, made a quick thrust behind the shoulder, jerked out the lance, rode to the next buffalo, and so on until his horse was winded. Sixteen buffalo were killed in a few minutes.[14] It was sport that quickened the blood of both hunter and horse, in colorful contrast to the businesslike slaughter by the Anglo-American, who "still-hunted" with a rifle.

Charles Goodnight, the noted pioneer who established the first ranch in the Panhandle, was making a trip from Colorado to his Palo Duro ranch in 1877. Near the junction of the Tierra Blanca and Palo Duro creeks he rode, late one evening, up to a *cibolero's* camp. The hunter's effects were packed upon a wagon, but his heart was with his horse, a fast pony, well kept. Love of horseflesh among men, whatever the diverse racial stocks, bespeaks a certain kinship, and prairie hospitality ever broke its bread and poured its black coffee with cordial abandon. The pioneer of more than one widely known cattle trail sat down in camp with a New Mexican who counted his horse his wealth.

Early the next morning six large buffalo bulls came by, headed north. The Mexican ran for his horse, saddled, and was quickly in pursuit. Within less than six hundred yards he pulled his pony up. Six dead buffalo attested the skill of the

[14] *Ibid.,* 54–58.

hunter and the quality of the steed.[15] In less than fifteen minutes his season's hunt was done. Soon dusky little tots would run from a squat adobe on the Pecos to welcome the hunter home, and the meat of the *cibolo*, mixed well with *chili*, would warm little Mexican stomachs long hungry for *carne*.

Such hunting was dangerous. A wounded buffalo might "horn" some too eager horse; a running pony might step in a prairie dog hole to receive a hard fall; and sometimes a man was killed when his lance failed to pull out. Once a Mexican named Trujillo, who lived at Tascosa, was on a hunt, and when he made the thrust, the handle of his lance splintered. His horse continued to run alongside the buffalo and pressed so closely against the animal's side that the sharp end of the handle pushed through the rider's abdomen. This was Trujillo's last hunt. His horse had been trained too well.[16] Though the Anglo-American hunters objected to the Mexican method of killing because it stirred the buffalo up and set them to moving,[17] the Mexicans continued coming to the plains as late as 1882, or until all the buffalo were gone. One party of hunters was seen on the Running Water that year, and in spite of the improvements in firearms, they continued to hunt with lances.[18]

While the *ciboleros* came to hunt, the *Comancheros* came to trade with the Indians for robes, for horses, and for cattle. As long as the Comanches enjoyed the freedom of the plains, the *Comancheros* plied their not especially voluminous but significant trade.

This trade had flourished for more than a century. The chronicler of S. H. Long's explorations of 1820 wrote that "The Indians of this region seem to have had intercourse with the Spaniards from a very early date." A man named Brevel, born among the Caddoes, told John Sibley in 1805 "that he had visited Santa Fé forty years previous." By 1820 there was an Indian trail to Santa Fé, supposedly from the Pawnee Picts vil-

[15] C. Goodnight to J. E. H., April 8, 1927.
[16] Wm. Balfour to J. E. H., July 29, 1926.
[17] George Simpson to J. E. H., July 18, 1926.
[18] Harry Ingerton to J. E. H., April 13, 1927.

lage on Red River,[19] when the trade seems to have been well established. Major Long met a party of Kaskaskias, or Bad Hearts, as the French called them, on their way from a hunt on the Colorado and Brazos to meet the Spanish traders near the headwaters of the Canadian.[20]

The first traders may have come for buffalo robes alone. But soon livestock proved an important item, and the Indians quickly learned how profitable it was to steal horses, and then cattle, from the western frontier of Texas as well as from the northern border of Mexico. During the decade of 1830–40, Gregg wrote that the traders, "usually composed of the indigent and rude classes of the frontier villages . . . collect together several times a year, and launch upon the plains with a few trinkets and trumperies of all kinds, and perhaps a bag of bread and another of *pinole*," which they bartered for horses and mules. Rarely the entire stock of a trader exceeded twenty dollars in value.[21]

In later years they brought ammunition, lead, paint, beads, knives, *manta* or calico, and other articles essential to the Indian toilet and boudoir. The Indian possessed little the trader desired except the stock he had pilfered from these two frontiers, which the Mexicans secured at very low cost. Goodnight knew two retired army lieutenants in New Mexico who furnished articles of trade to the Mexicans and received stock in payment, one of whom said that the cattle he received cost him about two dollars and a half apiece.

The poorer traders brought a few burro loads of goods and traded for but a few head, from ten to fifty. The more well-to-do brought their articles of trade in *carretas* and wagons, and sometimes traded for as many as five hundred head. Often the cattle received, well broken to the trail by the time the Indians delivered them, were driven on to New Mexico by Mexicans on foot.[22]

It appears that wherever the Indian and Mexican met, there

[19] James, *Account of Long's Expedition,* XVI, 95.   [20] *Ibid.,* 105.
[21] *Commerce of the Prairies,* XX, 137–38.
[22] C. Goodnight to J. E. H., November 13, 1926.

was the "stock" exchange, there the market place. It was sometimes Santa Fé and sometimes around the source of the Canadian. In 1839 Gregg saw that the trader was "content to wander about for several months," finally to "return home with a mule or two, as the proceeds of his traffic." [23] But when the trade in stolen cattle and horses assumed greater proportions, definite meeting places were established. Stealing in wholesale measure from the northwest fringe of Texas settlement began shortly before the Civil War. Both cattle and horses were stolen from the frontier ranches and driven northwest to meet the Mexican traders.

This exchange, according to Goodnight, began northwest of where Amarillo now stands, at a spring called Las Tecovas (perhaps a corruption of *techados*), a name of reputed Indian origin meaning "the tents." Later it became the headquarters of the Frying Pan Ranch, an eastern neighbor of the XIT, of which Henry B. Sanborn was one of the owners. The spring came to be called after him. According to tradition the valley of Tascosa Creek was once the scene of trading in cattle and horses.[24] But the principal place of meeting was shifted southeast to a fork of the Pease River, just below the caprock. Here developed the greatest trading ground in the history of plains cattle theft. For ten years after the close of the Civil War the trade continued.[25] While Washington theorized, cattlemen were losing their stock, reserving their driest powder for the Indians, and venting their choicest profanity on the politicians.

The head of the Brazos was a favorite camping place of the Indians as they returned from their raids into the San Saba and Llano country. There they stopped to rest and recruit their stolen stock before continuing into New Mexico or turning northeast to Indian Territory. This camping place was discovered by General R. S. Mackenzie's expedition of 1872.[26]

[23] *Commerce of the Prairies*, XX, 137–38; see Kendall, *The Texan Santa Fé Expedition*, I, 262.
[24] James H. East to J. E. H., September 29, 1927.
[25] Charles Goodnight to J. E. H., January 26, 1926.
[26] *Galveston News*, October 22, 1874.

When Goodnight came in to establish his ranch, "the roads of the Mexican traders were almost as big and plain as the roads of today." There was a north and south trade road. The north one left Las Vegas, where the traders outfitted, led northeast to the Canadian, and followed down it to turn southeast, about a day's drive from the Trujillo, near the state line.

The traders left the river and pulled for the Door of the Plains, a large gap in the caprock which could be seen for miles. They watered at the Trujillo and then at the extreme head of the Palo Duro, in the XIT range. The trail led down this stream to near the site of Canyon, and turned south to strike the Tule above the breaks at Mackenzie Crossing. It led southeast again to the head of Rock Creek, then to the foot of the plains, by some springs, and on to the Tongue River.

The southern trail came back by the same route to Mackenzie Crossing, from where it turned west to Las Escarbadas, where one of the divisional headquarters of the XIT was later located. The name means "the scrapings." Here the Mexicans scraped out little pits in the sand and thus secured water. From Escarbadas the trail led to Laguna Salada, thence to La Laguna, eight miles north of Fort Sumner, and eight miles farther to join the main government road from the fort to Santa Fé. From this road the traders dropped off to their homes.[27]

The Kiowas and Comanches found good sport in keeping all the horses stolen from the cowmen along the outer edge, and cattle could be stolen much more quickly than they could be raised. Down the trails from Santa Fé and Las Vegas came the New Mexican traders, across the plains to camp and await the coming of the Indians after the "light of the moon." [28] Indians of various tribes and dialects, Anglo-Americans, and Mexicans gathered at this great exchange ground below the caprock in the valley of the little stream. In order to carry on the barter, the traders or their interpreters were forced to speak several different languages or *lenguas*—tongues. So the stream came

[27] C. Goodnight to J. E. H., November 13, 1926.

[28] The Indians made their raids when the moon was full; hence the pioneer expression.

to be known as Las Lenguas. In time the name was anglicized, and today the river upon which so many stolen cattle changed hands is known as the Tongue.

In 1867 Goodnight found six hundred head of his own cattle in one bunch on Gallinas Creek, New Mexico. They had been stolen from near old Fort Belknap, several hundred miles to the east in Texas, and traded to the Mexicans. He went into court at Las Vegas in an attempt to recover them. Not only were his efforts fruitless, but it cost him seventy-five dollars to get out of court. He left with the "undisputed evidence" that at least 300,000 head of cattle had been stolen from the Texas frontier and sold to the New Mexicans during the war,[29] and, also, with a firmer conviction of what should be done with cattle thieves.[30]

An old trader named José Pena, once on the trail with Goodnight, told of a trip he made to the Quitaque. When he reached the rendezvous, no cattle were there. He met a chief who told him to let his Indians have the goods, and the cattle would be there shortly. Pena was afraid to refuse to let his Indians have the goods, though he supposed he would never receive the cattle once he turned over the goods. But in a week or two the cattle were brought in, and Pena happily went his way.[31] There were times, however, when the Indians traded and then forcibly repossessed the animals they had turned over to the Mexicans before those unfortunates had time to reach their homes.[32]

Stealing from the Texas frontier became difficult after the Indians were placed upon the reservations. The government, which is said to have encouraged the trade during the Civil War because of the harm it would do Confederate Texas, opposed it afterward.[33]

To what extent the depredations upon the Texas frontier were due to this Indian trade would be difficult to determine,

[29] Charles Goodnight to J. E. H., February 19, 1927.
[30] J. Frank Dobie, *Texas and Southwestern Lore*.
[31] C. Goodnight to J. E. H., April 8, 1927.
[32] Gregg, *Commerce of the Prairies*, XX, 137.
[33] C. Goodnight to J. E. H., November 13, 1926.

but certainly the traders furnished the Indians with the means of hunting and the market for their stolen stock. The animals trafficked away had to be replaced by new levies, and the greater the trade, the more serious the inroads upon the Texas settlements became.[34]

The traders usually made good guides, though Gregg does not agree. "They will tell you [he wrote] that you may arrive at a given place by the time the sun reached a certain point; otherwise, whether it be but half a mile or half a day's ride to the place inquired for, they are apt to apply *está cerquita* (it is close by), or *está lejos* (it is far off), to the one as to the other, just as the impression happens to strike them." [35] They may have been deficient in giving directions, but they were proficient in piloting a stranger upon the plains. General R. S. Mackenzie used some of these old traders as guides. One was a half-blood named Johnson whom he secured at Fort Concho.[36] Another who acted in like capacity was José Piedad. Goodnight said that he was simply "a wonder. He knew the plains from the Palo Duro to the Concho by heart. When the Mexicans know a country, they are great guides." [37]

The man who guided Mackenzie's expedition of 1874 to the Indian camp in Tule Canyon was another trader, named José Tefoya. He was out on a trading trip and was captured by Mackenzie. The old campaigner started to kill him, but decided he might be of help.[38] The old buffalo hunters report that Mackenzie propped up a wagon tongue and hanged Tefoya to it long enough to induce him to talk.[39] Hemp and a hangman's noose have long been conducive to speech, and the last time José was allowed to touch ground, he agreed to lead the troops to the Indians, with the result that the Comanches suffered a serious

[34] See Marcy, *Exploration of the Red River*, 105–106; C. Goodnight to J. E. H., November 13, 1926.

[35] *Commerce of the Prairies*, XX, 140.

[36] Charles P. Hatfield, Ms., "Account of the Mackenzie Battle," Panhandle-Plains Historical Society, Canyon, Texas.

[37] C. Goodnight to J. E. H., April 8, 1927.

[38] *Ibid.*

[39] Frank Lloyd to J. E. H., August 18, 1927.

defeat. Quanah Parker, one of the Comanche chiefs, heard that Tefoya had betrayed the Indians, and he told Goodnight he would broil the Mexican alive if he ever caught him.[40] Tefoya found the genial New Mexico climate preferable ever after that.

For hundreds of years wild mustangs roamed the plains in vast thousands, and among the Mexicans to visit the Llano Estacado were a few horse hunters whom the Texans termed "mustangers." The usual method of capturing horses was by "walking them down." Sometimes this was too slow for the Mexicans and they resorted to other maneuvers. A party of sixteen left Fort Sumner to steal horses from the Indians in 1875. Celedón Trujillo, an old horse wrangler who spent his last years at Fort Sumner, was with the party. They went by Portales Spring, Casas Amarillas, and south from there some eighty miles. When they failed to find Indian ponies, all but seven of the party returned. The others continued their search, but were discovered by Colonel W. B. Shafter while he was on his famous scouting expedition upon the South Plains. Shafter arrested the Mexicans and held them until he reached the Pecos, near the site of Carlsbad, New Mexico.[41]

The year before, an Indian band stole two hundred head of horses from the Maxwells at Fort Sumner. A party of seventy-three men, mostly Mexicans, set out in pursuit. The Indians headed southeast down another plainly beaten traders' trail that led by Portales and Salt Lake to Casas Amarillas. There the pursuing party caught the Indians and took four hundred head of horses from them.[42] But this was not the characteristic role of the "mustanger." His methods were less hazardous and more certain of results.

The region about the Yellow Houses, a South Plains landmark and later a part of the XIT Ranch, was a natural mustang country. In the early spring of 1878 eight Mexicans came from San Miguel to catch horses. They pitched camp at Laguna Rica, a lake some eight miles from the Yellow Houses.

[40] C. Goodnight to J. E. H., April 8, 1927.
[41] Celedón Trujillo to J. E. H., June 24, 1927.
[42] *Ibid.*

They wanted mares and brought twenty head of saddle horses to use in capturing them. The mustangs ran in bands, each led by a stallion that had fought his way to supremacy.

The Mexicans picked out a band and started two men toward them. They rode at a walk. When the wild stallion scented or saw the riders, he trotted out to examine them more closely. When assured of danger, he whirled and sped to his band, and by biting and squealing forced his mares into a run and then took the lead. Away they went, generally for three to five miles. The horsemen patiently fell in behind. After the band had stopped, the stallion again dropped to the rear, and when the riders came near, he started his mares again.

Mustangs had a favorite range which they would scarcely leave; therefore, on the second run they often described a big circle to swing back toward the point from which they had started, and thus might travel fifteen or twenty miles before they stopped the second time.

When the direction of the circle was determined, two other riders would start out and cross an arc of the circle. Another would do the same outside the circle; then one man would take two extra horses, hurry across the circle and intercept the first riders with fresh horses and a supply of *tortillas, carne,* and *agua* (bread, meat, and water). Another would station himself, with four extra horses, as near to the circle as caution and convenience would allow.

As the circle had once been completed, the horsemen adjusted themselves accordingly. The wild horses were kept on the move as much as possible both day and night.

The horsemen would drop in behind the wild horses at intervals; but they were always in a walk. Thus it was called walking them down.[43]

By the third day the old, weak horses dropped out, and by the fourth the others were becoming "leg-weary." At times the stallion, enraged by the persistence of the riders, turned upon them and was shot. As the horses grew more weary, they might

[43] Cook, *The Border and the Buffalo,* 254.

attempt to stop or lie down. The *vaquero*, using his riata as a black-snake, cut hair and hide and the animal struggled on. Usually the horses were kept moving through the fourth night, sometimes longer.

Upon this particular hunt all the Mexicans were on hand with their lariats when the morning of the fifth day came. Each mare was roped and thrown, and with a knife the Mexicans severed a small ligament in the foreleg of each animal and let out the joint-water. Then they were branded and turned loose. This treatment stiffened both forelegs so that one herder was able to care for the band and drive it to water and to grass. When the Mexicans had caught all they wanted, the horses were herded until the knees healed and then were driven into New Mexico. A Mexican named Valdez was in charge of this party, which secured thirty-five head of mares from eighty head of horses in the band that was walked down.[44]

The American mustangers, who came after the Mexicans, used a different method. After walking the mustangs down, clogs, usually made of short forked sticks, were tied around the mustangs' legs just below their ankles, which prevented the horses from running. These were usually substituted for the knee cut. But before the American horse hunter arrived, the sheep owners were to have brief but rather peaceful use of the grasses along the western edge of the plains.

Almost by the time the trading was over, and before the *ciboleros* had stopped visiting the plains, Mexican sheepmen were pushing down the Canadian into Texas. This movement seems to have gathered force in 1876. No sheep appeared in the Panhandle proper in 1875, but when Goodnight, moving down from Colorado that year, stopped at Rincón de las Piedras, a rocky bend in the river just above the state line, flocks totaling about 100,000 head gathered around him for protection from the Indians. Goodnight told his cowboys to hold range enough for his herd, but not to molest the sheepmen. One day when Leigh Dyer, the foreman, was away, a sheep herd came into the

[44] *Ibid.*, 254–55.

range which Goodnight held. Dave McCormick, one of the cowboys, had no love for anything that savored of mutton, and "wanted to drown the whole damn outfit."

"There was a Scotchman by the name of J. C. Johnston with my herd," Goodnight said, "who did not know anything about stock. As my men started to move the sheep, he asked McCormick where to put them. McCormick pointed to the river and said, 'Why, put them in here, of course.' "

Johnston faithfully followed instructions, and some four hundred were drowned. McCormick's understandable aversion to sheep had been served, but his employer paid the bill by reimbursing the owners in full.[45] Though neither cowman nor sheepman owned the country, Goodnight, who had previously decided to abandon the Canadian range, made an agreement with the Mexicans that he would leave this region to them, and they in turn were to stay off the Palo Duro. Only two Mexicans transgressed this agreement. Leigh Dyer took the double of his lariat and whipped one, and it is said on good authority that he never came back. An outlaw killed the other herder for his horses, and thereby hangs the legend of the naming of the Sierrita de la Cruz.[46]

The first sheep outfits formed no permanent settlements. They made great circuits, swinging out into the Panhandle from their New Mexican ranges, following good grass and adequate water. Many sheep were wintered on Cañoncito Blanco and the Tule, and even as far east as the Quitaque, until that country was taken as cattle range.

Other flocks ranged along the Canadian and its tributaries on either side. At times the New Mexican owners placed two or three big bunches of sheep on a circuit together in charge of a *majordomo*, a man who rode from one herd to another and directed their care and movements. Fine, ferocious dogs, apparently crossed with the wolf, aided the herders. At night the flock was thrown together, and the herders slept in the center of the herds. The dogs were left in charge, and no man or animal

[45] C. Goodnight to J. E. H., April 8, 1927.   [46] *Ibid.*, November 13, 1927.

could enter the herd without killing them. A cart was rarely if ever taken along. The *pastores* lived mainly upon meat, and pack burros carried what few provisions they had, together with their scanty bedding of skins and rags.[47]

The growth of grass and the supply of water determined their movements. Often the trip into the Panhandle began early in the year, and the flocks reached Texas by lambing time. In the fall they might be driven back to their old ranges. When the sheep were wintered in Texas, they were drifted back towards the settlements for shearing. Sometimes they were sheared fifty or sixty miles out, and large wagons transported the wool to market.[48]

One Padre Green built a big adobe wool storehouse on the Rito Blanco, in the XIT range,[49] and in 1880 a surveying party found flocks numbering 5,000 on the farther reaches of Red River, which were watered at pits dug in the bed of the stream.[50] An Englishman by the name of A. B. Ledgard had a big sheep ranch on the Alamocitos as late as 1882,[51] and the prominent Baca and Armijo families operated heavily in sheep, as did Mariano Montoya, the first clerk of Oldham County. Their flocks grazed the Panhandle and were driven to Dodge City to be shipped by rail to market. O. H. Nelson, pioneer breeder and dealer in registered Herefords, saw the Armijos there with 20,000 head in 1881.[52] Thus these early sheepmen used the Staked Plains ranges and were the precursors of Mexican settlement.

Three Mexican families settled on the river in Oldham County to start the town of Tascosa, where Juan Domingo and Victoria Ventura were the leading citizens.[53] About a mile and a

[47] C. Goodnight to J. E. H., April 8, 1927.

[48] *Ibid.;* J. E. McAllister to J. E. H., July 1, 1926.

[49] *Ibid.*

[50] *Frontier Times,* August, 1925, p. 14.

[51] *Prospectus,* 1882, p. 21; Alamocitos, or Little Cottonwoods, has been spelled "Alamositas" on the ranch maps.

[52] W. H. Ingerton to J. E. H., April 13, 1927; O. H. Nelson to J. E. H., February 26, 1927.

[53] J. Evetts Haley, Ms., "Old Tascosa," Panhandle-Plains Historical Society.

half down the river another *placita,* or little settlement, of four or five families sprang up on Arroyo Pescado, or Fish Creek, and assumed the Spanish name of the stream. Some three miles below was Casino, of like urban pretensions—the most eastern settlement of the Mexicans.[54]

Above Tascosa and just below the state line the plaza of Salinas held a more generous quota of Mexican families, perhaps twenty-five in all. It was located near a saline lake, where crude means of extracting the salt were in use, and to this point settlers came from much of eastern New Mexico to secure their supply.[55] Salinas had stores and saloons, attractions not possessed by most of the other settlements. To the east, at the mouth of Chaves Canyon, another plaza was founded, known as Chaves. Rude plows of forked limbs tipped with a shaft of iron barely stirred the soil enough to permit planting, and irrigation ditches carried the waters of Chaves to the fields. Between Chaves and Tascosa was the plaza of Joaquin. The inhabitants of these little settlements held their land by "squatter's right," just as did the first cowmen.[56]

Despite the popular impression, there was little hard feeling between the cowman and the sheepman in the Texas Panhandle. There might have been, but when cattle came, the sheepmen drifted back into New Mexico. There was no open conflict.[57] By 1883, or at the latest, 1884, the drifting outfits had ceased to visit the country,[58] and the plazas became deserted piles of adobe,[59] where the pack rat engaged in the occupation that gives him his name, where the norther whistled through rooms once resonant with the tunes of old Castile, and where silence no longer even echoed the melody of Latin voices once attuned to strumming guitars. The deserted villages of the Canadian were the last vestiges of Spanish influence but one.

The place-names of the country are essentially Spanish in

[54] W. H. Ingerton to J. E. H., April 13, 1927.
[55] *Ibid.*
[56] Frank Mitchell to J. E. H., December 1, 1926.
[57] J. E. McAllister to J. E. H., July 1, 1926.
[58] A. L. Turner to J. E. H., July 2, 1926.
[59] W. S. Mabry, Ms., "Recollections of the XIT Ranch," p. 16.

flavor, and form the last trace of a life long gone. All prominent landmarks, the creeks, rivers, and canyons of the plains country, were named by Spanish traders and hunters; and delightfully reminiscent of a romantic period are such names as *Los Brazos de Dios, Sierrita de la Cruz, Palo Duro,* and *Punta de Agua.* How striking in contrast the names of a few other streams—Dry River, Sod House, and Skunk Creek—how fragrantly American!

The great plateau was named *Los Llanos Estacados,* the Staked Plains. To the Mexicans it was an impediment to travel, but penetrable; to the pioneers from the Atlantic, it was a part of the Great American Desert, unknown and feared. At some early day the Mexican pathfinders of the Southwest named the region, and many stories account for the origin of the name.

Among the most common explanations is that which came to Josiah Gregg in the thirties.

I have been assured by Mexican hunters and Indians [he wrote] that, from Santa Fé southeastward, there is but one route upon which this plain can be safely traversed during the dry season; and even some of the watering-places on this are at intervals of fifty or eighty miles, and hard to find. Hence the Mexican traders and hunters, that they might not lose their way and perish from thirst, once staked out this route across the plain, it is said; whence it has received the name of El Llano Estacado.[60]

Of a similar nature is the unauthenticated story that Spanish *padres* came down from Santa Fé in 1734 "to establish a fort and mission" at San Saba, setting stakes along the way, upon which they placed buffalo skulls, that they might be seen at a distance.[61]

According to another legend relating to the Indians, a terrible feud once existed between the Pueblos and other mountain tribes of the West and the fierce Comanches of the plains. The war was long, devastating, and demoralizing to the mountain

[60] *Commerce of the Prairies,* XX, 239–40.
[61] Homer S. Thrall, *A Pictorial History of Texas,* 40; San Saba was established in 1757.

tribes. Finally the wise men of the Pueblos "made medicine" and caught the vision of a great chief who was to come from beyond the plains and deliver them from their blood-thirsty foes.

Thereafter the Pueblos journeyed to the western breaks of the plateau once each year and as far out upon the plains as common sense, sharpened by fear of the Comanches, would allow. At the end of their journey they buried with tribal unction and great ceremony the "social fire" brought from their sanctuary in the mountains. This done, they back-trailed to their mountain retreats, setting up stakes to guide the great chief who was expected to come out of the land of the rising sun. Early Spanish explorers are said to have found the stakes and to have named the plateau.[62] For the unimaginative and the coldly practical who wonder how the chief was to find his way to the eastern extremity of the staked trail, the legend does not provide.

The old guides localized the Staked Plains by calling the plains after the rivers that drained them. Around Yellow House Canyon there were *Los Llanos del Casas Amarillas*, around the Running Water, *Los Llanos del Agua Corriente*, and so on. All the country looked much alike to the average man, but in this way the old guides could describe any part of the plains well enough to direct a traveler.[63] A minor creek, the *Atascosa*, gave name to the first little settlement in this section, while *Los Rios Amarillos* provided that for the most prominent to follow. The names of some of the divisions and pastures of the XIT Ranch further illustrate the extent of the Spanish influence.

Where the South Plains vacillate between pampa and rolling sand dune country near the 103rd meridian, there arises one tributary of the Brazos, *Las Casas Amarillas*, the Yellow Houses—the location of one division of the XIT. Near the head of this canyon, which gashes across the South Plains, was an alkaline lake of like designation, an important landmark of the

[62] *The Midland* (Texas) *Gazette*, March 18, 1904.
[63] C. Goodnight to J. E. H., April 8, 1927.

Llanos fifty years ago. Bordering the lake are some high bluffs of yellowish hue, which may be seen at a considerable distance and which from certain points of view have somewhat the appearance of the walls of a great city, "especially when seen through a good mirage." This eerie appearance, coupled with some sheltering caves in the face of the cliff, suggested its name —the Yellow Houses.

Here Captain G. W. Arrington and a squad of Rangers, back from an Indian scout into the sand hills to the southwest, took refuge to escape being frozen to death in a blizzard of 1879.[64] And here too, by tradition, the "entire Sioux nation" came down from the north in the late forties to fight an alliance of the Comanche, Kiowa, and Arapaho Indians. At Casas Amarillas they fell to battle with a vengeance. In 1877, twenty years later, a stone breastwork might be traced crescent-wise upon the brow of the bluff. What more proof should legend demand![65]

Other names distinctly Spanish—*Ojo Bravo, Alamocitos, Las Escarbadas, Rito Blanco,* and *Punta de Agua,* all closely associated with the XIT Ranch—connote adventurous and hopeful *Comancheros,* hard-riding *ciboleros,* and great sheep herds tended by patient *pastores.* Long years have passed since the last of these disappeared, but happily the heritage of names will last down the years.

[64] J. Evetts Haley, "Lore of the Llano Estacado," from *Texas and Southwestern Lore* (Austin, 1927).
[65] Cook, *The Border and the Buffalo,* 208.

CHAPTER III

First Ranches
of the Panhandle-Plains Country

THIS STORY is one of the Texas plains, but the Texas cowboy originated in the southern part of the state. Barely had the Mexican rule been broken when adventurous souls, who rode like drunken Indians and fought like devils, were pushing into the country between the Nueces and the Río Grande, that strip which lay so long as a bone of contention between the two republics. The Mexican *rancheros*, fleeing after the defeat of Santa Anna, left their herds behind them. The Texans, then hating all Mexicans and disregarding the rights of any Mexican to hold property on Texas soil, raided down on these Longhorn cattle of the border, captured them, and began driving them to Louisiana to market. Thus in violent adventure the occupation and name of the Texas cowboy had its beginning.[1]

The Texas cattle industry was just taking form at the end of the Texas Revolution. It assumed definite shape in the forties, and made tremendous expansion between 1850 and 1855.[2] It rapidly pushed back the Indian frontiers of the state to the north and west so that at the outbreak of the Civil War the frontier approximated a direct line from Gainesville in North Texas to Laredo on the Río Grande. During the civil conflict,

[1] J. Evetts Haley, Ms., "A Survey of Texas Cattle Drives to the North, 1866–1895," pp. 51–56 (thesis, University of Texas).
[2] *Ibid.*, 68.

expansion gave place to recession, the frontier line wavered, and in many places fell back before Indian depredations. During this period the cattle industry went into chaos. With the close of the war, men who had won fame with Lee and Terry returned to find their stocks scattered, outlawry rife, government a farce, and their property worthless. Then they took the saddle for the "cow hunt," the rifle and six-shooter for the Indian, and the lariat and a short shrift for the outlaw. They blazed trails one to two thousand miles in length, and, driving millions of Texas cattle before them, extended the pastoral frontier to more northern states and territories. Out of chaos they brought order; out of outlawry, law; and out of poverty, prosperity.

Again the pastoral frontier of Texas pushed out, and, as the decade of the seventies passed the meridian, it pressed against the caprock of the plains. Within a few years, ranches were established upon the Llano Estacado. Almost immediately it was seen that this climate exercised some magic alchemy as cattle grew larger than upon any other occupied Texas range.

When the first "saddle-warmers" reached the plains, the Indian problem, which had worried Texas since the beginning of settlement, was just a thing of the past. Even the Comanches were forced to the reservations, and men with longhorned beef could now possess the land with moderate comfort and little danger.

Before the Panhandle country was settled, Texas cowmen, advancing along the Goodnight Trail, had located ranches through eastern New Mexico from the lower Pecos Valley to the farther waters of the Cimarron. Among those to cross the Raton Range and push into Colorado was Charles Goodnight.[3] He located in Pueblo County on the Arkansas River in 1869, as the first Texan to enter the cattle business in the southern part of that state. There the outlaws became numerous and vicious, and he and other cowmen brought order by vigorous measures, as most of them were vigorous law and order men. Eventually the

[3] W. R. Owen to J. E. H., August 12, 1927; O. H. Nelson to J. E. H., February 26, 1927; James Jones to J. E. H., January 13, 1927; Charles Goodnight to J E. H., November 13, 1926.

country became overstocked and some of the Colorado cowmen looked towards the Texas Panhandle.

Goodnight, again the first to move, was schooled to the frontier. He had scouted over much of the plains country as a Texas Ranger and realized its grazing possibilities. He moved his herd from Pueblo, Colorado, in 1875, and wintered on the Canadian below the site of Tucumcari. Leigh Dyer, the boss of the outfit, was sent to scout out the country to the southeast and choose the best range he could find. A Mexican guide accompanied him, and his own qualities as an excellent frontiersman were supplemented by the counsel of Goodnight, imparted before he left the Canadian.

Dyer rode over much country, chose the Palo Duro, and in November of 1876 the herd of 1,600 head was placed on the new range—a marked event in the history of Northwest Texas. Other seekers of grass rapidly followed. Cattle grew fat on ten thousand hills, and soon the rustler flourished at his chosen calling.

Among the cowmen, Thomas S. Bugbee was the second to come. He left the Arkansas River in extreme western Kansas, and came to settle upon the creek that now bears his name, a few miles from the Canadian.[4] There he built a dugout with a buffalo hide for a door, and he and his cowboys used their six-shooters to keep the buffalo scared off their range, while Goodnight, to the south, was maintaining a line which his cowboys rode daily, turning back from a thousand to fifteen hundred buffaloes, and thus saving the grass for their cattle.[5] Thus the way had been opened from the north, and shortly more cowmen followed.

"Deacon" Bates and David T. Beal, millionaire shoe manufacturers of Boston, felt the lure of the open range, for at that time the bawl of a steer was akin to the jingle of silver. They built up the great LX Ranch with first headquarters on Pitcher Creek, about twenty miles north of the site of Amarillo. Their

[4] T. S. Bugbee to J. E. H., July 17, 1925.
[5] Ms., "Recollections of Charles Goodnight," Panhandle-Plains Historical Society.

range expanded with the growth of their herds, and they sold at the peak of the boom to the American Pastoral Company in 1884, and retreated to their Boston homes to enjoy the culture of the Hub.

To the west, up the river from the LX's, the LIT outfit, owned by George W. Littlefield, a Texas cowman of the old order, came in. His first herd of 3,500 head of Texas cattle was turned loose and the ranch headquarters was established at a dugout about four miles below Tascosa. Soon a Mexican's place on the Cheyenne was bought, and the ranch was then located two miles above the little town.[6] Still farther up the river came Old Man Ellsworth Torrey, another who left the baked beans of Boston for the *frijoles* of Texas. Above him, just inside the Texas line, the LE Ranch was located by W. M. D. Lee and E. A. Reynolds, extensive buyers of buffalo robes and noted Indian traders and freighters of the Southwest.

At the same time cattlemen were settling farther down the river. In 1878, W. T. and G. T. Reynolds came in from Las Animas County, Colorado, wintered on Chicken Creek, and sold their cattle next spring to Charles Goodnight. Hank W. Cresswell, a Canadian and a remarkable character, came from Pueblo County, Colorado, the same year, and located about twenty-five miles east of Adobe Walls to start the well-known Bar C's Ranch.[7] In 1879, R. L. McAnulty came from near Fort Griffin with the Turkey Track brand,[8] later bought out by the Hansford Land and Cattle Company, and W. E. Anderson released his Scissors cattle near by,[9] and started the Adobe Walls Ranch. Huff, Mell, and Frank Wright crowded into the Canadian country of the central Panhandle, farther to the east, Nick Eaton appeared from central Texas during the same year, and Robert Moody trailed in from Colorado to locate near the future site of the town of Canadian with the PO brand.[10]

[6] J. Phelps White to J. E. H., January 15, 1927.

[7] C C   [8] V   [9] ⊶

[10] O. H. Nelson to J. E. H., August 15, 1925; C. Goodnight to J. E. H., September 16, 1927.

As steers long shut in a corral eagerly take to water and grass when the bars are let down, so the cattlemen stampeded into the country along the Canadian. In a few years the adjacent ranges were occupied from New Mexico down into Indian Territory. At first in the Panhandle-Plains country the lines of settlement were scattered, predetermined by the living water supply. Near the northwest corner of the Panhandle a cow camp at Buffalo Springs, maintained by cattlemen along the Cimarron and the Beaver, consisted of some adobes which had been built either by Bill Hall of Kansas City or Dan Taylor of Trinidad, or perhaps by both. There they kept winter line-riders to push back cattle drifting to the south.[11]

To the east of Buffalo Springs, the North Palo Duro loops south into Texas from what was then called No Man's Land, and then swings back to join the Beaver. Berry and Boice located the 777 Ranch along it in 1881.[12] One of the first "improved" herds was that owned by the Snowden brothers from McMullen County, Texas. They settled on Grapevine, a tributary of the Blue, in Sherman County. Just when they came in is a matter of speculation, but they were ahead of Bates and Beal, running the SNO brand upon cattle graded up by good Shorthorn sires. They sold out to the LX's in 1877.[13] In the northeastern corner of the Panhandle the four Bartons—Henry, Clay, Doc, and Dick—ranged a fertile scope of country where nearly ten years later Old Ochiltree was to boom to life with expansive ideas and soaring real estate.

To the south of the Canadian in the eastern Panhandle, Nick T. Eaton, from Central Texas, with the U—U, and Tobe Oden, with the T—T, enjoyed, in the later seventies, the ranges of North Fork and McClellan Creek.[14] Perry LeFors was there with a small herd in 1878, and a great many "little men" exercised the prerogative of squatter sovereignty for their cattle along the valleys of the Washita and the Sweetwater. Among

[11] Dixon, *Life of Billy Dixon*, 136.
[12] O. H. Nelson to J. E. H., August 15, 1925.
[13] James East to J. E. H., September 27, 1927.
[14] O. H. Nelson to J. E. H., August 15, 1925.

them were Henry Frye, Billie Miller, G. W. Arrington, Cape Willingham, Mark Huselby, Henry Fleming, and others who pushed out the borders of settlement and helped to temper the Mobeetie country with law and order.[15]

The year after he helped Goodnight locate the "Old Home Ranch," Leigh Dyer started the first ranch west of it on the Palo Duro, just above its junction with the Tierra Blanca and north of the townsite of Canyon. Here in 1877 he built a log house which stands today, the oldest building in the Panhandle. For several years this place was the extreme western ranch of that country south of the Canadian. Dyer sold it to Jot Gunter, Munson, and Summerfield, and when Summerfield's place was taken by Jule Gunter, it changed from the GMS to the T Anchor Ranch, by which name it is known today.[16]

The first man to range cattle to the south of Dyer was L. G. Coleman, who came from southern Colorado in 1878 and located upon the Tule. The next year he went to Hall County, chose a range along Red River, sold a one-fourth interest in his herd to Dyer, and started the Shoe Bar Ranch under the firm name of Coleman and Company.[17] Curtis and Atkinson released their Diamond Tail cattle [18] on Buck Creek in Hall and Collingsworth counties; Morrison brothers with the Doll Baby brand located near where Giles is; and Alfred and Vincent Rowe, two Englishmen, brought in the RO cattle along the Salt Fork.[19]

Along the base of the Plains south of the Palo Duro the Baker brothers came from the Ratons in 1877 to be the first cowmen of the Quitaque. Their two thousand head, under the

[15] R. A. LeFors to J. E. H., October 24, 1925; O. H. Nelson, "First Panhandle Stockmen's Association," *The Southwest Plainsman* (Amarillo), February 20, 1926.

[16] C. Goodnight to J. E. H., April 8, 1927; W. H. Ingerton to J. E. H., April 13, 1927. The T Anchor brand looked like this: ⊤⊔.

[17] O. H. Nelson to J. E. H., February 26, 1927; S. A. Bull to J. E. H., February 27, 1927.

[18] ◇̆

[19] O. H. Nelson to J. E. H., August 15, 1925.

management of J. Wiren, were in the Lazy F brand.[20] Their
ranch was soon bought by Goodnight and Adair, and became
a part of the JA holdings,[21] which, with the Tule Ranch to the
west, composed the range of one of the greatest pastoral establishments of the West. Colonel McCoy likewise found the
Quitaque country to his liking and brought the Hat brand.[22]
Below the Quitaque, Bob Wiley and Tom Coggins brought
some eight thousand head of cattle to settle in the Matador
country and on a fork of the Pease. They came from the Pecos
in November of 1878 with their Jingle-bob herd—some of John
Chisum's cattle which the owners had taken on a mortgage. The
next year these cattle were bought by Campbell, and the Matador outfit launched into the range business in Texas. In the
spring of 1879, a man named Hall located some eight miles
north of Roaring Springs, and the same year an outfit of four
thousand head, with George Brady as foreman, located on
Tepee Creek.

Early in 1877, before any of these Matador country outfits
came, Charles P. Tasker, a young Pennsylvania spendthrift,
was opening the eyes of old Fort Griffin to lavish ways and having Hank Smith select a site for a ranch in Blanco Canyon.[23]
Smith located the first ranch on the South Plains, and Tasker
gave it the high-sounding name of Hacienda Glorieta. But even
frontier hospitality was at last worn thin by the impositions of
this scion of the smoky atmosphere who rarely if ever paid an
account, and suddenly C. P. Tasker, his Negro coachman, and
his fine hounds left for parts unknown, and Hank Smith exercised his liens and came into possession of this glorious estate—
a cow camp in Blanco Canyon.[24] John and W. B. Slaughter
came to Bull Creek, above Colorado City, in 1878, and moved

[20] ⊓   [21] A

[22] C. Goodnight to J. E. H., September 16, 1927; O. H. Nelson to J. E. H.,
August 15, 1925. The hat brand looked like this: ⋂

[23] Dick Bussell to J. E. H., July 19, 1926.

[24] Letters from C. P. Tasker to H. C. Smith, Panhandle-Plains Historical
Society.

to Crosby County late in the same year, locating just south of Mount Blanco.[25]

Naturally, excellent ranges adjacent to plentiful water were taken first. Back upon the plains where water was scarce, some good ranges lay idle for several years after the beginning of settlement as the illusion of aridity, cherished by Pope and Marcy of presettlement days, was but slowly dispelled. Even as late as 1880, Joseph G. McCoy, the man who opened Abilene, Kansas, as a cattle depot, after a careful examination, declared that not more than seven million acres of the Panhandle were an absolute desert. Yet, at the very time he made his survey, Texas solons were about to trade three millions of acres of this land for a capitol, and men born to the saddle were trailing their herds to those rolling swells of grass.

Up the Tierra Blanca they went, and west along the Tule and the Yellow Houses. The old trail that the Indian traders and buffalo hunters had used from Fort Sumner to Casas Amárillas lifted its eddies of dust to the saddle gait of a cow horse by 1881, as Doak Good and Ben Webb carried the scanty mail from Colorado City to the old fort.[26] They "kept camp" at Portales Spring beneath a natural porch, and Doak raised a small bunch of cattle to supplement his none too bounteous wages. Except for stolen cattle gathered here, either by Indians or such outlaws as Billy the Kid and his gang, and a few drift cattle from the Canadian and the Palo Duro, these were the first to graze the Portales sand hills.

As the buffalo became scarce, a party of hunters pushed up the canyon to the Yellow Houses and pitched camp at a seep spring near by. The Causey brothers, George and John, and another hunter by the name of Frank Lloyd, with their skinners, after having killed and skinned 7,500 buffalo along the Yellow Houses and the Running Water Draws in the winter of 1877, built, in 1879, an adobe camp near the spring.[27] A mere remnant of the once great herds had been driven from its native

[25] W. B. Slaughter to J. E. H., October 9, 1926.
[26] Sid Boykin to J. E. H., June 23, 1927.
[27] Frank Lloyd to J. E. H., August 18, 1927.

haunt along the breaks back into the plains country,[28] and these hunters, holding on after most men had left the range, followed them. Some few remaining hunters killed coyotes, wolves, and skunks for their fur—a really prosaic ending to an epic hunt. This party stopped just long enough to build a little house of sun-dried brick—but permanent. That action represented an entire movement in plains life. It depicted the passing of the transient Indian and hunter; it prophesied the day of settlement. It marked the end of the extreme mobility of the range; it marked the beginning of the era of homes.

Meanwhile the ranges of the Sweetwater country were becoming crowded—as they always became when someone settled within an easy day's ride of the old-timers who craved some forty miles of "elbow room"—and Jim Newman came to the Yellow Houses and bought the buffalo camp for sixty dollars. Since it had been built on what was known as the Capitol Tract, of course Newman bought no land, but he paid for the house and the intangible "range rights" which belonged to the original settlers by virtue of priority. He turned his herd of 1,054 head loose on the Fourth of July, 1882, and held his range until the XIT began fencing. In the spring of 1886 he moved his cattle to the Salt Lake Ranch, about twenty miles east and north of Portales.[29]

The year before the Causeys moved to the Yellow Houses they built a sod house on a tributary of the canyon, which has since been known as Sod House Draw. About the time Newman arrived, the Estes boys—Green, Tant, and Sanders—brought their herd to that range and kept bachelors' camp in the little sod house, moving south about 1885 as the XIT began fencing. By 1882 a Las Vegas outfit owned by a man named Lynch had located at Spring Lake, which later became the headquarters of the largest division of the XIT.

Some of the first settlers along the Canadian in the XIT range held over until the ranch began to stock. In 1882 when

[28] C. Goodnight to J. E. H., September 3, 1927.
[29] Sid Boykin to J. E. H., June 23, 1927.

A. C. Babcock, one of the original owners, examined the land to check the report made upon the tract by State Commissioner N. L. Norton, he found several outfits running cattle upon the XIT range—Terry's, Simpson's, the LIT, the LE, the LS, and others.[30]

Among the interesting characters of every frontier are a few who live by barter. The traders, the early merchants, of the western Panhandle were not exceptions, and two stores upon and adjacent to XIT lands were once interesting landmarks, but are now forgotten. To the southeast was one run by "Old Man" George W. Singer. He came west in 1879, catering to the buffalo hunters yet upon the range. At the last water in the Yellow House Canyon, two and one-half miles northwest of the site of Lubbock, Singer made camp and built a store some eighteen feet square.

Besides being the head of running water on the Yellow House Canyon, this point was at the crossing of two military roads, one from Fort Sumner, New Mexico, to Fort Griffin, and the other from Fort Concho to Fort Elliott. A few travelers along these trails contributed to his business. About the same time a Frenchman by the name of DeQuazy built a store a hundred yards from him. Supplies came from Fort Griffin prior to 1882, and later from Colorado City. This humble mercantile house of Singer's was known far and wide as "Old Man" Singer's Store.

When the cowboys pushed up the canyon with their cattle, he was there. When the roundups drew to a close and jingling spurs struck music from the floor of his store, "Old Man" Singer was in his glory. Pack horses were hobbled out, bed rolls thrown upon the floor, and when night came the old man left the cowboys in charge and went to bed. Until far in the morning the good old game of poker held forth in earnest. When a cowboy's money was gone, which did not take long, he reached up and pulled down a box of stick candy or a plug of tobacco from a shelf, "sweetened the pot," and the game went on. As

[30] Prospectus, *3,000,000 Acres of Land in the Panhandle of Texas,* 21.

others went broke, down came a pair of California pants to be bet against a couple of shirts. Singer appeared in the morning after the struggle was over. Never did a padlock fasten his door, and never was his confidence betrayed to the loss of a cent by these men who gambled in zest but who would have shot at a word.[31]

Another frontier store of note was that owned by two Germans, the Sperling brothers. They came to the western Panhandle by 1880 and settled on Trujillo Creek to start the little settlement by that name, to contend with the Mexican toughs who gave life to the near-by plaza of Salinas, and to sell out their property to Lee and Reynolds, who, late in 1880 or early in 1881, started the LS ranch.[32]

If the western Panhandle had been as well watered as the eastern portion, its settlement would have taken place more rapidly and many cowmen would have been upon its ranges before the XIT was stocked, in spite of the fact that the Capitol Reservation was rapidly becoming patented land. But the barbed wire fence was drawing its prickly lines across the open range, and the days of free grass and drifting herds were coming to a stormy close. Eastern and foreign capital had been attracted to the cow country, and the Panhandle was getting its share.

In no section of the world has the pastoral pursuit of cattle raising flared to a more magnificent scale than here, when the Prairie and Hansford cattle companies, the JA's, the Matadors, the Spurs, the American Pastoral Company, and others were "cornering" staggering amounts of land and counting their cattle by the tens of thousands. It was the day of enthusiastic appraisal, of "book count," of hasty investments and leisurely repentance. And then, as most of the companies were floundering in the net of speculation which they had helped to spread, the XIT Ranch, generally recognized as the largest in the United States, began to stock its ranges.

[31] R. C. Burns to J. E. H., September 23, 1927; J. B. Mobley to J. E. H., September 23, 1927; Sid Boykin to J. E. H., June 23, 1927.
[32] James H. East to J. E. H., October 8, 1927.

CHAPTER IV

The State Capitol and Its Builders

As the cattle frontier of Texas pushed west and north, as immigrants poured into the state to convert grazing land into fields, as the railroads replaced the freight trails and promoted commerce, the functions of the state government enlarged, and the growing need of adequate state buildings at Austin became apparent. The one expedient of meeting the need of a magnificent state house was through the reservation of state-owned lands as a building endowment. At the Constitutional Convention assembled in Austin, J. R. Fleming of Comanche offered a resolution on November 1, 1875, "requesting the Committee on Public Lands and Land Office to consider the propriety of setting apart five million acres of the public domain for the purpose of building a State Capitol." [1]

There is no telling what might have stood on Capitol Hill had this resolution carried, but five million acres for a state capitol would have been more than Texas needed.

Ten days later W. H. Stewart, of Galveston, offered a similar resolution but pared the amount to 3,000,000 acres. The Committee on State Affairs reported recommending an ordinance "substantially embodying the second resolution," and after one attempt to increase the figure to the first amount, and another to decrease it to 1,000,000 acres, it passed the convention on November 17, by a vote of 48 to 14. The constitution

[1] *Report of the Capitol Building Commissioners,* 3.

containing this section was submitted to the people of Texas late in November, and ratified at an election in February, 1876.[2]

This provision opened the way for legislative action, but the mill ground slowly and it was not until February 20, 1879, that a law was passed appropriating 3,050,000 acres, and on April 18 the act to provide for the actual building went through.[3] N. L. Norton, of Salado, was appointed commissioner to supervise the survey of the Capitol Reservation, which consisted of over 5,000,000 acres lying in Dallam, Hartley, Oldham, Deaf Smith, Parmer, Castro, Lamb, Bailey, Cochran, and Hockley counties, beginning at the northwest corner of the Panhandle and extending south adjacent to the New Mexico line for over two hundred miles.[4] From this reservation 3,050,000 acres were to be selected.

The law provided for a board to be composed of the Governor, O. M. Roberts, the Comptroller, the Treasurer, the Attorney General, and the Commissioner of the General Land Office to contract for the survey of these lands. Roberts wrote Norton in the summer of 1879, instructing him to bear "in mind the fact that first-class arable land cannot probably be secured in any large amounts and that all land available for pasturage should be secured." Norton was to exercise such discretion as to secure the "best land in the reserve for the State,"[5] and he was to prepare a report indicating the character of the soil, topography, and water, or "nearest water," of each league surveyed.[6]

The board, as provided by law, advertised for bids for surveying the land into league tracts.[7] Twenty were submitted. These ranged from approximately $6,000 to $37,500. The lowest bidder failed to provide bond, whereupon the contract was let to the next lowest, J. T. Munson, an able man schooled in law, who had come from Illinois to launch into business at Deni-

[2] *Ibid.*, 4.   [3] *Ibid.*, 4–9.

[4] *Ibid.*, 4; Prospectus, *3,000,000 Acres of Land in the Panhandle of Texas,* 3.

[5] *Report*, 7.   [6] *Ibid.*, 5.   [7] *Ibid.*, 7.

The Capitol of Texas
built in exchange for 3,000,000 acres of land
(Mears photograph)

C. B. Farwell

Spring Lake Headquarters

John V. Farwell, Sr.

The grass on the original range

Abner Taylor

XIT General Headquarters at Channing

A. G. Boyce

son. His bid was $7,440.[8] Norton and the surveying party set out in the fall of 1879,[9] but were forced to abandon their field work because of a drouth. They resumed operations the following spring, and the report, with field notes and maps, was in the Land Office early in September, 1880.[10]

Wandering bands of Indians sometimes crossed the plains at that late day, and outlaws maintained strongholds in some few remote spots. Therefore the provision made for protection of the surveyors may have been a wise one.[11] In returning to their work in the spring of 1880, the party, of which A. G. Wiley was head surveyor, came upon the High Plains by Blanco Canyon. A detail of five Texas Rangers was sent forward with it. By the first of May they reached the Canadian and work was renewed. Good water was not always plentiful and recourse to the alkali lakes was sometimes necessary. Pits were dug at a distance from the lakes, and the water that filtered through the sand was hardly so brackish. At one time the surveyor's horses became mixed with a band of mustangs and, if they had not been both hobbled and sidelined, would have been driven off by the mustangs.[12]

Late in January, 1881, Commissioner Norton submitted his report to the board.[13] The tract was not cut into sections, but divided into Spanish leagues of 4,428 acres each.

Fifty thousand acres of the reservation were provided to meet the costs of surveying. By the law of 1879 it was the duty of the board to sell the lands for cash, or one-fourth cash and the remainder in annual quarterly payments, "in such size tracts as will enable them [the board] to realize for the whole reservation the best price possible." None of the land was to be sold for less than fifty cents an acre.[14] Bids upon these fifty thousand acres were received December 10, 1880. The bidders were privileged to specify the boundaries of the land, but the board reserved the right to reject any bid. The great boom of the cattle industry had not gained sufficient force to create a

[8] *Ibid.*, 7.   [9] Prospectus, 3.   [10] *Report*, 8.   [11] *Ibid.*, 4.
[12] *Frontier Times*, August, 1925, 14.
[13] *Report*.   [14] *Ibid.*, 5–6.

decided demand for the lands, and only two bids were received. Both were rejected. Again the land was advertised and sold to the only bidder for fifty-five and one-half cents an acre,[15] which was actually an excellent price at the time.

Eleven building plans for the capitol were submitted. N. Le Brun, an architect of New York City, was engaged as an expert to recommend the best design, and after a study of the plans he chose that of E. E. Myers, of Detroit. His selection was endorsed by the building commissioners, Joseph Lee and N. L. Norton, and approved by the Capitol Board on the seventh of May, 1881.[16]

On the ninth of November of the same year the old capitol burned, making imperative the need that had been urgent. The first day of January, 1882, was set for bids for the new building. Mattheas Schnell of Rock Island, Illinois, and A. A. Burck of Rockdale, Texas, were the only bidders, and the contract was awarded to the first, ten days later, upon the presentation of $250,000 bond.[17] In return for the building he contracted to erect, he was to receive the 3,000,000 acres of land.

In accordance with the contract, dirt was broken on the first day of February, 1882,[18] though the first building material was not placed upon the ground until eleven months later.[19] With the consent of the state, Schnell assigned a three-fourths interest in the contract to Taylor, Babcock and Company, composed of Abner Taylor, A. C. Babcock, John V. Farwell, and Charles B. Farwell, of Chicago. On May 9, 1882, he assigned the remaining one-fourth, and in June this company reassigned its interest to Abner Taylor as its representative, "the more effectually and properly to carry out the provisions of the said contract," [20] with the Farwells standing as sureties.[21]

[15] This land was located in Oldham County and netted $27,750, one-half of which was placed to the credit of the common school fund, as provided by the law. *Ibid.*, 8–9.

[16] *Ibid.*, 13–21.   [17] *Ibid.*, 29–31.   [18] *Ibid.*, 52.

[19] *Third Biennial Report of the Capitol Building Commissioners*, 89.

[20] *Report*, 31 and 181.

[21] Taylor, Babcock & Co. to N. L. Norton, June 9, 1882, XIT Papers, Panhandle-Plains Museum, Canyon, Texas.

This matter of building the Texas state house was no easy undertaking. The company was forced to build a short railroad to the quarries in Burnet County, and when work began upon the capitol, enough American masons were not available. The contractors sent to Scotland for granite experts and then found themselves in the United States court charged with importing labor under contract.[22]

The cornerstone was laid on the forty-ninth anniversary of Texan Independence, March 2, 1885. This stone of red Texas granite, weighing 16,000 pounds in the rough, had been hauled fifteen miles from the quarries to Burnet by fifteen yoke of oxen, and shipped by rail to Austin. Past and present commingled in the transportation of this stone. Before a large gathering of notables it was slipped into place, and the symbolic trowel of a Mason cut away the excess mortar.[23]

By the original contract the building was to be delivered to the state on or before January 1, 1888. But changes in specifications necessitated an extension of the time, and it was not completed until the middle of April.[24]

Original estimates of its cost were placed at about $1,500,-000,[25] but the materials and labor alone totaled $3,744,630.60.[26] The Syndicate Company did not have to bear all this expense, but its expenditures reached the sum of $3,224,593.45,[27] for which full title was given to the 3,000,000 acres of land, a certain per cent being conveyed as the work progressed.

By contract the state bound itself "to convey . . . the complete and perfect title" to this land.[28] Then, when patents to the first leagues were issued, a charge of fifteen dollars each was made. Abner Taylor wrote to the Capitol Board, pointing out the fact that this was a breach of the contract. That body

[22] Forrest Crissey, "The Vanishing Range," *The Country Gentleman*, March 1, 1913, p. 3.

[23] *Third Biennial Report,* 88–89.   [24] *Fourth Biennial Report,* 105.

[25] Crissey, "The Vanishing Range," *The Country Gentleman*, March 1, 1913, p. 3.

[26] *Final Report Capitol Building Commissioners,* 3.

[27] Transcript from office of Capitol Reservation Lands, Chicago.

[28] *Report,* 5, 101.

unanimously adopted a resolution, which was submitted to Governor Ireland, recommending the refund of these fees and their discontinuance in the future.[29] Somewhere amid the convenient mazes of administration this resolution must have been lost, for the company paid over $10,000 for the title to its land, because the state had not time to check up its loose business items.

The capitol is an imposing structure, said to be second only to the Capitol at Washington among the state houses, and, for a long time, it was claimed to be seventh among the world's largest buildings. It is 566.5 feet long, and over 288 feet wide. It is taller than the Capitol at Washington, towering 311 feet from the grade line to the top of the symbolic figure of justice surmounting the dome.

There was, no doubt, criticism of the legislature for the passage of the original law. Soon after letting the contract, the Capitol Board offered this defense, sound enough in logic and history:

The few criticisms which have occasionally appeared on the policy of this appropriation have generally come from those who originally pronounced the reservation a desert waste, and the effort to utilize it in exchange for a consideration of value as little better than fraud. It is safe to say that these lands have been sold for more than the rate established by law for similar lands. . . . The risk of creating a monopoly . . . in authorizing the sale or exchange of these lands in a body is not greater than that taken by former Legislatures, which have gratuitously bestowed multiplied millions of acres of the same domain on railroad and other corporations. The Capitol lands will represent money actually expended in a business venture. . . . It is, therefore, to the interest of the contractors to sustain and advance the value of these lands by every proper expedient. This can be done more effectually and speedily by a strong syndicate personally interested, than by the . . . State. It is clear that any increase in the value of the Capitol lands . . . will appreciate other Texas realty in a corresponding degree. The building of the Capitol may, then, be regarded as a profitable business engagement for Texas; and the Constitution

[29] *Fourth Biennial Report,* 9–11.

could have devised no more effective means for the development of the material resources of the State.[30]

Thus, despite the possible political aspect of their defense, we may credit the board with some little appreciation of the significance of this biggest land swap in Texas history. As to relative values, it is worthwhile to look again at the record.

On the second call for bids on the survey tract of 50,000 acres, the highest bidder offered 55.5 cents an acre. This was a better price than the state had been realizing on its western lands. But in the end the Capitol Syndicate Company paid to Texas more than double this price. Only a few years previously Gunter and Munson, surveyors of and dealers in land, were buying certificates issued by the Reconstruction government and were locating land in the Panhandle to which the certificates entitled the holders. It is said that they paid only $16 per certificate and each certificate called for a section of land. Goodnight understood that Munson returned to Illinois, raised $100,000 and bought up every unlocated certificate that was on the market. Assuming that he spent the entire amount, he had in his possession 4,000,000 acres of land.

As late as 1883, Goodnight bought 170,000 acres for twenty cents an acre. When the contract with the Capitol Syndicate was made, almost any land in the Panhandle away from water could have been bought for twenty-five cents, while Gunter and Munson were selling well-watered land along the Canadian for fifty cents an acre, "and glad to get it." [31]

Thus, while the original estimate of the cost of the capitol was a million and a half, the actual cost made the 3,000,000 acres of land come to practically $1.07 an acre, about twice as much as the state had been offered in competitive bidding for the best-watered and choicest part of the 3,050,000 acres set aside for building the capitol, and four times the price at which unwatered lands were selling. Some citizens unversed in simple calculation prated that Texas had *given* away her birthright,

[30] *Report*, 50–51.
[31] C. Goodnight to J. E. H., September 3, 1927.

and worried themselves into a ferment over the dangers of a land monopoly.

Meanwhile the Capitol Building Commissioners reported that

The design which has been secured for the Texas Capitol, combining, as it does, all the essential elements of proportion, dignity, size, adaptability, and modern improvement, is believed to be a fair reflex of the enlightenment of our age. As such we respectfully commend it to the people of Texas.[32]

Over forty years later the Texas Legislature passed a resolution addressed to Mr. John V. Farwell, Jr., expressing the gratitude of Texas for the "magnificent and splendid Capitol" which the company erected.

Development of the ranch was started before the capitol was complete. The men developing the ranch had helped transform Chicago from an overgrown western town into a metropolis. With but two of these is this story primarily concerned. Among the English families of the seventeenth century to come to America was one by the name of Farwell, which settled to farming near Painted Post, New York, and became financially independent. Among the children born from the union of Henry Farwell and Nancy Jackson were two sons named Charles B. (1823) and John Villiers (1825).

In July, 1838, the Farwell family left Big Flats, New York, in a covered wagon, and joined the westward migration to Illinois. They passed through Chicago and settled in Ogle County, again to follow the plow.[33] In Chicago, May 24, 1900, at a banquet honoring Queen Victoria, John V. Farwell, the guest of honor and the principal speaker, told of that trip:

It was my privilege to see Chicago in July, 1838, from the deck of a prairie schooner. We entered the then incipient city of say 3,000 people, via the Michigan Avenue–Lake Shore Drive, then a succession of sand ridges. . . . Being bent on a farming life, we

[32] *Report,* 49–50.
[33] John V. Farwell to Samuel H. Roberts, June 28, 1927.

commenced our westward journey in said prairie schooner and passed over the Chicago river at Randolph St., on a ferry boat, little thinking that within seven years I should come back to Chicago for a permanent home.[34]

John V. and C. B. Farwell grew to manhood in Illinois on a farm of 160 acres. Then they entered Chicago and for years were associated in what eventually became an immense mercantile business. They were in their sixties when they undertook, with business colleagues, the experiment of developing the 3,-000,000-acre Capitol Tract upon the frontier of Texas. Colonel A. C. Babcock, of Canton, and his son-in-law, Colonel Abner Taylor, of Chicago, were the other members of the Taylor, Babcock Company.[35] Their first act towards establishing a ranch was to order a careful inspection of the land they were to receive.

[34] *Reminiscences of John V. Farwell* (by his elder daughter), 17–18 (Chicago, Ralph Fletcher Seymour, 1928).
[35] "The Capitol Syndicate or XIT Ranch," 1, Chicago files.

CHAPTER V

Babcock's Inspection
and the Texas–New Mexico Boundary

THE CAPITOL COMPANY assumed the contract to build the
state house without so much as inspecting the land it was to
receive. Notwithstanding the fact that the contractors were
hard-headed businessmen, they evidently reposed exceptional
confidence in Commissioner Norton's report. However, inquiries
for ranches and lands at once poured in upon them, and A. C.
Babcock was soon on his way to make a thorough inspection of
the Capitol Tract.

Through the influence of Senator Charles B. Farwell, Babcock carried a letter from General Sheridan to the commanding
officer at Fort Elliott, on the eastern border of the Panhandle.
It secured for him a four-mule ambulance, a wagon, wall tent,
and camp equipage. Thus supplied, he took the trail for Tascosa, a rollicky little cow-town in Oldham County. There he
sought W. S. Mabry, surveyor for the Oldham County Land
District, for whom he had a letter of introduction from A. W.
Spaight, commissioner of insurance and statistics for Texas.
Mabry agreed to help inspect the lands. They added a two-
mule wagon to the equipment, hired some cowboys to help with
the work, and a Mexican to do the cooking.[1]

Babcock wished to start his inspection of the tract from the

[1] W. S. Mabry, Ms., "Recollections of XIT Ranch," 1–2, Chicago files.

north end. Upon learning that Buffalo Springs was near the northwest corner of the Panhandle, the party of ten men, not one of whom had been there, set out for the place. Though Mabry was surveyor of the district that included most of the counties of the western Panhandle, he was late from Alabama and wholly unacquainted with the region. However, he had a transcript of the surveyor's field notes of each league of the tract, and once the initial starting point of the reservation surveyor was found, the lines of the leagues could be followed out. The notes upon League Number 1 described it as beginning of the northwest corner of the state, as established by the John H. Clark survey of 1859.

The cowboys on their saddle horses, Babcock in his ambulance, the Mexican cook, Felix, driving his mess wagon, and the four-mule wagon with the necessary equipage set out from Tascosa along the road that led to Springer, New Mexico, March 23, 1882. They turned northwest at the Punta de Agua and for some distance made fair progress with their unwieldy outfit. Between Tramperas and Perico creeks the party came into a heavy belt of sand, where the bumpy sagegrass and the sand hills made travel extremely difficult. The man with the least experience is usually the first to fear that he is lost.

Here Colonel Babcock lost faith in me as a guide [Mabry wrote] and he became very restless and impatient and asked a great many questions as to how far it was to Buffalo Springs, questions we could not answer. After a very tedious and tiresome day pulling through this heavy sand with our unwieldy outfit, we made a dry camp in the sand hills, put up the wall tent for the Colonel and made him as comfortable as possible, but he was so impressed with the idea that we were lost I don't think that he slept any that night. He was a poor sleeper at best. The next morning we lost several hours over our maps. He wanted to be shown on the map what league we were camped on, which could not be done as we had found no corner by which we could locate our position. After much talk Vivian and I left camp horseback to find Buffalo Springs.

About mid-afternoon they reached the place. The Prairie Land and Cattle Company had a camp there in an adobe house, and kept two cowboys to ride the range and look after their cattle that grazed the northern end of the Capitol Tract. Neither cowboy was there, but a quarter of a beef was hanging near, coffee and bread were in the house, and soon the two had a hot meal. After feeding their horses, they started back to report that the Springs were found.

We knew from our course up [Mabry wrote], that the Colonel's camp must be about due south; so on our return we took a south course. It soon became dark and we needed some guide . . . so I told Vivian to ride south two or three hundreds yards and place himself in line with me and the north star, when he did this I selected a star due south of him, knowing it could not move enough in the distance we had to go to throw us much off of the course . . . one could watch the star and the other the lay of the land we had to travel over. As we rode along we wondered whether everyone in camp would be asleep and the camp dark, and that we might pass near . . . and not see it. About ten o'clock much to our delight a light loomed up in the distance. Changing our course but little we rode straight to . . . our camp. Everyone asleep but the Colonel. He had not even considered going to bed. He was so pleased with the news we brought him, that we had found Buffalo Springs and could land him there safely the next day, that he got out a bottle of Chapin & Gore's best and made us a long toddy, which seemed just what we needed. We spent about half an hour in pleasant conversation and went to bed happy.[2]

From the Springs, Babcock struck out northwest across a plains region almost devoid of landmarks in search of the northwest corner of the state, as established by Clark and "adopted by J. T. Munson, the contract surveyor for the capitol lands." In 1859 Clark had marked the corner, supposedly the intersection of the 103rd meridian with the 36°–30′ parallel, by digging a circular trench and setting up a large cedar post. Babcock came upon a sandstone post, the corner established by

[2] *Ibid.*, 2–4.

the survey of Richard O. Chaney and William W. Smith, who had sectionized No Man's Land in 1881.

Evidently this was not the point established by Clark, and, with further search, his location was at last found 4,131.5 varas west and 131 varas south of the sandstone post. Mabry had no way of deciding which was the true location, but he pointed out the significance of the two corners to Babcock. They knew that Munson began his survey from the Clark corner, but should, in the future, the Chaney-Smith corner be established as the true one and the 103rd meridian projected south from it as the western boundary of Texas, then a strip of land more than two miles wide and about three hundred and ten miles long would be cut off and placed in New Mexico.[3]

It is an open and gently rolling country, and Munson's lines were easily followed. Babcock rode in his ambulance with Norton's report spread out before him. An odometer, attached to a wheel of the ambulance, indicated to the party where to stop and look for the corner of the next league. As they moved along, a mounted man was sent out a mile or two to either side to return and report the character of the land. In this way, practically the entire tract was inspected and each league compared with the description given in the report Norton had made. The limits of the tract seemed a little erratic in places, since Norton had rejected about fourteen leagues in Dallam and a strip of land in Bailey and Lamb counties because of a belt of sand hills.[4]

Colonel Babcock was unused to camp life. His wall tent was set up every night with a Sibley stove to warm it and drive away the evening chill of the High Plains. Instead of rolling his bed upon the ground as the others did, he slept on a cot. "Before leaving Chicago he bought a large drummer's trunk . . . filled . . . it with a great variety of canned goods, such as boneless chicken, canned beef, canned cheese of various kinds, and a good supply of crackers. . . . At each meal a camp table was set for the Colonel, in his tent." He wanted Mabry

[3] *Ibid.*, 4–5.   [4] *Ibid.*, 5–7.

and Vivian to eat with him, but they, with a better knowledge of the democratic niceties of western camp life, declined the invitation, reminding him that they would eat up his store of delicacies and that they were accustomed "to eating around the campfire."

C. B. Vivian, a one-armed cowboy who was clerk of Oldham County at the time, "was familiar with camp life . . . had seen a good deal of the world, and was an entertaining, useful fellow in camp." Vivian saw to it that the Colonel's table was reinforced with edibles from the campfires of the boys. Vivian was an expert at broiling a steak, and he carefully laid in a supply of wood to use as the party traveled through what was, for the most part, a timberless country, while cow chips, gathered in sacks as the party passed along, furnished fuel for many meals prepared by Felix. But

the Colonel had a very strong dislike for anything cooked with cowchips [Mabry said]. His dislike for this fuel furnished the camp with a good deal of amusement and they soon began to refer to it as Babcock coal. He was a very early riser, was up every morning before daylight with lantern lit, calling the cook and getting the men up to feed the teams, so we could get an early start. This early rising and watching the cook so closely gave him a disgust and dislike for Felix . . . and he got so he would not eat anything . . . Felix cooked. He was not cleanly enough to suit the Colonel. I do not know what he would have done had it not been for Vivian and his trunk of canned goods. In the best regulated establishments it is not best to watch the cook too closely. We have to take our food largely on faith. The balance of us thought Felix was a good cook. His sour dough rolls cooked in a Dutch oven were excellent. They would rise until they would almost lift the lid off the oven, [were] thoroughly done and brown and had a very appetizing odor.

As his prejudice toward Felix grew, Colonel Babcock reached the point where he would eat nothing that the Mexican prepared. But after a month in camp his appetite improved, and one day on the South Plains, he called Mabry into the tent and said in a low voice: "Go out there and get me two or three of those rolls and bring them in here, but don't you let that Mexican cook know you are getting them for me." The incident furnished the boys no little amusement and proves that active camp life finally spurs the appetite past the point of fastidiousness.[5]

The inspection came to an end at the Yellow Houses in Hockley County, April 27, 1882, thirty-six days after the party left Tascosa. It had traveled over 950 miles to inspect all the land except that in Castro County and to find that Norton's report "as to soil, grass, water, timber, rock, and shelter" was correct.[6]

The party met the veteran hunters, George and John Causey, in their camp at the Yellow Houses, but the only buffalo seen on the trip were two calves that these hunters had captured and kept in their corral. Babcock continued south to the fresh and extreme frontier village of Colorado City, there to take the train for Chicago. The others drove back to enjoy the urban advantages of Tascosa and quench the accumulated thirsts of a month.[7]

Aside from verifying Norton's report in respect to the lands, Babcock discovered discrepancies in the surveys of the western boundary of Texas. In 1850, Texas, then a state, relinquished her claims to land in eastern New Mexico, western Kansas, and southern Colorado for the consideration of $10,-000,000. She accepted the 103rd meridian and the parallel of 36°–30' as the western and northern boundaries of the Panhandle.[8] Therefore the northwest corner of Texas was formed by the intersection of these lines. This intersection was first established by Colonel Joseph E. Johnston in 1857, but the boundary was not surveyed.

In July, 1858, John H. Clark was appointed as a federal commissioner and surveyor to aid in establishing this boundary, while William B. Scurry was appointed to represent Texas and

[5] *Ibid.*, 6–7. [6] Prospectus, 21. [7] Mabry, "Recollections," 7.
[8] *Report No. 1186,* 59 Cong., 1 sess., pp. 1–2; *House Reports,* Vol. I, February 13, 1906. Henry Gannett, *Boundaries of the United States* (third edition); *Bulletin No. 226,* Series F., Geography 37, Washington, 1904.

assist him. Clark worked east from the vicinity of El Paso, marking the 32nd parallel to its intersection with the 103rd meridian, roughly north of the site of Kermit, Texas. He then turned north and surveyed the 103rd for about twenty miles. Upon running short of water, he gave up the work from that end of the line in May.

About that time sectionalism seems to have penetrated to that isolated portion of the wilderness and caused trouble before the Civil War broke. Partisanship found zealous champions in Anson Mills, Scurry's principal assistant, and John E. Weyss, topographer of the Clark party, and such a serious quarrel took place that the Texans withdrew and refused to take part in the further marking of the boundary.[9]

Clark then went up the Pecos through New Mexico, crossed to Rabbit Ear Creek, and in September, 1859, located the northwest corner of the state. He ran a line 156 miles south, when, it is said, his water gave out again and the Indians became so troublesome that he withdrew.[10] This left a gap of about 130 miles between the ends of his two lines. He made his report, which, on account of the impending war, was not adopted, and for a while the boundary question was completely lost to sight. Again in 1874, John J. Major, and in 1881, Richard O. Chaney, made locations for the northwest corner of the state, but no two of these four different locations agreed.[11]

In 1882, after Babcock saw not only possibilities but probabilities of litigation over these various locations, he had Mabry write letters to Governor O. M. Roberts of Texas and Senator C. B. Farwell "explaining in detail the confusion as to the proper location" of this corner,[12] but no decisive action was taken until nearly ten years later.

Then Clark's survey of the 103rd meridian was approved by Congress through an act passed March 4, 1891, with Senator C. B. Farwell and Colonel Abner Taylor, both in Congress

[9] *Bulletin,* United States Geological Survey, No. 194, Series F., Geography 30, Washington, 1902, pp. 14–21.

[10] John V. Farwell to Col. R. D. Bowen, July 7, 1926.

[11] Mabry, "Recollections," 1–2.   [12] *Ibid.,* 5.

at that time, taking an active part in passing the bill. The Chaney corner, about two and one-fourth miles east of Clark's, had not been established in 1880 when Munson surveyed the Capitol lands. Except for this, Munson might have started his survey from that point, in which case Farwell and Taylor would have had no interest in the Clark survey, nor in saving this land to the state of Texas, and the strip from 36°–30', the northwest corner of the Panhandle, to the 32nd parallel might have gone to New Mexico.[13]

But the boundary question was not settled. It developed from later surveys that Clark's line, as approved by Congress in 1891, was not the 103rd meridian, but lay about one-half mile west of it. In selling her lands and in deeding the Capitol Reservation to the Farwells, Texas naturally made her assignments by the Munson survey, which started from Clark's initial corner. Thus, when the Capitol Company began selling portions of the XIT Ranch prior to 1910, there seemed to the sellers, who received the land direct from the state, and to the buyers, no chance of flaw in the title, no question of equity.

But now, to add to the confusion, it was found that besides the failure of Clark to run his line along the meridian, there was a discrepancy in his two lines as run from north and south. The line he ran from the north and the one he ran from the south, neither of which was completed, did not coincide and would not have met had they been projected. The Syndicate sent James D. Hamlin to Washington in the interest of an equitable settlement of the boundary question in 1907, and he attended every session of Congress until 1911, when the matter was finally settled. Shortly before New Mexico sought admission as a state, Congressman Stephens from Texas introduced a bill having for its purpose the connecting of the two ends of Clark's surveys by a diagonal. It failed to pass.

Then the New Mexico constitutional convention of 1910 took up the issue. It contended that the eastern boundary of the state, as then established, was not upon the true 103rd

[13] *Ibid.*, 8.

meridian, but west of it "a little over to considerably less than 3 miles," and that the land between the two lines "of right" belonged to New Mexico.[14]

William H. Andrews, as territorial delegate in Congress from New Mexico, engineered the introduction of an "enabling act" for the purpose of making his territory a state. On June 20, 1910, the Enabling Act was approved, but the New Mexico constitution had not been submitted to the President. Among its provisions was a statement of the boundaries. Andrews knew that the boundary, as already established, was not the 103rd meridian, but this bill so designated the eastern boundary of New Mexico. Thus at last it looked as though this strip of land would be taken from the Texas owners, placed in New Mexico, and, as generally understood, left vacant and open to filling. The Capitol Company took action that saved for Texas this strip, one-half mile wide and more, and 310 miles long, and thereby saved its owners much litigation. John V. Farwell, in a letter to R. D. Bowen, of Texas, gave an account of how the question was finally settled:

When we discovered what this would mean to the State of Texas and to ourselves, we communicated with Senator Bailey, Senator Culberson and Congressman Stephens, and also wrote to Speaker of the House Joseph G. Cannon. While Congressman Stephens was much interested, we got no satisfactory response from any of the other gentlemen. I, therefore, had our attorneys, Tenney, Harding & Sherman, make up a brief of our case, which I took to Washington, and showed to President Taft. . . . I had known Mr. Taft very well during our undergraduate days at Yale, and had kept up my friendship with him ever since.

I met him . . . at the White House, and told him I knew he was always interested in preventing unnecessary litigation, and that I had a case in which I thought he could be of great service along that line, if I were right in my contention. I then told him the . . . facts, and gave him the documents covering them. I said to him that we only wanted what was right, and if he thought we

[14] *House Report* No. 1883, 61 Cong., 3 sess., p. 4.

were not right in our contention we would make no further protest to the proposed legislation. . . .

He said he would be glad to read over the documents, and let me know his position later on. . . .

He telephoned me the next morning, saying he would like to have me meet himself, two senators from Texas, Representative Andrews and Congressman Stephens, at the Cabinet Room of the White House, at about eleven o'clock. . . . When I got there, these gentlemen were all present, and President Taft stated the case as I had represented it to him, and said as a judge he had decided many such cases, and he had gone over the question very, very carefully, and had come to the conclusion that our Company was right—that it was an outrage for New Mexico to attempt to get this land away from Texas, and, as far as he knew, nobody had made any particular effort to prevent it, up to date. Representative Andrews then said he would do anything the President wanted. President Taft inferred that he had not done very much as yet to show a right disposition towards the question. Stephens explained his Bill and his position.

The President then said he was going to direct Attorney-General Wickersham to draw up a special message to Congress, which would provide that, when this Enabling Act was passed, the eastern boundary of New Mexico should be on the original line of the survey made by Clark, except in that portion where the two lines did not meet, and that a joint commission of the United States and Texas should decide where the diagonal connecting these lines should be.[15]

The message was sent and the bill passed with these provisions. President Taft wrote Mr. Farwell upon its passage, February 18, 1911, that he was "glad the Texas–New Mexico boundary business went through." The old school tie had really helped.

The joint resolution in regard to the boundary was approved on February 16, 1911. It declared that the United States and Texas had patented land along the line of the John H. Clark survey, and any provision of the constitution of New

[15] John V. Farwell to Col. R. D. Bowen, July 7, 1926.

Mexico that "in any way tends to annul or change the boundary lines between the State of Texas and Territory or State of New Mexico shall be of no force or effect." [16] Thus the Capitol Syndicate was largely instrumental in the settlement of the boundary controversy with New Mexico.

It was not a disinterested matter for the Capitol Company and other land owners, but it was a question of considerable importance to Texas and should have commanded the active interest of her senators and congressmen. And, while all mixed up in Babcock's mind with cow chips and Mexican cooks, it was one of the really far-reaching ramifications of his initial inspection of the Capitol Reservation lands.

[16] "Report upon the Resurvey and Location of the Boundary Lines between the States of Texas and New Mexico," pp. 1–2 (Texas Land Office, 1911).

CHAPTER VI

The First Cattle

THE CAPITOL RESERVATION, or the range of the XIT Ranch, was over two hundred miles in length, a waving sea of nutritious grasses. On the plains proper, grama, buffalo, and mesquite grass made an unbroken turf, furnishing excellent range for the wild animals of the plains—buffalo, antelope, and mustangs—and the scarcely less wild Texas cows that replaced them.

In the undulating sand country there was sideoats grama, and the sagegrass grew tall and rusty, furnishing shelter for prairie chickens and tinder for prairie fires. The buffalograss, closely resembling the curly-top mesquite, has been claimed as the best.[1] By early tests conducted at Manhattan, Kansas, it proved "considerably superior to Kentucky blue grass and very much better than timothy." These grasses cured in the summer and fall, and the old, unpampered Texas Longhorn cattle wintered well with no other feed. Babcock inspected these grasslands and was favorably impressed.[2]

Our lands examined by me [he reported] are generally well adapted to agriculture. There is no question but they will produce fine crops of all kinds of grain adapted to that climate. I found our lands and the climate admirably adapted for grazing purposes,

[1] *Land Booklet*, 15; *The Tascosa Pioneer*, June 12, 1886; Marcy, *Exploration of the Red River*, 40.
[2] *Land Booklet*, 14.

69

the prevailing grass being mesquite, which is exceedingly nutritious, said to be not excelled in fat producing qualities. Stock in that climate require no other feed winter or summer.[3]

Babcock was told, and correctly, that yearling steers brought from Southwest Texas to the Panhandle would in a year weigh from one to two hundred pounds more than if kept in the lower country. He was told that both cattle and sheep were "very profitable," and that the JA's had realized a 98 per cent calf crop in 1881. He was told that ranches of the Panhandle paid 25 to 40 per cent annually "and generally with very slack management"; and that, on account of state laws and the system and organizations of the cowmen, the business was "as legitimate and secure from loss on account of drifting, straying, theft or other causes, as the raising of cattle or sheep in Illinois." [4] In fact, he was told a lot that looks good in print but is hard to prove out on the ground.

But the boom was on, and it was natural that Babcock should hear tales of prosperity. He did not recognize that even in the cattle business depression dogged the footsteps of unnatural expansion. The wildly speculative early eighties were but the prelude to the hard times of the late eighties.

Thrilled by ideas of the "cattle bonanza," Babcock returned to show "on paper" what the profits of the range would be from grazing 150,000 head of cattle. He estimated the purchase price at twenty dollars a head and an annual calf crop of 90 per cent, whereby in five years the purchase amount of $3,-000,000 would net $4,561,031, or an increase of a little over 30 per cent annually. And Babcock gave this as a "conservative estimate." [5] Yet such reports as this were at the time commanding the attention of the speculators of eastern North America and were attracting many investors, among them canny financiers from as far away as Edinburgh. The investment made, the investor had time to consider the rarity of 90 per cent calf crops on million-acre ranges, the hazards of drought and blizzard, and the possibility of a disastrous decline in market value.

[3] Prospectus, 21–22.   [4] Prospectus, 21–22.   [5] *Ibid.*, 23.

Nevertheless Babcock came back all fired up with the expansive prospect of the plains of Texas, and wrote his recommendations:

I would advise placing cattle and sheep on our lands—cattle on northern and sheep on southern portion. I would suggest fencing our lands in ranches. The cost of wire fence, when enclosing large tracts, I ascertained to be less than ten cents per acre.

He pointed out that fencing would save expense of many line camps and obviate the annoyance of drifts from other herds.[6] Even as he wrote there was a clamor for the land.[7]

The Capitol Company considered the possibilities of immediate sale and of colonizing its land. But finding colonization impossible at that early period in Panhandle development, it followed Babcock's advice and established the ranch as a temporary institution to secure the use of the land until the time of the farmer should come.[8]

Even then, to fence three millions of acres, to provide watering facilities for cattle where little live water existed, to build houses and barns, and to buy thousands and thousands of cattle required much money. To begin such an immense enterprise when the cattle business was going into the decline of the middle eighties and money was becoming scarce called for a lot of courage. American banks refused to lend on anything not quoted upon the stock exchange, and, finding the raising of sufficient capital in the United States impossible, John V. Farwell went to Europe. His connections there were ample. As large buyers of merchandise the Farwells maintained offices in Paris, Manchester, and Belfast, and were known therefore to capitalists in those cities.

In order to borrow money in England Mr. Farwell found that he must form an English company. After extended nego-

[6] *Ibid.,* 21–22.

[7] See Taylor, Babcock & Co. to R. W. Cameron, March 16, and to D. N. Rowan, December 5, 1882, XIT files.

[8] Crissey, "The Vanishing Range," *The Country Gentleman,* March 1, 1913, p. 4.

tiations, in 1885 the Capitol Freehold Land and Investment Company, Limited, was organized,[9] and incorporated under "The Companies Acts" of England. Its authorized capital was 3,000,000 pounds sterling, or approximately $15,000,000, two-thirds of which was subscribed by October of 1888.[10]

Acquisition and development of the Capitol lands as a cattle ranch was the expressed purpose of the new organization.[11] As the Capitol Company, the American organization, received its land from the state, it transferred it to the trustees of the Capitol Freehold Land and Investment Company, whose offices were in London. The latter organization borrowed money through the sale of debentures, which bore interest not to exceed 7 per cent. The first debenture issue reached 1,000,000 pounds sterling, in certificates of fifty pounds and above, bearing interest at 5 per cent. Each debenture was negotiable anywhere in Britain. Interest coupons were payable semiannually, while the debentures matured in periods of five, seven, and ten years, but might be called and redeemed by the company upon six months' notice by the payment of a bonus of 2.5 per cent for each year of the unexpired term.[12]

The directors of the company were men of distinction, chosen not without regard for business psychology. The Earl of Aberdeen and Quintin Hogg were the first trustees for the debenture holders. The Marquis of Tweeddale, governor of the Commercial Bank of Scotland, was chairman of the board of directors. The four other foreign directors were the Honorable Lord Thurlow, Edward M. Denny, a London merchant, Sir William Ewart of Belfast, and Henry Seton-Karr, a member of Parliament. In America, John V. Farwell, Charles B. Far-

---

[9] Walter Farwell to J. E. H., September 22, 1927.

[10] *Debenture Prospectus,* 1888, p. 2.

[11] *Ibid.,* 6.

[12] *Ibid.,* 4–9. John V. Farwell had first agreed to go to England in 1883 to study financing as original plans to sell portions of the tract were not carried through. In London in July, he was still pondering the advisability of selling 500,000 to 700,000 acres.

A. Taylor to A. C. Babcock, March 20 and April 21, 1883, and Taylor to Farwell, July 7, 1883.

well, Walter Potter, a Boston banker, and Abner Taylor completed the board.[13] The National Provincial Bank of England, London, the Commercial Bank of Scotland, Edinburgh, and the Importers and Traders National Bank, New York, were the company bankers.[14]

The ranch was turned over to John V. Farwell as managing director, and the Capitol Freehold Land and Investment Company had almost nothing to do with its operation. The Capitol Syndicate, made up of the American owners, took the properties under lease from the British company and operated it on their own. Annual reports giving the conditions of the ranch, number of cattle, sales, and values were made to the directors by Mr. Farwell. The debentures constituted "a first charge on the freehold land and improvements, cattle, equipment, and all other property of the Company." In offering these bonds for sale, the directors felt that they formed "an exceptionally well-secured and desirable investment." [15]

The XIT Ranch was often thought of as an English institution because of the English capital used in its development. The organization in London constituted the necessary technical machinery for securing needed loans, raised through the sale of interest-bearing bonds, secured by a mortgage upon the lands under development. Foreign buyers of bonds were not shareholders in the ranch, only in the company, as they received interest upon their money whether the ranch was paying dividends or not. When, in 1909, the directors completed the redemption of the bonds, the foreign company went out of existence. Then, in 1915, the Capitol Reservation Lands, a real estate trust, was formed for the disposal of unsold land.

Annual meetings of the directors were held in London until the British company was dissolved. The reports and results kept the foreign bond-holders satisfied with their security, and met the English legal technicalities governing such companies.[16]

[13] *Ibid.*, 2.   [14] *Ibid.*, 3.   [15] *Ibid.*, 9.
[16] *Ibid., Abstract of Capitol Lands*, 24.

Comparison of the Syndicate's dealings with the English directors and the dealings of no few other companies of like nature is interesting. The stories of "book counts," by which foreign investors paid for thousands of cattle that were not upon the range, of "padded" tally lists, of failure to report losses, and of misrepresentations of range and market conditions yet find currency in regions where foreign syndicates briefly flourished.

But, in making his first report in November, 1886, Mr. Farwell deducted the losses from the total of the herd, "something," he observed, "cattle companies have not usually done on their first year's business. In most companies the losses are carried along unreported as long as it is possible to do so. We, however, took great pains to ascertain our loss and report it to you, and have done so as far as it was possible, as we wished to face our losses from the beginning."

Furthermore, a low evaluation of the cattle had been made, one "much lower than is usual in similar cases," he continued, "although they are at least equal in value to any in the vicinity. My object in so doing has been to avoid any possible overestimate of the value of the herd, and my anxiety in this matter has been thus great, as I well know the total results of overvaluation in other companies, and my present valuation is thus undoubtedly low." [17]

That portion of the ranch extending north from Deaf Smith County, some 1,500,000 acres, is more rolling than the southern half and was considered a better cattle country.[18] The Canadian River cut the ranch about midway between the north and south ends. To the north, the topography changes from rolling to gently rolling, then to high rolling and to gently undulating, or plains country. South of the river, rolling land gives way to gently rolling to meet the caprock in Deaf Smith and Oldham counties, which marks the northern boundary of the Llano Estacado. From this irregular line of bluffs, plains

[17] John V. Farwell, *Report of the Managing Director*, 1886, p. 8.
[18] Prospectus, 3.

land lies swell upon swell to the Yellow Houses and the south-line fence. The altitude of 2,000 feet in the south gradually rises to 4,700 feet at Buffalo Springs.[19] Except for scattering cottonwoods along the Canadian and its tributaries, and scrub hackberry, mesquite, and cedar scattered throughout the breaks, the region was barren of timber.[20]

After deciding to stock its lands, the company located its headquarters at Buffalo Springs. The north end was the first to be stocked. George Findlay, a Scot who had spent more than ten years with the Farwell interests in Chicago, began the stupendous task of directing the business details of the ranch from that office. The Texas ranch became his life work.

Almost at once the owners got in touch with Colonel B. H. Campbell, usually called "Barbecue," because of his brand Bar B Q.[21] At first they considered cutting the tract into several ranches and taking "Barbecue" in as a partner. Eventually they brought him down from Wichita, Kansas, and made him general manager of the ranch. As a cowman in Indian Territory he became noted for his parsimony, traditionally antagonistic to the code of the cow camp. But inversely proportionate to his penuriousness on his own ranch was his extravagance on the XIT.[22]

Berry Nations, who had come up the trail from South Texas with a herd of George West's cattle, became range foreman, though a man named Collins was the boss at first. By the spring of 1885 the organization of the outfit was under way. Cattle were contracted and improvements at Buffalo Springs were being built. With the growth of grass, over on the Punta de Agua, the general roundup, with fifteen to twenty wagons, gathered for the "spring work," and Ruck Tanner became wagon boss for the XIT.[23]

When Campbell was away on business W. S. Mabry took control. After his services were required to survey the fence

[19] *Land Booklet*, 7–8.   [20] *Ibid.*, 15.   [21] B̄Q̄
[22] A. L. Matlock to J. E. H., December 1, 1927.
[23] Frank C. Irwin to J. E. H., September 24, 1927; M. Huffman to J. E. H., November 3, 1927.

lines in Hockley and Cochran counties, far to the south, Walter
de S. Maud, fresh from England and a jolly good fellow, took
his place. He represented the English investors in the Capitol
Freehold Land and Investment Company. He was unversed in
the ways of the range, but not at all overburdened by responsi-
bilities. Between drinking highballs at the ranch and gambling
in Tascosa, he really put in full time. Shooting craps was just
coming into form at the little frontier town, and Maud followed
the game with zest.[24] This group of men directed the initial
organization of the XIT Ranch.

Campbell contracted for cattle in southern and western
Texas, and the first herd, driven by Ab Blocker, came north
from the Fort Concho country, reaching the ranch in July,
1885. From the drivers of each herd, Collins, the range boss,
hired all who wished to stay, and Campbell bought the wagons
and camp equipment of every outfit that would sell. Mac Huffman, one of the cowboys coming up the trail from South Texas,
said he never saw so many bull's-eye lanterns in his life as they
had on hand at Buffalo Springs.[25]

Thousands of cattle were contracted for delivery in July
and August. Some herds were late, and "Barbecue"—"big
faced, overbearing, and loud mouthed—gave the owners a
pretty hard cussing." A big corral and a large chute capable
of holding twenty-four head of grown cattle had been built. In
considering what brand to put on the company cattle, Campbell had settled on a brand representing a frying pan. But
when Ab Blocker, bubbling over with knowledge of the range
and trail, suggested the XIT, Campbell accepted it.[26] At once
the ranch became known as the XIT wherever stray beef was
eaten or mavericks were branded.

Wherever men rode the ranges of the cow country, they
talked of cattle and of horses, and they talked too of the heral-
dic marks of ownership, the brands these cattle and horses wore.

[24] H. F. Mitchell to J. E. H., June 10, 1927; E. C. G. Austen to J. E. H.,
November 7, 1927.
[25] M. Huffman to J. E. H., November 3, 1927.
[26] *Ibid.;* Marvin Hunter, *The Trail Drivers of Texas,* I, 432.

Perhaps from the fertile mind of some "sweater" or chuck-line rider, whose daily bread depended more upon his ability to lie engagingly than upon his inclination to work, the legendary significance of the XIT brand emerged into Plains folklore. Almost any embryo cowboy who has perched upon the top rail of a corral knows that XIT means "Ten [counties] in Texas" and that the brand was chosen because XIT "waddies" rode into and over that many counties without leaving the home range. Commission men of the stockyards of Chicago, between measured expectorations of the juice of the weed, told the story when XIT steers came in by the trainload from Montana,[27] and the story is still being told wherever reckless riding and good cow work mark the Texas cowboy.

Ab Blocker knew that a good brand must be easy to make but difficult to burn or alter, and it is doubtful if his mind dwelt upon any county in Texas, much less the ten that embraced the Capitol Reservations lands. The XIT brand, though a large one, was easily made with one five-inch bar, but was difficult to alter, or as the range hands say, to "burn out."

Campbell asked Blocker to take charge of the branding, but the trail driver wished to set out for Camp Supply, in Indian Territory, where John Blocker's north-bound herds were blockaded along with many others. When Campbell asked him what method he would follow in branding the incoming herds, Blocker, with good-humored bent, said he would show him. He called "Goat," his Negro cook, to get a horse and follow him. "Goat," who was no mean cowhand, left his dough and came with his rope. After Barbecue's Mexican hands had built a fire, Blocker called for the boys to turn a cow out at the gate. He took after her, swung a regular "Blocker loop," picked up her front feet, and the cow horse did the rest. Hardly had the cow hit the ground when the cowboys were upon her, an iron was brought, and she was branded. "Goat" roped the next cow, Blocker followed, and so on until they had roped about twenty, "never missing a throw."

[27] L. Gough, Ms., "History of the XIT Ranch."

Then Blocker rode up to the manager and, "just putting on," said, "Colonel Campbell, that is the way we brand in Tom Green County—the way John Blocker has taught us."

"Barbecue" looked at him and roared, "Well, Mr. Blocker, you surely are mighty good, but you can't brand any cattle for me." [28]

This suited Blocker exactly, for he did not want the job. He gathered his remaining riders and headed his wagon and remuda east toward Supply, with "Goat" again among his pots and skillets and sourdough.

Branding began in earnest when the first chute-full of cattle was jammed in and the bars put up behind. Four or five men did nothing but handle branding irons. Following each was a man with a pole about five feet long. He thrust one end of this under a bar of the chute on the opposite side, and with the lever thus formed drew down across the cow's neck to keep her from jumping about when the hot iron was applied. This gave dispatch to the branding and saved time. When all the cattle in the chute were branded, the bars in front were drawn, the cattle passed out into the pasture, and the chute was filled again with cattle from the corral.

An old mule skinner, with sixteen mules "strung out," hauled cottonwood and piñon from the head draws of the Corrumpa, in No Man's Land, forty miles away. He plied his axe and his bull whip day after day to keep the Mexicans who tended the fire supplied with wood. When the iron in use became cold and would not sear the hide, the brander yelled, "hot iron," and a Mexican brought one from the fire at a trot and returned with the cold one. "Coosie" [29] had breakfast for the boys before day, and branding began by daylight. After a short respite for dinner the work continued until dark. Daily the chute poured forth its bovine flood, while the corrals behind

[28] M. Huffman to J. E. H., November 3, 1927. Mr. Huffman went to the ranch with Blocker's herd, began work under George Collins, and stayed with the company as a division foreman for many years.

[29] A corruption of the Spanish word *cocinero,* meaning cook.

it received a stream of cattle from the south—from the over-flowing ranges of Texas.

Day after day this routine, killing in hours and effort but never growing monotonous, went steadily on as other herds drifted down the grassy slopes to welcome water at Buffalo Springs. Daily, cattle to be branded were driven from a large corral into a small one, the "crowding pen." Yelling, sweating, and plying quirts, the cowboys drove the cows into the chute until they jammed it full. Amid dust from thousands of hoofs and through acrid smoke from burning hair and hide, the branders walked alongside the chute upon ground packed like hardened cement until their feet were raw. The hills about Buffalo Springs for miles around looked like one immense "day herd." After the work commenced, 22,000 head were run through the chute before the branding ended.[30]

During the spring and summer of 1885 contracts were made for 65,000 cattle. While in England, Mr. Farwell let contracts for 40,000 of these to agents of American cattlemen. For various reasons the contractors failed to deliver about 45,000 head, fortunately for the company. Adequate preparations for handling this many cattle had not been made in 1885, and when cattle went down in price by 1886, the company saved money by letting new contracts.[31]

While most of the XIT cowboys were busy receiving cattle at Buffalo Springs, Ruck Tanner had an outfit, a chuck wagon and a crew of cowboys, with the general roundup, "working" [32] the surrounding country. About that time Frank Irwin quit punching cattle in Indian Territory and set out for Arizona. He crossed the Panhandle and one day rode up to the Buffalo Springs ranch and met his old friend, Berry Nations.

Nations told me he wanted a man about my size to go to the Canadian the next day [Irwin said]. I told him he would have to

[30] M. Huffman to J. E. H., November 3, 1927.

[31] John V. Farwell, *Report of the Managing Director,* 1886, p. 2.

[32] "Work" is the inclusive term applied to handling cattle. To round up stock, to brand calves, and to gather beeves is "to work" cattle.

go a long way to find one, as I was going to Arizona to get rid of the chills and fever that had been bothering me down in the Territory. He lied to me, saying I couldn't get through, as there was no water. He sent out some men to bring in the horses. He cut out twenty-one head of small Texas horses for me. They all had the itch, and had very little hair upon them.

The next day I told him I would go to work. He told me where I would meet Ruck Tanner, who was over on the Punta de Agua waiting for the general roundup to start. I went over and laid up about a week with the XIT outfit. There were fourteen wagons [33] when I got there. We waited for others to come in. Cattlemen from southern Colorado, from northern New Mexico, the Strip, and from Texas met there for the general roundup. Some outfits sent men but no wagon. The OX, ZH, Cross S, TWT, Seven Up and Down, 7HL, 101, Pitchfork, and the LIT outfits were represented. That year the XIT sent wagons out to work through the surrounding ranges. Later they just sent "outside men," as they had the best fence in the world, and not many cattle got through. The Colorado and New Mexico men got a good many of their cattle out of the XIT that year, as they had drifted in and had then been fenced up.[34]

Early in August of 1885 the last of the cattle received at Buffalo Springs had gone through the chute and had the XIT burned wide upon their right sides. An outfit, consisting of about six cowboys and a chuck wagon, began drifting the cattle away from Buffalo Springs to different waterings to relieve the pressure on the grass on the north end of the ranch. Cowboys "loose herded" the cattle for several days "to locate" them, turned them loose, and went back to Buffalo Springs after another herd as the rush of work went on in preparation for the first winter.

Fall came and the grass matured and dried. Prairie fires broke out. The worst swept south from the Cimarron into the LE range along the Canadian, destroying some thirty miles

[33] These were chuck wagons, indicating that at least that many ranches were represented.
[34] F. C. Irwin to J. E. H., September 24, 1927.

of that outfit's newly built fence and killing some of the LE cattle before burning itself out in the breaks. E. A. Reynolds, one of the owners, threatened suit, but Abner Taylor disclaimed responsibility for the XIT's.

In spite of the efforts of the cowboys to check it, it burned the Buffalo Springs country clean, and destroyed most of the grass in the Middle Water and Rito Blanco ranges. Collins pushed four thousand cattle across the line into New Mexico to drift far and wide before the severe blizzards of the winter that followed. The bulk of the cattle were thrown south to the un-burned country along the Canadian.[35] By the next summer losses had depleted the herd to 16,813.[36]

During 1885 all cattle received went north of the Canadian. In 1886, 16,000 head of "grown stuff" were branded at Rito Blanco, and many were placed in the Alamocitos, Alamoso, and Trujillo country just south of the river. By November, 1886, a total of 110,721 cattle had been bought and contracted for. The value of the cattle, horses, and mules was placed at $1,322,-587, and that of the entire holdings at $5,589,522.[37]

During the dry year of 1887, dust cloud after dust cloud rose above the horizon of the South Plains, heralds of north-bound herds bearing a hundred brands, all trailing to the ranges of the XIT. Many of these herds were delivered at the Yellow Houses. During the thirty days following June 7, 1887, the tally at the Yellow Houses headquarters increased by 30,-000, as thirty different brands were transferred to the Capitol Syndicate. At this time in western Texas many men were anx-ious to sell, and the stocking of the Syndicate land furnished them the needed outlet. Through parched country to the south and over trails notable for their frequent dry camps, cattle came pouring in, gaunt and weak from long, hot days across the plains.[38]

[35] M. Huffman to J. E. H., November 3, 1927.
[36] Farwell, *Report,* 2.
[37] *Ibid.,* 3–11.
[38] J. E. Moore to J. E. H., February 26, 1927; F. C. Irwin to J. E. H., November 3, 1927; James H. East to J. E. H., September 29, 1927.

About the first herds to arrive [W. S. Mabry said] were those purchased from D. H. and J. W. Snyder; A. G. Boyce was their trail boss. Gus O'Keefe was the trail boss in charge of the cattle bought from C. C. Slaughter. William Ragland was another prominent trail boss who brought up a herd for Rachell Brothers, from Refugio County. All three of these were life-long cowmen. In receiving these cattle it was necessary to class them, as the ones, twos, and threes all differed in price. When a yearling approaches a two, it is difficult to draw the line and say whether it should be classed as a yearling or a two and the same is true as to twos and threes and so on. Experienced cowmen can tell their ages by examining their teeth. When a dispute arises the only way to settle it is to throw the animal down and examine its teeth. There seemed to be little or no trouble classing the different herds until they began to receive the Slaughter herd. When the disputes began to arise as to ages, Colonel Campbell called on William Ragland to help him class this herd. Ragland and O'Keefe began to clash so often and got into [such] heated controversies that Colonel finally called on Mr. Boyce to help in classing. Many of the disputes could only be settled by throwing the animal and examining the teeth. After so long a time the cattle were all received and carried the XIT brand.[39]

Such was A. G. Boyce's first connection with the XIT Ranch. He was soon to become its general manager and would continue as such for nearly eighteen years. A frontier cowman of commanding presence and of vast experience, Boyce was a native of Travis County, Texas. He had fought with Terry's Texas Rangers through the Civil War, had driven the long cattle trail to California in 1869, had engaged in the cattle business with the Snyders in West Texas for several years, and became manager of the Syndicate in 1887. He was described by a ranch visitor as a "wonderful combination of activity, fearlessness, principle, and purpose." And while he had seen something of the world, his Southern prejudices never left him.

I was entertaining Colonel Boyce one time when he was in Chicago [said Walter Farwell]. We went to see a prize fight. We had

[39] Mabry, "Recollections," 14.

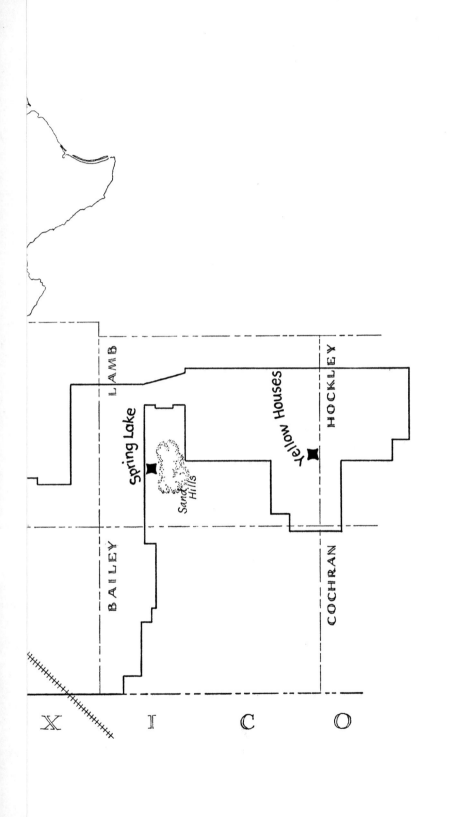

no more than got to our seats when a fist fight started between a white man and a Negro. We happened to be right in the middle of it. The Negro began getting the better of it, which was more than the Colonel could stand. The place did not share his Southern sentiments, but he yelled out advice to the white man so loudly everybody there heard him: "For God's sake leave his head alone and kick him on the shins!" [40]

This was the extremely positive man in whom Gus O'Keefe met his match in classing cattle at the Yellow Houses—a dominant character almost to the point of being domineering.

Many of the first herds came from South Texas, but those contracted in 1886 and 1887 were to be of better quality. All were supposed to be bought from above the quarantine line, which meant in West Texas, where stock was larger and of better grade. Many came from the country tributary to the Texas and Pacific Railway, and were better than the average Longhorns,[41] though compared with the stocks of today they were of decidedly "indifferent quality." [42] The carrying capacity of the ranch had been estimated at 300,000 head, but ten acres to the animal was far from enough when allowances for droughts and fires were made, and the herd as maintained totaled from 125,000 to 150,000 head.[43] No great movement of cattle to the ranch took place after 1887.[44]

Shortly thereafter, work began upon the improvement of the herd already accumulated, and stocky Hereford, Durham, and Polled Angus sires were imported from Illinois, Iowa, and Missouri to grade up the Texas Longhorns into a stock more tractable and heavier, though less hardy and picturesque. The gruelling job of converting the plains to the production of beef was under way.

[40] Walter Farwell to J. E. H., September 22, 1927.
[41] George Findlay to Charles Gray, May 20, 1910.
[42] Ms., "The Capitol Syndicate or XIT Ranch."
[43] *Debenture Prospectus*, 8; *The Tascosa Pioneer*, June 8, 1889; *The Southwestern Reporter;* Farwell, *Report*, 3–11.
[44] George Findlay to Charles Gray, May 20, 1910.

CHAPTER VII

Fences, Windmills,
and "Barbecue's" Bad Men

WHEN THE XIT began to stock its ranges, Tascosa was the only town in the western Panhandle. All supplies offered for sale there by Howard and McMasters or Cone and Duran were freighted over trails from Springer, New Mexico, and Dodge City, Kansas. "Bull" and mule teams "leaned against" heavy loads along the 242-mile rutted course that joined Tascosa and Dodge. Mexican bull drivers, to whom a shuck-rolled cigarette was comfort and coffee with sugar a luxury, patiently drove these trails, bringing to Tascosa the provisions demanded by the scattered ranches.

The trail to the nearest railroad point led to Springer, 176 miles away. Therefore, the Tascosa merchants explained that it was the high freight rate alone that caused ordinary sewing needles to sell for ten cents each.[1] But instead of buying its supplies at Tascosa, the Syndicate contracted with freighters to deliver direct from the merchants to the ranch.

Great quantities of supplies and building materials were needed at Buffalo Springs late in 1884, before the first cattle were brought in. The fencing contract for the north end was let to Bill Metcalf, an old buffalo hunter and frontiersman. Abner

---

[1] W. S. Mabry to J. E. H., April 27, 1928; E. C. G. Austen to J. E. H., July 7, 1927; see appendix for logs of the Tascosa-Dodge and Tascosa-Springer trails.

Fences, Windmills, and Bad Men

Taylor wrote W. S. Mabry early in the winter of 1884, requesting him to meet Metcalf at Buffalo Springs and survey this fence line. Because of the permanent water at Buffalo Springs, Perico, and Agua Fria, the erection of windmills and reservoirs was not immediately necessary, and plans were made to stock the north end of the ranch first. On reading the fencing contract, Mabry said:

> I found it required the posts to be of cedar and thirty feet apart, and Metcalf had caused them to put in the contract that the surveyor should mark the place for each post by driving down a stake every thirty feet. . . . Metcalf would furnish the crew necessary to do this surveying. Knowing that country as I then did, with no timber in miles of Buffalo Springs, I was amazed at that clause in the contract, that I should drive a stake in the ground every thirty feet. As soon as I saw Metcalf I had him agree . . . that in lieu of a stake I could throw up a small earth mound every thirty feet. I organized my surveying party and commenced the survey.
>
> The winter of 1884 and 1885 was a very cold winter. It began snowing and freezing soon after I began the survey and most of the time the ground was frozen so hard the mound builder could not put his spade into the ground . . . and had to use a pick. On this survey I had only a small "A" tent, large enough for only one man besides myself. The balance of the party slept out in the open. The only fuel we could get was cowchips and the roots of the grease weed, which we later had to dig for. We were very much delayed in our surveying by the snow storms which caused us to lay up. This weather caused Metcalf to lay up too. . . .

In the winter antelope generally collected in good size herds, with a hundred or more to the herd. Days when we would have to lay over Metcalf and I would saddle our horses and ride out to find an antelope. He taught me a new way to hunt antelope. The plan I had always pursued . . . was . . . to slip upon them under cover, if possible. But he . . . would run his horse at full speed toward a large herd, and when in gunshot, dismount, throw the reins over his horse's head, and shoot at the lead antelope. This would turn the herd, another shot or two would get them confused and all bunched up together, and he would usually kill two or three before the herd got beyond gunshot range.

I managed to get this fence line surveyed and marked without causing Metcalf any delay. The pasture fence was completed late in the spring.[2]

Mexican laborers cut the posts from the Canadian breaks. Barbed wire for the four-wire fence was delivered at El Moro, a station near Trinidad, Colorado, on the north side of the Raton Range. Despite this, it was freighted to Buffalo Springs in two-horse wagons. Since wire is put up in eighty-rod spools, Metcalf's contract with the freighters stipulated that they should unload four spools of wire every quarter of a mile along the fence line. Supplies were bought from Forbes Brothers, merchants at Trinidad, who became the receiving and forwarding agents for the ranch. Porter and Clothier, merchants at Springer, shared the Syndicate trade when the freight trains loaded there. For the most part, these two railroad points supplied Buffalo Springs with articles needed from the outside world.[3]

During 1885 construction of fences on the north end went forward, and 162 miles were built. Mile after mile of barbed wire was reeled off as the fences stretched south to the Canadian and beyond. Bands of mustangs, thousands of antelope, and small bunches of buffalo were enclosed, while cowboys "threw" thousands of cattle upon the range to crowd these wild creatures from the grass. From where the northern caprock of the Llano Estacado falls away to the Canadian breaks, south to the Yellow Houses in Hockley County, the XIT range was mainly prairie land and presented greater need for fencing. The contractors kept at the job.

Late in 1885 the contract for fencing the southern portion of the ranch was let to Ben Griffith and J. M. Shannon, a Scot who was herding sheep over the hills and flats of Mitchell County, and at times working for Coman and Shear, merchants

---

2 Mabry, "Recollections," 9–10.
3 W. S. Mabry to J. E. H., December 27, 1927.

of Colorado City. A man of tremendous frame, energy, and purpose, Shannon, a true Scot, became one of the richest men in West Texas. A. T. Clarkson and Ben Griffith were to aid Shannon in building the fence. Clarkson had a big string of ox teams that he intended to use in freighting the wire from Colorado City, and Griffith was to help. About Christmas time of 1885, another serious prairie fire struck the South Plains and burned the grass from a scope of country a hundred miles square. Griffith, discouraged, is said to have left for Arizona. Water became scarce. Clarkson's oxen, dependent upon grass, were worthless, and he secured some fine mules.

> With mule teams [said Shannon], the drivers could put a water barrel on each side of their wagons and haul some hay and do pretty well, but you had to have grass and lots of water for oxen. We hauled water thirty-six miles for use in some places in fencing the Yellow House. There was no grass and we had to keep our horses tied up to our wagons.
>
> We had to hire all our materials freighted from Colorado City, and they cost us $1.25 a hundred pounds. Clarkson was to have hauled them for a dollar. The freighters would not scatter them along the fence line, but dumped them all in one place. Lots of them threw the material off at Singer's Store, thirty miles from where we wanted it. . . . This meant that we had to re-haul it before we could use it. I never worked so hard in my life as I did there for eighteen months. We put in sixteen hours a day and seven days a week. I erected eighty-five miles of fence at $110 a mile, and lost about thirty dollars a mile on the contract. But that fence was different from anything in the country—it was put there to stay always.[4]

Until this time, Texas had never seen anything to compare with this immense venture with wire. By the fall of 1886 the Syndicate had contracted and put up 781.25 miles of fence.[5] The west line, with all its "jogs," was 260 miles long. It began at the northwest corner of the state and ran south 150 miles

[4] J. M. Shannon to J. E. H., November 27, 1927.
[5] Farwell, *Report,* 4.

without a turn. The east line was 275 miles long, and line-riders watched 575 miles of outside fence. Estimates place the material in this fence at over three hundred carloads. It cost $181,-000. All Syndicate land was enclosed late in 1886 except about 35,000 acres, which were not fenced immediately because of the hope of exchanging for state land lying inside the enclosed Syndicate land.[6]

By the late nineties cross fences cut the XIT into ninety-four pastures, making a total of about 1,500 miles of fence, which, in single strand, would have stretched for over 6,000 miles. Besides the wire, over 100,000 posts, five carloads of wire staves, and one car of staples were required. So many gates were necessary in the corrals and along the fences that the first general manager just ordered a carload of gate hinges.[7] Line-riders rode these fences periodically. Some of the divisions kept "fence wagons" running all the time, and regular "fencers" kept the lines in repair.[8]

Telephones were extremely rare in the cow country, but a line was erected from Tascosa to the general headquarters on the Alamocitos in 1888. In the early 1900's a great many telephones were placed upon the ranch. Where possible, the top wire of the fences was used for a telephone line, thus effecting economy in initial expenditure if not in maintenance, though the "service" was atrocious.[9]

In the Buffalo Springs country there was an abundance of water, and the country was stocked with little worry over wells and windmills. Nature was not so prodigal throughout the southern half of the XIT Ranch, and, before cattle were placed there in great numbers, artificial reservoirs, tanks, and windmills were necessary. "Barbecue" Campbell let a contract to two well drillers, Marshall and Jones, for a number of wells to be completed by the time the cattle arrived in the summer of 1887.

[6] *Ibid.*   [7] L. Gough, Ms., "Sketch of the XIT Ranch," 2–3.
[8] H. W. Eubank to J. E. H., July 1, 1926.
[9] *The Tascosa Pioneer*, January 14, 1888; J. P. McDonald to J. E. H., June 25, 1927.

Fences, Windmills, and Bad Men

W. S. Mabry and W. D. Twichell, his young assistant, after having run the surveys for the fence lines, made locations for the wells. Marshall and Jones shipped their machines to Big Spring and brought them out to the ranch. Their freight mules were young and green and, by the time they reached the Yellow Houses, were fagged out and almost useless from sore shoulders. Marshall pitched camp, and, after many difficulties, began drilling in high hopes of striking artesian water. Instead, he struck adverse formations, the hole went down crooked, and as the time for the delivery of the cattle approached, there began to be serious worry since there was no water at hand.

Colonel Campbell complained to Marshall about his being so far behind with his drilling contract. Marshall replied, with the saving grace of humor, that he came out "to bore for water and did not expect to have to bore for tea." Finally, while he was drilling in the valley just south of the Yellow Houses, water began flowing from the well at the rate of about three gallons a minute. Everybody was elated. Marshall moved his machine about a mile farther south and drilled again. At about the same depth a flow of a gallon and a half a minute started, and the flow in the first well was reduced one-half.[10]

With the coming of spring and time for the delivery of herds on contract from down in Texas, blustery old "Barbecue" got back to the Yellow Houses with his hands. At that time, Marshall had discovered no gusher of water—not even a good seep. Thousands of cattle require lots of water, and there was still time to divert the herds to the creeks of the Canadian—to ample water farther north, as any conservative cowman would have made plans to do short of heavy rains and a surface supply in the plains lakes. The rains did not come, but under the dependable Texas trail outfits the cattle did.

The fences had been completed and the herds were rigidly held in the woefully inadequately watered pastures. Meanwhile the water hands were feverishly digging great pits or

10 Mabry, "Recollections," 13. One of these wells was still flowing 5.5 gallons a minute, from a depth of 102 feet, five months after completion. General Manager's *Report,* 1886.

wells in the Sod House Draw. Carpenters were put to work
building troughs, and the first herd was actually watered by
bucket and by hand—by the diligent use of a double row of
men formed from the well to the troughs, much like an old-
fashioned fire-bucket line. Surveyor Mabry, much concerned
with the entire problem, never got over the fact indelibly impressed on him as he watched famished cows fighting about the
troughs for hours and individually sucking up water, not by
the bucket, but "by the barrel."

It was a killing experience for both men and cattle, especially since the season was uncommonly dry and the last sixty
miles on the trail to the Yellow Houses was a dry drive, off
which cattle came on the verge of perishing. Frontier ingenuity
quickly improved on the bucket line as Williams contrived a
long, hollow, wooden box with an endless chain through it. At
regular intervals upon this chain he fixed blocks of wood which
just fit the box as the chain pulled through, something like the
carriers on a grain elevator. Then by means of a wheel and a
"Fort Scott horse power, he rigged his scheme . . . as to
throw water in the trough as rapidly as the cattle drank it."

Other wells were dug by hand, one of which—18 feet wide,
26 long, and 12 deep—was capable of producing 8,000 gallons
an hour when powered by the horse-driven, homemade pump.
Still the cattle piled into the pastures. General Manager Campbell had left the ranch and headed south for the railroad as the
news scattered far and wide that the company's cattle were
dying in bunches. Yet he had made no provision with his hands
to relieve the pressure by the shifting of herds to water on the
north, but left orders to keep throwing them into the pastures
of the Yellow Houses. Early in June, Campbell had asked an
experienced Texas range man, Colonel A. G. Boyce, to "take
charge of the XIT cattle." After a month to put his affairs in
shape at home, Boyce returned by way of the Snyder outfit.

While at the Snyder ranch, on my way to the Yellow Houses
[Boyce wrote], I heard from one of my men there that 28 head of
XIT cattle had died on the east fence of Yellow House pasture;

this was attributed to the fact that there were no fence-riders there to drive them back on water.[11]

When Boyce reached the Yellow Houses, he asked Williams, whom Campbell had left in charge of water, about conditions, but got no particularly alarming reports. Then he inquired if Campbell had left any letter of instructions for him. He was told that Campbell had relayed orders through Billy Ney, the wagon boss, to move on to Spring Lake to take care of the branding there and get a beef herd ready for market. "Barbecue" reported back by hurriedly written notes, and Boyce did as directed.

Before leaving the Yellow Houses, however, Boyce pressed the urgency of water on Williams and took some steps to alleviate the danger, though he did not personally ride the south end and learn half the story. As it eventually unfolded, threatening dire calamity, he took the reins over despite his orders, while Campbell was still far away. In the fall Boyce summarized the situation for George Findlay as it had developed during the past July:

I asked Mr. Williams if the dry well, known as the Chinese well, just southeast of branding pens, was in running condition, and he answered it was. I then asked him to send a man down with a horse to pump water for the "Q" herd. The men returned soon after, and said the well was full of mud and the pump would not work. I told Mr. Williams then to send an outfit down there, but they failed to get the pump running for three or four days.

Meantime I had the "Q" herd driven over to big dam, on the morning of the 26th, where there was a little water, so that they could get water enough to enable us to brand them. We cut off a little bunch of them there and brought them back to branding pens, where they were received and branded. I received them and kept Mr. Ney there, to attend to the branding, in order that it might be hastened along, so that we could get the "Q" horses which the Chi. Tex. Cattle Co. refused to turn over, until their cattle had all been

---

[11] Boyce to George Findlay, December 3, 1887, Matlock Papers.

received. Mr. Yearwood had to have most of the horses to move the beef herd and we were very scarce of horses at Yellow Houses.

While this bunch of cattle were being received, I started Earl Wright, with what men and horses I could scrape up, with instructions to take the cattle that had drifted from different parts of the pasture and gathered around the little Artesian well, and drift them north to water at Elevator at Sod House Draw, gathering what cattle they saw by the way, and, after watering them at the Elevator on Sod House Draw, to slowly drift them north to Spring Lake pasture.

During the night, or next morning, Wright and some of his outfit returned to Yellow Houses, and said the cattle were so dry and so hard to control and his help and horses so few that he could not manage the cattle, and that they had broken away from him and most of them had drifted back to the country of the little artesian well. He started with from 3,000 to 5,000 head of cattle.

In order to spare Wright and the men with him from the branding pens, I had to hire the Standard's tanking outfit, which happened to come in that evening.

On the morning of the 27th, I prevailed on Stuart, who was in charge of the "Q" herd, to let me have part of his horses, and these I turned over to Ney, and told him to take them and what men he could spare, and gather all the cattle, and drift them north to Sod Houses, and there water all the cattle he could; leaving such as he considered too weak to travel, and taking the balance on to Spring Lake.

About this time Blocker came up in charge of Jim Newman's outfit. Newman is a neighboring ranchman on our west line, and I am well acquainted with him, and I told Blocker that, if Newman was here and saw the condition the cattle were in, I was satisfied he would give me what assistance he could, and give me his outfit to help move the cattle. Blocker thereupon said he would go himself and turned over his outfit to help move the cattle.

Ney succeeded on this trip in moving about 5,000 head to Spring Lake, a few cattle dying by the way.

On the same day, I sent H. W. Taylor with instructions to Yearwood to turn the beef cattle loose on water, wherever he might be, and travel night and day and spare no time or horses in getting back to Yellow Houses, to help move cattle north.

Mr. Yearwood got back to Spring Lake about the time Mr. Ney got his herd watered and turned loose there, and they arranged that Mr. Yearwood should only go as far as Sod House, and there gather and move north another herd, and Mr. Ney should return to the Yellow Houses for a herd.

On or about the 30th, Mr. Yearwood moved north a herd of about 6,000 head, and Mr. Ney came to Yellow Houses and started, I think, from near the big dam with a herd of about 5,000, which were also moved to Spring Lake.

Ney then returned, as soon as possible, and took another herd of about 3,000 or 4,000 head from around the flats about artesian well, and it also was moved to Spring Lake.

The number of cattle in each herd is given from the estimates by the men in charge, and they amount together to 19,000 head; but I think a safe figure would be about 16,000 head. Cattle were moved later from time to time from Spring Lake and Escarbada pastures to the pastures north of them, to make room for the new cattle.

We finished branding the "Q" herd about August 3rd, and I remained around Yellow Houses and branding pens all the time, and received the cattle.

The "Q" herd numbered about 2,500 or 2,600 head, and under ordinary circumstances could have been received and branded in a couple of days; but they had been and were so starved for water that they were constantly scattering and getting away from the herders, and we were thus delayed, having to wait for them to be again collected and brought in.

About nine or ten o'clock on the night of the 27th, while I was in bed at the branding pens, Mr. Larrabee came down from Yellow Houses and woke me up to say that word had just come in from Sod House Draw that a great many cattle were falling into the dug wells, and that Mr. Williams, who was in full charge of the water supply, did not appear to think it necessary to do anything that night. I told Mr. Larrabee to go back and tell Mr. Williams to get a team, load it up with lumber to fence the well, and send a man out with it that night, with instructions to go at once to the windmill outfit near the Sod House well, and have it help pull the cattle out of the well, and then fence in the well. This was done.

Next day, the 28th, or 29th, Mr. Williams claimed that his wife was very sick, and that he must move her to Colorado City. I insisted on his not leaving the ranch just at this time, urging, as my reasons, that he was in charge of the water supply, and that the cattle were dying for want of water, and that it was his duty to stay on the ranch at this, above all other times, particularly as he was the only man on the ranch entirely familiar with each watering place. But he said that his wife was sick, and that it was his duty to consider her case before that of the cattle, and he started with her for Colorado that day. I understood she had been complaining of being sick for some time.

Upon my return from Spring Lake, 25th of July, seeing the condition of the cattle, I made inquiries of Mr. Williams if there were any horse-powers and elevators that could be set up at once to add to the supply of water. He said, as near as I can remember, that there were four or five elevators with horse-powers at Escarbada, not put up, and one in Running Water draw, in Spring Lake pasture: for all of which, I understood, wells had been dug last winter, but that they had never been mounted. I said that these elevators should be put up immediately, as we would have to move cattle through that pasture very soon; and he sent instructions at once to have this done.

I also asked him if there were any horse-power pumps or elevators that could be put up in Yellow House or Silver Lake pasture, and he replied that there was a horse-power at Yellow Houses, but no well to put it at. Ney told me of a dug well on the edge of Silver Lake, and I mentioned it to Mr. Williams, who replied that there was such a well but that it was so situated at the foot of a hill that you could not put a horse-power down at it. After Williams' departure, and under my instructions, Murphy took the horse-power to Silver Lake, and put it at work on the well, where it did good service.

From the fact that Colonel Campbell had only a few days before my arrival left Yellow Houses and left Williams, according to my understanding of it, in full charge of the water supply, I naturally concluded that, before the keeping of all the new cattle in Yellow House and Silver Lake pastures had been decided upon, the question of water-supply and safety of the cattle had been fully discussed and considered; and I therefore literally followed Colonel Campbell's instructions to go to Spring Lake and attend to calf-branding and gathering of beeves, and did not look into the water supply as I would have done had I considered it in my province, or had I been fully apprised of the real condition of it. The real state of affairs did not break in on me until on my way back from Spring Lake, when I saw the condition the cattle were in.

Mr. Williams had never intimated that there was any danger of a shortage of water, and did not even send me word to Spring Lake during the few days the cattle were suffering before I returned.

Upon my return, I immediately took steps to move the cattle to Spring Lake pasture for temporary relief, intending to move them further north, from time to time, as opportunity afforded. This movement was carried on with all possible haste, but was considerably retarded by a shortage of men and horses, and the poor condition of the latter, and having to receive and brand the "Q" herd at the same time.

The bulk of the cattle died during the days from the 26th to the 30th of July. [Seventy-six were pulled out of the Sod House well.]

Other wells were dug and in time a number of horse pumps were placed in operation over the southern half of the ranch. They were practicable only where water was shallow—from ten to twenty feet below the surface. Two work horses, used on alternate days, furnished power for these pumps. The water was lifted to the surface by an endless chain carrying half-gallon buckets a few inches apart. Their production was prodigious as each pump would easily water a thousand head of cattle. One such pump was on the Frio, two were on the Blackwater, and two were on the Sod House Draw.[12]

Surveyor Mabry continued making locations for wells and for dams across draws. Many artificial reservoirs were formed by impounding the drainage after heavy rains, and soon scores of windmills spun above deep and shallow wells, varying in depth from 10 to 400 feet, but averaging 125. The towers averaged 34 feet high, and the windmill wheels were 12 to 18 feet across.

Water was pumped into cypress tubs twenty feet in diame-

[12] J. E. Moore to J. E. H., February 26, 1927.

ter, and conveyed from them to earthen tanks. These tubs were used almost exclusively at first and cost from $700 to $1,000 each. No one had experimented with earthen tanks, and there was a general supposition that they would not hold water. The first the Syndicate built were lined with coal tar or with a thin layer of cement. The cement cracked, allowing the water to seep through, and tar was equally unsatisfactory.

About 1892 experimentation showed that the tanks would hold water with little loss from seepage if thoroughly tramped by cattle and horses. After this discovery several two-hundred-pound sacks of stock salt were placed in the bottom of each tank as soon as it was completed. By the time the cattle had eaten the salt, the tank-dump, the sides, and the bottom were well packed. When the water was turned in, there was little seepage. By 1900 there were 335 windmills and 100 dams upon the ranch, artificial facilities enough to supply 150,000 to 200,-000 head of cattle with water. These represented an estimated expenditure of a half-million dollars.[13]

As preparations for the first fencing were being made, the company began building ranch houses, barns, and corrals. The locations for these were made by the surveyors. At first, Buffalo Springs served as the headquarters for the ranch north of the Canadian. In the spring of 1886, the company began erecting buildings at the Yellow Houses, but only the improvements absolutely necessary were erected that year "owing to the great cost of transportation" in freighting 150 miles from the Texas and Pacific Railroad.[14]

Coman and Shear, contracting agents for the company at Colorado City, supplied the Yellow Houses with groceries, windmills, barbed wire, and other building materials. They kept a number of freighters on the road continuously. During the construction work at the ranch, these freighters struck for a higher rate. Coman and Shear refused to grant it, and the matter began to look serious for the ranch, as building materials

[13] Gough, "Sketch," 3–4; Ms., "The Capitol Syndicate or XIT Ranch," 1; *Land Booklet,* 8; B. P. Abbott to J. E. H., June 24, 1927.
[14] Farwell, *Report,* 5.

were needed. By that time, a number of settlers had come into Jones County to the east, and were trying to make a living by farming. Their efforts in 1887 met with failure on account of the drouth. These nesters, in dire straits, heard of the strike, swarmed to Colorado City in their two-horse wagons, and applied for the freight at the old rate. Thereafter the freighters gave no more trouble.[15]

In time the ranch was cut into seven divisions, each of which was handled from separate headquarters. The ranch houses were well-improved residences, and cellars, bunkhouses, storerooms, barns, and corrals were built at each location. Eventually the XIT came to be known as one of the best-equipped and most systematically arranged ranches in the country.[16]

The need of a centrally located, general headquarters became apparent. One of the XIT's immediate neighbors, the LS Ranch, was located on the Alamocitos, south of the Canadian, almost in the center of the XIT range. After an exchange of land late in the summer of 1886, the LS outfit moved over to the Alamoso Creek, about twenty miles east, leaving the XIT in charge of the Alamocitos country. Soon the Syndicate built a fence between the two ranges.[17]

After the Fort Worth and Denver Railroad built into the Panhandle in 1887, the company erected a large warehouse at Tascosa. All supplies were bought wholesale. Stock salt by the trainload was stored there, and charged out to the foremen of the different divisions. Then the town of Channing arose on the brow of the caprock of the North Plains overlooking the Canadian, and about 1890 the company moved the general headquarters there.[18] Freight wagons beat trails from the new town on the railroad to the headquarters at Buffalo Springs, Middle Water, Ojo Bravo, and Rito Blanco—the divisional headquarters north of the river. Then Spring Lake, Yellow Houses, and Escarbada were supplied from Amarillo, the town which was

---

15 Mabry, "Recollections," 15.
16 Gough, "Sketch," 3.
17 James H. East to J. E. H., September 27, 1927.
18 Gough, "Sketch," 7; H. W. Eubank to J. E. H., July 1, 1926.

started on the edge of the breaks south of the Canadian. With the building of the Pecos Valley and Southern Railroad, years later, and the formation of another division, a warehouse was built at Bovina, and the four divisions south of the Canadian came there for supplies.

Each division had a freight outfit of its own, consisting of six or eight mules and two wagons. One wagon was fastened behind the other and was known as a "trail wagon." The freighter carried a camp outfit, prepared his own meals while on the trail, fed his teams, hobbled them out, and slept upon the ground. He was never inside a house except when he stopped in town to load and at the ranch to unload. He hauled ten to eleven thousand pounds of ranch supplies at a trip, with which load he daily covered from twenty to twenty-five miles. He freighted month in and month out, every day of the year.[19] And so the Capitol Syndicate transformed the open range of the western Panhandle into what was probably the best-equipped ranch in the Southwest—a range dependent on fences, windmills, freight wagons, and the ingenuity of men.

But in the administration of the ranch all was far from well. In 1887, Colonel Campbell had contracted cattle from a cousin, M. C. Campbell, who went down in Texas far below the tick line, to Lampasas and Burnet, and even to Lee and Milam counties, for herds. There he bought stock some four dollars cheaper than the better stock to the west. The farther east he went, the cheaper he could buy. He contracted with men in these counties, who in turn furnished him with a big string of very inferior East Texas cows.[20] Thus, geographically, and quite profitably, he stretched the terms of his contracts, which called for cattle from above the tick line. But he delivered 16,-751 head of these cattle at the Yellow Houses at the contract price.

As the summer of 1887, the time for the delivery of the cattle at the Yellow Houses, approached, Nations and Maud

[19] W. A. Tate to J. E. H., October 31, 1927.
[20] J. Frank Yearwood to J. E. H., December 9, 1927.

started 180 head of horses down from Buffalo Springs to be used in receiving the herds. Nations sent Frank Irwin with them, telling him to remain and help receive the cattle.

They sent two shorthorns along to help me [Irwin said]. I had never been farther south than the Torrey dugout on the Canadian, where I had spent two winters, but Mabry told me to go as nearly south as I could from there. I put these two shorthorns with the horses and I rode in front. . . . The Plains were bare and there was not even a bush to go by. We had canteens of water, provisions, and a little tepee, a sheep herder's tent that we carried on a pack horse.

After riding all morning we stopped, and I got down and faced south. When the other two came up they put the tent pole down on the ground pointing due south, so that we could have it to go by if it was cloudy when we got up the next morning. We would gather a few buffalo chips, make some coffee, eat, and then we would go to hobbling horses. We would work from then until night at this, as we had to hobble every one of them. Without unsaddling our horses, we would stretch ropes from the saddle horns, and, with each man holding the end of a rope, form a three-cornered corral out of which we caught our horses. After we had hobbled all of them, we staked out our saddle horses. We carried no stake pins but dug holes eight or ten inches deep, put our pocket knives through the knots in the ends of our ropes, slipped these into the holes, turned the knives across, and filled the holes up with dirt. With a long rope a horse could not pull them up. The first night out we heard a roar like thunder. The country was full of mustangs and a bunch of them ran right through our horses trying to carry them off. That was why we had to hobble.

They had received no cattle at the Yellow Houses when we got there. They had some men out gathering cow-chips and digging mesquite roots to use in branding. There were three or four big old awkward boys there from the timber down in Texas and they wanted to know where we came from. We told them Buffalo Springs, and they wanted to know where that was. I had been sent down to have charge of one wagon, but I didn't like the outfit and I pulled out for Old Tascosa.

On the way back I rode at night, as my eyes had almost gone

99

out on the way down. I stretched the tent about daylight every morning, and slept all I could until along in the evening. Before I got to the breaks I saw something away ahead of me, and coming nearer I saw it was a horse. It looked thirty feet high at first [on account of the distortions of the High Plains mirages]. I got within about 300 yards of him and saw it was a mustang asleep. I got down and tightened up my cinches and moved up as close as I thought I could to him easily, and then made a run and was on him before he fairly woke up. I roped him and he fought terrible. He was old and his teeth were worn off. I throwed him and put a "swaller-fork the right," the XIT ear-mark on him, and turned him loose. I went on to Tascosa and Buffalo Springs. . . . Nations wanted to know what I was doing back up there. I told him I would not stay with those cotton-pickers down on the south end. He said that if I had stayed there I would soon have had more money than I ever had in my life. I asked him how. He replied that the contractors would be there to turn over some cattle . . . and that they wanted me there to help do the counting and the tallying . . . and the plan was for us to tally three or four head for every animal that went through. The Company did not know of the crooked deal until about a year later.[21]

Nor was this graft all. By fast work and loose management, yearlings were being tallied as two-year-olds, thereby costing several dollars more a head; cowboys were "hair branding" [22] cattle to be rustled out of the pasture later and branded as their own. "Barbecue" exercised slight control over his men and allowed the ranch to become a rendezvous for rustlers, outlaws, and hard cases of all kinds.[23] At last realizing that something was wrong, John V. Farwell wrote to A. L. Matlock, a prominent lawyer of Montague, asking him to make an investigation.

Matlock was a member of the Texas Legislature when the Capitol Reservation was set aside. The letter from Mr. Farwell announced the coming of George Findlay, a trusted young man

21 F. C. Irwin to J. E. H., September 24, 1927.
22 In hair branding, the iron was held against the animal just long enough to burn the hair, not the hide. The hair grew out, effacing the signs of brand, and a rustler could then put his own brand on the animal.
23 A. L. Matlock to J. E. H., December 1, 1927.

from Chicago, who would accompany him to the ranch and in whom he might confide if he wished.[24] Findlay came to the John V. Farwell Company in 1872, and from then until his death, on January 24, 1927, he served the Farwell interests with faithful efficiency.[25] These two men came to the Yellow Houses in the summer of 1887, the former under guise of looking after near-by personal property, the latter as a representative of the company.

We got to the Yellow House [said Mr. Matlock] and found three men there, the range boss, the bookkeeper, Rollen Larrabee, and D. B. Braid, the surveyor. We asked where the manager was and they said he was down near Colorado City. Findlay asked who was in charge and they said that the range boss was. I knew then that I had a job on my hands. I was District Attorney at Vernon some years before and had kept a mob from hanging this same man on condition that he would leave the state and never come back. Now he asked me if I thought he ought to leave the ranch. He said that he supposed that I was after him. I told him no, and asked him why he thought so.

"Well," he said, "I had to leave Vernon. I reckon I ought to resign now."

"Not on my account," I told him. "If you suit Colonel Campbell, you can stay."

He seemed satisfied at that and walked off. I told Findlay what he was, and that his being there was evidence that something was wrong. Directly a man walked by whom I recognized as the brother-in-law of the range boss and a horse thief. I pointed him out to Findlay and said that the ranch must be harboring thieves. Campbell returned in a few days and I presume the boss told him that I was there, and that he guessed I was after him. Findlay and I were sitting on a wagon tongue talking when he and Campbell walked up.

"You know this man?" Campbell said.

"Yes," I answered.

"What about him?" he continued.

"He is a very good cowman," I replied.

[24] *Ibid.*
[25] John V. Farwell to W. S. Mabry, January 25, 1927.

Campbell repeated his question and I answered him as at first. Then I turned to the range boss and said:

"Did you bring Colonel Campbell over here to get a recommendation?"

"No," he said, "but I told him that you knew me."

"Well," I said, turning to Campbell, "he is from a family of thieves noted for horse theft, cattle theft, and the like; but if he suits you, all right." [26]

Matlock talked with the cowboys, saw men working there— or upon the payroll—who had been run out of other sections of Texas, saw the ranch harboring horse thieves, saw lax business management, evidences of theft, and general lawlessness.

Upon his return to Montague he reported his impressions and received a wire, brief, but expressive enough: "Go take charge of the ranch and run it as though it were your own." He went. At Colorado City, 150 miles from the Yellow Houses, he met R. M. Bourland of Cooke County, whom he had decided to make general range manager. But that individual, as became one judicious, had already looked the situation over. In effect, he said that in good health he was worth much more to a wife and children back in the settlements than he could possibly be worth to the XIT cows after being shot full of holes.

Matlock went on to the ranch where the range boss, whom he had once saved from the rope, was now threatening to kill him. In casting about for a general range manager, Matlock chose A. G. Boyce, who, after delivering the remnant herds of the MOS and Horseshoe T Cross cattle of the Snyder brothers, was then out on the XIT range trying to keep the cattle from perishing for water. Matlock sent him a note. He came, excited over the threats being made against Matlock's life. They made the trade for Boyce to take the job. These two men vigorously began the reorganization of the XIT.

With few exceptions, every cowboy and foreman upon the ranch was ousted. Then the old range boss, Matlock's acquaintance of old, rode up with ten of his gunmen, to bring an end to

[26] A. L. Matlock to J. E. H., December 1, 1927.

the administration of this lawyer who had given up the pursuit of Blackstone for the pursuit of cattle. They met at the Yellow Houses, and old-timers tell that soon thereafter the population of New Mexico was slightly increased by several horsemen who wore their guns low and left their reputations behind them. Matlock was still on the range.

"Barbecue" Campbell did not wait to receive all the cattle. Before Matlock arrived, he had been uneasily sleeping in his tent, a shotgun by one side of his "roll," a Winchester by the other. Then a "tough hombre" named Spencer, who fed his private horse with company feed, was reported by a boy working on the ranch, and Campbell fired him. Spencer whipped the boy, and Campbell, becoming frightened, fired the boy for doing his duty and reinstated the tough cowboy.

Events were moving too rapidly for Campbell. He had a fine team "hooked" to a buckboard, and with a special bodyguard, mounted upon a cow pony, left the ranch behind him and whipped his team south to the railroad. The bodyguard accompanied him only a part of one day, it is said, but they had traveled so swiftly that it took him two and a half days to get back with his jaded pony.[27]

With Campbell gone, Spencer, of individual horse-feeding note, lorded his way over the Yellow Houses camp. A passerby, disillusioned after going to the Nogal mines to pick up nuggets, stopped on his way back to gather cow chips for the branding fires. It takes a lot of chips to heat an iron, but this miner was energetic and heaped up a pile by the corral fence ten feet high. Mounting a bronc, Spencer spurred him to the top. Then with a cowboy yell he caught his pony with his rowels and came down amid a show of "prairie coal."

Boyce, who was present and who had contended with outlaws along the hard cattle trail to California in the late sixties, was never known to run from trouble. He told Spencer to keep a-riding until he had left the XIT range behind him, and he handled other undesirables in the same way. Gradually they

<hr>

[27] J. Frank Yearwood to J. E. H., December 9, 1927.

were moved off the range, and working hands took their place.

Findlay, Matlock, and Boyce were bringing system and splendid organization to the ranch. From Buffalo Springs to Casas Amarillas, approximately two hundred miles, where no telephone or advanced means of locomotion operated to annihilate distance, where the fastest communication was the flying feet of a cow pony and the only messenger a puncher of cows, where law was so distant as to be impotent, "the Syndicate" was bringing development, law, and a measure of promise out of the desert.

CHAPTER VIII

A Long Fight for Law

WHEREVER CATTLE have been grazed extensively on the open range, the rustler has always swung a wide loop. But rustling never became quite as profitable upon the plains as in broken or timbered country, where ravine or forest offered seclusion from watchful cowboy eyes and protection from flying lead.

Though the plains country in general had enough cattle theft to give added zest to range life, the central portion of the XIT Ranch was the scene of the heaviest depredations. Here the Canadian breaks, with their creeks, canyons, hills, and scrub timber offered protection for such outlawry. Now, in the cow country, next to horse rustling, cattle theft ranked high in the category of crime, and at one time along the western line of the XIT, men were inclined to shoot first and ask questions afterward.

Above personal comfort and above personal safety for the cowboy was the welfare of the herd that he had in charge. Attesting adherence to this unwritten law of the Texas ranges are cowboy graves, unmarked and unknown, along forgotten trails from south of the Río Bravo to north of parallel forty-nine. Next to the cowboy riding range, the greatest enemy of the rustler was the barbed wire fence. Cattle thieves, to be successful, must be mobile. The XIT was fenced, but across its west line in New Mexico a great open country stretched northward to the headwaters of the Canadian and the Cimarron, and southward beyond the Pecos to the Capitan Mountains. One fence could be but slight restriction to the movement of cattle into this wide area. Topography conspired with the rustlers of eastern New Mexico to give the cowboys of the Escarbada Division much trouble.

A third big factor favoring profitable cattle theft was the remoteness of law, the lack of judicial force. There were courts and sheriffs at Las Vegas and Tascosa, but both were remote from the Escarbada. But even when a cow thief had been brought to the bar, it was almost impossible to convict him. Many of the jurors, used to the less exacting days of the range business, were loath to sentence a culprit for eating a neighbor's beef or branding his overgrown calves. The grand juries indicted, the petit juries acquitted, as is their wont, and so rustling flourished.

Cattle were stolen in many different ways. Bold and powerful rustler bands sometimes rode upon a range and drove off small bunches or even herds. Favored by natural conditions and a thinly settled country, they often made good their escape to sell the stolen cattle or place upon them a brand of their own before the owner discovered his loss. At times their operations were known, but they were powerful enough to steal openly and with impunity.

The practice of eating a neighbor's beef was once general upon the ranges of Texas. Hungry men killed a fat beef wherever they found one, regardless of owner, and in those days of lax business methods and open-handed hospitality, such action seemed above reproach. But foreign capital came, the barbed wire fence confined each brand to its own range, the happy-go-lucky pastoral ways of the seventies became a business of exacting methods, and killing strays came to be regarded as theft.

Brand burning, another method employed by the rustlers, required skill and was always risky. Brand burners simply burned the original brand into another figure or symbol.

But the most general form of theft practiced upon the **XIT** was that of mavericking, which usually took the form of stealing large, unbranded calves. Mavericking, along with "beefing" and brand burning, is sometimes designated "petty stealing." But losses may be very heavy from such rustling. They were for the XIT since this broad range was particularly open to the practice.

Calves large enough to live upon grass continue to follow their mothers until "kicked off"—until weaned by them, or are separated from them by the cowboys, which became the general practice under the new order of wire fences. Unbranded, the calf's ownership is clearly established by the brand of the cow it follows. Weaned and cast upon its own resources, it becomes a maverick—an animal whose ownership is undetermined because of lack of mark or brand, whether six months or six years old. In the days of open range, the maverick belonged, theoretically and in practice, to the first man having cattle upon that range who roped and applied his iron to him. The man with 100 head of cattle often branded more mavericks into his own title than the man who had 5,000 head upon the range—obviously an unjust distribution, but often allowed. With fences, clearly the mavericks found within an enclosure belonged to the brand ranging therein, and the man from the outside who burned his heraldry into the hide of a maverick had committed an act of theft. Thus progressed the ethics of the range.

Maverickers would ride over into the XIT pastures, find large unbranded calves, cut them off from their mothers, and run them over to their homesteads. Mother cows and their calves, upon becoming separated, back-track for miles to reach the spot at which each last saw the other. The old Texas Longhorns would travel farther, guided by an uncanny sense of direction and smell, than cattle of better blood. Because of this instinct, the rustler was forced to wean the calves he stole before he applied his brand, or have them so secured that they could not return to their mothers.

A calf that showed up on the home range switching its tail over a fresh brand told a more vivid story than human tongue, and often precipitated a six-shooter and Winchester-draped cavalcade upon the trail of the owner of the brand. Some rustlers kept big stolen calves in a corral a short while, cut the muscles which supported their eyelids so that they dropped closed, and at last turned them loose. Thus separated from their mothers, they "bawled their heads off" for a few days. Getting no response and not being able to see to return to their mothers, they became hungry, groped around for food and were soon weaned. The muscles of their eyes healed, but the lids always drooped slightly.

Another method employed by the rustlers was to burn the calves between the toes with a hot iron, making their feet too sore for them to walk. A few rustlers followed the even more brutal practice of splitting their tongues so they could not nurse. Safely weaned from parental milk and attention by the time these wounds healed, they ceased bawling for their mothers, the rustler placed his own brand upon them, and they were his by right of dangerous industriousness and legally registered brand.[1]

If a calf so stolen happened to find its way back to the home range and its mother and was there discovered, the rustler explained that in branding his own calves this one, at the time among them, had been branded by mistake. To be doubly cautious, he often employed several maverick brands. These fictitious brands were used to throw a watchful rider off his guard. When all danger seemed past, the rustler's brand appeared upon the animal, and, if any one questioned its ownership, he named an original fictitious owner of some distant place. Winter time was open season on the rustler, as then he was busiest. Then, evading the range riders, he "still hunted" through the grazing cattle, picking up big calves that had been missed during the summer and fall brandings.[2] By these methods did thieves around Tascosa and, more extensively, the rustlers along the New Mexico line depredate upon XIT calves. But

[1] R. L. Duke to J. E. H., July 6, 1927; Ira Aten to J. E. H., February 26, 1928; C. R. Smith to J. E. H., August 11, 1927.

[2] Ira Aten to J. E. H., February 26, 1928.

they were hard to catch and hold; harder to bring to justice.[3]

Yet the most serious problem of law and order confronting the XIT originally arose on the ranch itself. This unfortunate internal situation largely grew out of the gross carelessness if not the sympathy of the first general manager. The condition was encouraged by the convenient anonymity insured by this vast new venture on the borders of Texas. It was abetted by the bustle and confusion incident to its early development. Within two years it grew to grave proportions.

At this point the owners, as already observed, called on A. L. Matlock, the tough-fibered and stubborn-minded young lawyer from the Texas Senate, to take this perverse bull of lawlessness by the horns and "go to the ground with it." In October, 1887, Matlock reported on the conditions that he found:

> There is no avoiding the fact that the ranch, until I came here . . . has been, for eighteen months before, the stopping place and rendezvous for a large number of bad men and criminals. Some of these men have been in the employ of the ranch, while others have been harbored by those employed. The consequence has been that the reputation of the ranch has been very much below par with the neighboring ranches, who have been spending large sums of money for years to rid the country of the very class of men, many of whom were employed on this ranch.
>
> Colonel Campbell was informed of the class of men he had . . . but I find no evidence whatever that he made any effort to rid himself of them, but, on the other hand, I have evidence that he encouraged some of them to remain and was very abusive toward those who gave him the information.[4]

In his report Matlock listed the names and records of many unsavory characters on the ranch. With such bad company, practices other than theft contributed to the owners' troubles. Upon this score, Matlock continued:

[3] R. L. Duke to J. E. H., July 6, 1927.
[4] A. L. Matlock to George F. Westover, October 9, 1887, Matlock Papers, in files of the author.

Gambling was another very constant practice on the ranch, and it was not altogether unknown to Colonel Campbell. The gambling that was done here (without permission, of course, but not suppressed when made known) has cost the company much loss of time, provisions, neglect of business and consequent loss of cattle.

At Escarbada last winter they had a regular monte bank, where men from distant parts of the ranch, and from long distances off the ranch, came to gamble, and stayed for days at a time, at the expense of the Company.

The gambling was not confined to the men, but included the bosses. Kyle, who was at Escarbada in charge, says that Ney and his men came up there and gambled all night, and were coming in to their breakfasts as late as eight o'clock. Mr. Williams, who was in charge of the water supply here (at Yellow Houses), states that Ney and his men gambled at Spring Lake. Dan Cole says that while he was in charge of the outfit, his men would get right down in the road, or around a cow herd and gamble, and that he could not prevent it, because he was not allowed by the manager to either employ or discharge any man and they did as they pleased. Mr. Braid says that the regular gamblers used to go down from Tascosa to Escarbada to gamble with the men. . . . Boyce says that . . . as much gambling was done at the Yellow Houses as anywhere on the ranch.

Besides this, a lot of the men were still wearing guns, which Matlock called a "common occurrence," all of which, he insisted, "could not do otherwise than destroy all discipline and organization on the ranch, and could result in nothing else but loss to the Company." [5]

A reputed gun-fighter was named as one of the first foremen of the Escarbada. Jim Cook, wearing his two six-shooters and his ill-boding reputation with equal grace, rode in to do battle with the cow thieves to the west. Aggressive and overbearing, it is said, he was eternally at odds with the riders across the line. Not only that, but he had trouble with one of his own men, and when Cook started to draw, the man protested that he was unarmed. Pulling his gun on the left, Cook pitched

[5] *Ibid.*

it across to the cowboy and told him to pick it up and defend himself. Had he made a move to follow the suggestion, Cook would have killed him before his hand reached the gun. He was an imaginative, colorful character, but women, not outlaws, caused the fall toward which Cook was riding.

Over to the east the little town of La Plata had grown up to become the county seat of Deaf Smith. Cook forsook doing battle with cattle rustlers and entered the jousts with cupid when a young lady from Kansas City visited there. When she returned to Kansas City, he succeeded in having the Escarbada Ranch designated a post office in order that he would not have to suffer the delays of uncertain trips to La Plata for mail.[6] Femininity and cattle mix poorly; so in his place came good-humored, whistling, hard-working and hard-riding Mac Huffman.[7]

Within a year Spring Lake needed a foreman and Mac was placed in charge of that fine range. Jim McLaren, comical Jim, who bought such delicacies as butter and eggs on the trail and charged them up to the company as potatoes, took the place he left. Jim was not the type of man needed and was replaced by the sheriff of Castro County, a former Texas Ranger of power and force, who, in handling lawless elements, believed strongly in the efficacy of fear. Under the ten-year administration of Ira Aten, who took charge in 1895, the Escarbada was operated with a minimum of loss. "I controlled them through fear," he said, and his methods were efficient.

As a Texas Ranger upon the frontier he had formed associations which now proved of much value. From El Paso he brought Wood Saunders, another Ranger seasoned in border service, and from the company of Captain W. J. McDonald, he secured for detached duty "Big Ed" Connell.[8] With modesty commensurate with his size, Connell gave his complete story of several years service with the ranch: "Stealing wasn't so bad;

6 M. Huffman to J. E. H., November 3, 1927.
7 J. W. Stevens to J. E. H., November 23, 1927.
8 Ira Aten to J. E. H., February 26, 1928.

they just had us there as a preventive." ⁹ Saunders was placed at Trujillo Camp to watch the New Mexico line. Connell was placed at a camp named Tombstone, to watch the men of "The Strip." ¹⁰

Once each day a rider, armed with six-shooter and Winchester, rode the fences from these camps, and it became extremely hazardous to be found along one without evident legitimate business. The situation in the west became so tense that the riders began taking a shot at every man seen near the line in New Mexico, not so much with malicious intent, but just "as a preventive." The rustlers often tore the fences down so that it appeared to have been done by cattle, and drifted a bunch of cows and calves out. Whenever this was discovered, Aten called his two main fighting men, Connell and Saunders, and with an armed outfit of cowboys, crossed with his wagon into New Mexico as quickly as possible and rounded up the country. By fast work he was usually able to gather most of his cattle before the rustlers had picked up the calves.

Confidently expecting to be killed when he went to the ranch, Ira Aten doubled his life insurance but kept his six-shooter oiled.¹¹ In making his rides about the ranch, he never traveled the same trails twice. Riding out by one course, he returned by another. The windows at the Escarbada were painted a dark green and heavy shades hung over those at Trujillo. In camp, Aten always sat back beyond the light of the fire, and if a stranger came to the wagon, he never slept until he identified him or ascertained his business.¹² At Trujillo the line-rider never stepped from camp without his six-shooter. If a rider appeared at night, the cowboy was certain of his identity before admitting him, and, if uncertain, he maintained the advantage. Eternal vigilance was the price of life.¹³

In order for the foreman to be in close touch with the men

⁹ Ed Connell to J. E. H., October 31, 1927.
¹⁰ Ira Aten to J. E. H., February 26, 1928.
¹¹ Ira Aten to J. E. H., February 26, 1928.
¹² C. R. Smith to J. E. H., August 11, 1927; *ibid.*, March 20, 1928.
¹³ Ira Aten to J. E. H., February 26, 1928.

at Trujillo and Tombstone, a camp diary was kept under lock in a small box. The foreman carried one key to the lock, the cowboy keeping the camp carried the other. Daily entries were made. Upon the fly-leaf of one of these diaries is this note:

Tombstone Camp,
January 1st, 1902

To Camp Men

Keep the name and date of every man who stays all night, passes camp, or seen on range. If the person is a suspicious character take a full description of man and color & brand of horse where from & where going, etc. The above instruction must be closely carried out. This book must be kept in lock up in box for that purpose. [Then a supplementary note was added in pencil.] Also date of each ride number of dead cattle mills out of fix, etc.

Ira Aten Foreman.[14]

Choosing at random from among its many entries, one may read in the Trujillo Camp Diary of 1902 and 1903:

Dec. 29th. I rode the Mexico fence—
Jany—4th. Frank Cavender came over to have small pox—
Jan. 26. [In Aten's handwriting] Ira Aten came to camp at dinner today. . . . I want dates, passing of people & circumstances reported more closely.
Feby. 13th. Bad day sleeted all day, we soaked.[15]
Feby. 19th. Greased mills chopped ice, rode Mexico fence and rounded up bulls! . . .[16]
Jan. the 4—1903. Rode to Caps dam then to Holy dam then to the Mohairs & to Chalkey and down the Mohairs to Henry the first, from their to camp found the cow dead that we dipt
9. Sand Storm done nothing.[17]

The Tombstone Diary, of the same years, likewise gives intimate glimpses of cow-camp life:

[14] "Tombstone Camp Diary, 1902–1903."
[15] A cowboy expression for loafing.
[16] During the winter the cowboys cut ice from frozen troughs and tanks so that cattle might drink.
[17] "Trujillo Camp Diary, 1902–1903."

Aug. 25. Two wagons loaded with chickens & Kids passed Camp from Tucumcari. . . .

Aug. 17 Skined—3—cows came on to camp found the tombstone mill out of whack. fraters [freighters] past by.

April 23—1903 rode Phone line then rode bog Skined—4—cows one with ticks Came back found that an unnoen friend had been at camp prised into grane house taken one sack of grane.

Ma 30 1903 One man past Camp driving to black asses with a long whip in Buggy Concord Springs on it he looked suspicious he come and watered and went to feed and just got up and drug it.[18]

June 22—1903 Three men passed here on foot back, going from Rag Town to Hereford at the rate of   miles an hr They looked kinder lank in the sinch [through the girth] and week in the hine legs.[19]

27. Sept. Old Dynimite was bitten by rattle snake

28 of Feb. . . . 20 calves died with Black leg during Feb.[20]

When Aten, riding over the ranch, reached the camps to find the line-rider away, he opened the box with a key which he carried and made an entry of his visit, leaving any orders he wished, often telling whence he came, but rarely his destination.[21] Among his significant entries is this:

Aten ate dinner here today. I dont want the Glasscock [trail] outfit showed any courtesies whatever. Make them go out of pasture as soon as possible. They tied the phone wire down yesterday morning on Mex line . . . where they had stayed all night. . . . Look through there cattle good. . . . I expect to go & meet them to day and demand an explanation. You better stay at camp tomorrow. Be at Correll Lake Friday night.

Aten.

And so the daily entries ran, sometimes significant, often of little import. When a new man replaced an old line-rider, an

18 In cowboy parlance "to drag it" is to depart precipitately, or without ado.

19 "Tombstone Camp Diary, 1902–1903."

20 "Tombstone Camp Diary, 1902–1903."

21 Ira Aten to J. E. H., February 26, 1928.

Escarbada Headquarters

Picket Corral, Rito Blanco Division, 1898
(Panhandle-Plains Historical Society)

Roping and branding on the range

XIT chuck wagon on general roundup
on Buch Horn Ranch, New Mexico, in 1888
(Panhandle-Plains Historical Society)

W. S. Mabry, about 1884

A windmiller's chuck wagon — his only home

John V. Farwell, Sr.
holding Sunday morning services for the cowboys at Spring Lake

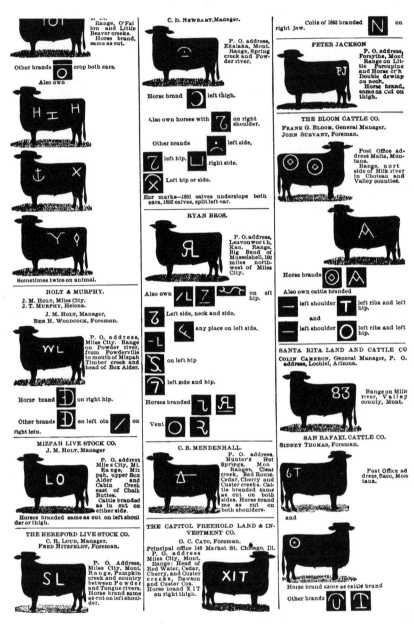

Brands of the XIT and neighboring ranches in Montana
as they appeared in an early Miles City newspaper

inventory of items about the camp was made. W. S. Kirk took
charge at Tombstone, April 14, 1903, and wrote, with rather
picturesque spelling, his own inventory:

1 hatchate
1 ax
1 saw
1 spade
1 post auger
1 schisle
1 wrench
1 pare nipers
1 oil can
1 skinning knife
9 hens and one ruster [22]

Nobody but the line-rider and Aten was to see these camp
diaries. The practice was peculiar to these two camps on the
Escarbada and was one means of many by which the foreman
attempted to keep track of the cattle rustlers and of his own
men.[23]

I happened to be at Tombstone Camp one night [said the vigilant
Aten] when a fellow came along and stopped to stay all night. I
had never seen him before. He had his six-shooter on and talked
ugly all night. I found that he was a cow thief. The next morning
I said to him: "Now get your horse, saddle, and go. Take that road
and never come back. When you start, don't even look back. If you
do," I added as I picked up my Winchester, "I am going to shoot
you right through the middle."
He went, and never looked back.[24]

Careful to see that neighboring riders respected its property, the XIT management, after cleaning up its own initial
mess, was even more careful that its own cowboys rode trails
that were straight. Findlay and Boyce drafted a code in Janu-

[22] "Tombstone Camp Diary, 1902–1903."
[23] Ira Aten to J. E. H., February 26, 1928.
[24] *Ibid.*

ary of 1888 called "General Rules of the XIT Ranch." The twenty-three requirements of this code constituted a radical departure from old range etiquette and practice.[25] From the first, cowboys were told: "Don't steal a beef for us! If you do we'll fire you."[26] Cowboys were forbidden to carry six-shooters, to keep private horses at their camps, to gamble, or to run mustangs and antelope with XIT horses.[27] There was much infringement of these rules, particularly the one concerning the carrying of guns, but those governing liquor and gambling were rigidly enforced.[28]

Another innovation introduced upon the ranges at the insistence of John V. Farwell was the observance of Sunday as a day of rest.[29] But in theory alone was Sunday observed. Cow work, once started, went forward seven days a week for seven or eight months of the year, during which time the Lord was sadly neglected.

Few diversions broke the daily routine of winter work. A little reading matter was a welcome addition to any camp. Practical jokes were perpetrated upon unsuspecting tenderfeet, and, as a respite from the real thing, kangaroo courts sometimes imposed sentence upon the transgressor of Western etiquette. One such is described in *The Tascosa Pioneer*, August 6, 1887:

> Kangaroo court opened at the LX ranch Monday with one case on the docket. Dick Cross had been summoned to answer before that august tribunal for a glaring misdemeanor—lying idle about the ranch while he should have been out rustling for a job. James Wyness wore the judicial purple and tioga of judge, J. D. Bain represented the commonwealth in the responsible position of prosecuting attorney, James Gober was Sheriff and his honor appointed Mr W. D. Lard, Esq., to defend the accused. . . . But for

[25] *The Fort Worth Gazette,* September 25, 1892.
[26] M. Huffman to J. E. H., November 3, 1927.
[27] Ms., "General Rules of the XIT Ranch" (Chicago files). See appendix for these rules.
[28] McClure, "Among the Cowboys of Texas," 15; J. E. Moore to J. E. H., November 8, 1927.
[29] *The Tascosa Pioneer,* May 26, 1888.

all the wonderful efforts of Counsel Lard, who is said to be something of a real attorney, the verdict was against the defendant. The evidence, it seems, was really overwhelming, and the prosecution carried the day. The prisoner was sentenced to eighteen licks with the leggings on the back, which Deputy John Watkins administered with a will. This responsible duty over, court adjourned and the late prisoner pulled his freight.

Yet real trouble dogged the boot heels of the general manager of a ranch that took an arbitrary stand for law and order. Over on the Rito Blanco, two cowboys were breaking horses for Henry Kimball in 1891. Boyce, wishing to see the country rid of them, was instrumental in their being discharged. They rode into Channing during the late fall, evidently intent upon shooting Boyce. They first got drunk and for a while practiced shooting at the bolt heads that held the bar of the hitching rack in place.

Then they went to the office of the general headquarters of the ranch there in town. One went in, expecting to find Boyce, but instead W. S. Mabry sat at the desk writing a letter. Perhaps not knowing the difference, perhaps not caring, one of the boys threw down on Mabry but missed him, even though his gun was so close that the powder burned Mabry's face. Mabry jumped up and ran over to the home of Jim East, the rugged former cowboy sheriff of old Tascosa.

"Mabry wasn't armed and this made him pretty mad," East recalled. The two armed themselves with .44 Winchesters, and set out after the cowboys, who, after plundering Humphrey's store, had taken refuge in Kimball's blacksmith shop. They had "taken in the town" so completely that someone had wired Tobe Robinson, sheriff of the county, at Hartley, that he had better come down. Tobe hopped a freight train and got into Channing as drunk as a lord, but thoughtfully brought a Texas Ranger by the name of Owens with him.

The boys had gone from the blacksmith shop into a pump house near by. Robinson and the Ranger came up as Mabry and East started after them.

"Come on," Robinson said to Jim East. "You and Mabry go to one end of the house and Owens and I will go to the other. If they run out at the front door, you and Mabry shoot them and we will attend to the back door."

Almost immediately one appeared at the back door, and Robinson, about fifteen feet away, called: "Throw up your hands and surrender." Robinson was armed with a double-barrel shotgun and a six-shooter, and Owens carried a Winchester.

But this cowboy, a fearless fellow, shouted: "Go to hell! I won't surrender to anybody," and, drawing his six-shooter, fired one quick shot, hitting Robinson just below the hip. Meanwhile, much to East's disgust, as he later described the fight, Robinson had stood there like a "gawk" and hadn't fired his shotgun, but as he fell he jerked his six-shooter and shot the fighter, giving him a scalp wound that "didn't knock him down."

"Then Mabry and I heard the other and a tramp, who had thrown in with them, start out at the front. We ran back around to the front. Both of us opened fire, shooting this one through the side and thigh, and the tramp didn't offer much resistance. I called my brother Bob to take Robinson down to the hotel, as we thought he was bleeding to death.

"By this time it was dark, the other cowboy had run down to a windmill tower about fifty yards from the house and taken shelter behind it. We exchanged several shots and then he called: 'Jim, is that you out there?'

" 'Yes,' I answered.

" 'Don't shoot any more, Jim,' he said. 'My brains are shot out and I want to surrender.'

" 'All right,' I answered, 'Leave your six-shooter there and come out with your hands up.' He did. Mabry and I took him to the hotel where the others had taken Tobe. Then we got him into the light. The blood from his wound was running down through his eyes. He kept rubbing his hand through the stream and looking at it.

" 'Aw, hell,' he said, 'that's not brains. If I had known that, I wouldn't have surrendered.'

"There was no jail at Hartley or Channing, and we took them to Tascosa. The grand jury met and indicted the worst of the two—not for attempted murder, but for breaking into Humphrey's store. The only regret Mabry and I had was that we didn't finish him up that night." [30]

Mavericking upon the ranch continued for many years. In 1906, after Aten had left the ranch and R. L. (Bob) Duke had charge of the northern portion upon which cattle were yet being ranged, rustlers were still stealing as many as twenty-five head of cattle at a time. Bob rode into Endee one evening and had supper at the hotel. Across the table from him sat a man and woman who, in collusion, raided upon Texas brands, and at the ends of the table sat two men who had that day conspired to kill him.

A daughter of the hotel owner, with whom one of the Syndicate cowboys was enamoured, overheard the plot and told Duke of it. Originally these two rustlers planned to get him into a poker game, start a row, and kill him. Finding he did not play poker, they conspired to get into a scuffle in the hall, break his door down, and, in the melee, shoot him. Duke saddled his horse after dark and rode out for Escarbada, and that night the door was broken in.

At that time just "a kid of a boy" was attempting to live upon a claim across the line. As he had worked a little with the XIT outfits, Duke hired him in 1907 to keep his eyes open and discover what he could about any cattle thieves. When XIT cattle got through the fence, the New Mexico farmers around Endee would put them in a corral, and by the herd law of that state the ranch was forced to pay damages. Some of the farmers almost made a business of drifting cattle upon their land so that they might collect damages. This boy was to "ride sign" unobtrusively and discover the parties guilty of this fraud and of cattle theft. Suspecting the kid, Mart McCracken

[30] James H. East to J. E. H., September 27, 1927.

and another cowboy rode up to his dugout and told him they were going to kill him. His precocious belligerency surprised them.

Opening fire, he shot McCracken through the arm and ran both of them off, but that night he left the country and Duke never heard of him again. He feared to stay after the open break. Duke always paid him in currency, never by check, and though the boy worked off and on for nearly a year, Duke never knew his name. When the Escarbada was closed out as a breeding range in 1906, the XIT began using it as a steer pasture, and its troubles from mavericking became a thing of the past.[31]

In history, as in legend, the trails left by the mavericks are trails blazed with human blood. Scarcely less sanguine were those of the brand burners, though the extent to which brand burning was practiced has frequently been exaggerated. The ingenuity and skill necessary to its successful pursuit have flushed the already colorful stories of cattle theft. Fittingly, the most widely told legend of brand burning of the Southwest is of this brand of one of the world's largest ranches. Almost as far as the brand is known, cowboys tell the tale of the Star Cross burn. Around their fires at night, or as they sit in the shade of a corral fence by day, someone will tell the story, and others, tracing the XIT in the sand between their bowlegs, will attempt to convert it into a Texas star with a cross in the center.

Uncertainty as to the rustler who performed this work of art is an attribute of each recital, but little doubt that it was done shakes the believer's faith. One old-time cowpuncher tells how the man who stole so heavily under this manorial coat of arms was brought to trial at Lubbock. The jury acquitted him upon the ground that the conversion of the XIT into a lone star was an impossibility. Now cow thieves are smart, the story honestly holds, and are aware of their constitutional guarantees against being held in jeopardy twice for the same offense. Once acquitted, the rustler took a piece of paper, called the jury

[31] R. L. Duke to J. E. H., March 21, 1928.

around him, and with the pride of a master craftsman in his work, proceeded to show that such was not an impossibility.

The Syndicate brand was made with one straight bar about five inches long. By turning this bar in the relative position of the lines of the three letters, the entire brand was stamped upon the animal with five applications of the iron. Haste in the work or the hide of a calf drawn a little from its natural position, often resulted in a brand not altogether symmetrical, and this legendary rustler searched until he found such a brand,[32] of which there were a great number among the thousands of Syndicate cattle. After roping and tying the animal, he took his running iron or ring, and traced the lone star cross upon it.[33]

Another old-timer recalls that it was not a Texan but a New Mexico rustler who executed this burn.[34] However, the matter of geography is unimportant, because wherever the vivid imagination of the storyteller may wander around the ranges of the XIT, there rides this mythical rustler with a running iron upon his saddle. Looking across the glowing remains of "coosie's" fire after the day's work is over, the cowboy, hearing this tale, gazes upon a moonlit plain where the pungent odor of burnt hair yet lingers. Somewhere a calf calls to its mother, and in the breeze a swaying trace chain tinkles against a wagon wheel. The half-dozing cowboy jerks himself to life, for in these sounds from across the prairies comes the muffled jingle of a rider's spurs, the "beller" of a calf in pain, the unmistakable aroma of burning hair and hide.

In the mysterious spell of a land that fires the imagination so much, even the fantastic seems quite possible, and the ordinary cowhand often settles back on his heels and smiles to himself for a moment before hunting his "suggans." Thus, in retrospective moments this legendary horseman still rides through the ranges of cowboy imagination, still, with bold stride, bursts

[32] X/T

[33] In this way: ⬠ Harry Ingerton to J. E. H., April 13, 1927.

[34] A. L. Turner to J. E. H., July 2, 1926.

from danger to live among the heroes of folklore. Thus frugal Nature balances the scales with her incalculable compensations.

But such "foolishness" is lost among the balance sheets of business. The veteran business manager of the ranch, George Findlay, explained the origin of this widespread tale.

With reference to the burning of the XIT brand into a star cross [wrote Mr. Findlay], I have to say that while this story was given circulation by several reputable publications, it is purely a myth and never occurred in fact. I was living on the ranch about the time, and the XIT being a new brand in that country, the cowboys used to amuse themselves around the campfire by showing how many different things it could be altered to, and I remember this star cross was one of them.[35]

Yet where legend is so prolific, there is usually a basis in fact, and more than one rustler burned out the XIT brand. In the Yellow House country it was burned into Boxed XITF and Boxed XITE.[36] Again it was burned into Eighty barred out.[37]

While the Escarbada and the country to the north were having trouble, out upon the plains to the south a few rustlers kept their irons smooth.[38]

An XIT steer was burned into 4 Box P, a steer branded with C. C. Slaughter's Long Lazy S wore an ace of clubs, and a JA animal was burned into DA connected.[39] Often brand burning was so skillfully done that the alteration could not be detected. Though the cowman could not succeed in bringing a thief to justice before regularly constituted courts, he matched

[35] George Findlay to J. E. H., December 3, 1926.

[36] R. C. Burns to J. E. H., February 22, 1927. ⊠ |Ϝ and ⊠ |Ɛ

[37] S. A. Bull to J. E. H., July 6, 1926.

[38] A branding iron must be smooth, free from rust and scales, to give satisfaction.

[39] Ira Aten to J. E. H., March 1, 1928; B. P. Abbott to J. E. H., June 24, 1927. The drawings below show these brands: (1) 4 Box P; (2) Long Lazy S, which was changed into an Ace of Clubs; (3) JA, which was changed into DA connected. (1)   (2)   (3)

his wits against the most clever of rustlers, and in some way usually defeated him at the game. In the case of the last-named XIT steer, the X had either been applied carelessly, or in handling the calf had been twisted around so that the brander made almost a cross instead of an X, and its burning was simple.

Brands usually "hair over," but the hair ruffles to show the brand distinctly. A brand applied after the animal becomes old may fail to "hair over," but often leaves instead a whitish, calloused scar. In burning a brand, the rustler traces his iron over the entire old brand in order to give it the same freshly branded appearance as the new parts. In the instance of the 4 Box P steer, the old brand left a scar, the newly branded portions "haired over." The 4 Box P was distinct when viewed at close range, but from a distance the XIT stood clear from the alteration. Thus a trick of nature proclaimed this steer a stolen one and the man holding him a thief.[40]

Not often did Nature thus conspire to defeat the rustler. When unable to prove a suspected animal burned, cowboys sometimes shot it down to be skinned. The old brand shows more plainly than the new when viewed from the flesh side of the hide. As the hide begins to dry, the original brand stands out against the light more distinctly than the alteration and is incontestable evidence. A hide that has been dry for months may be soaked in water until pliable, held to the light, and the brand inspected in the same way with almost as unerring results.

Where the rustler killed a beef, he usually destroyed or threw the hide in an out-of-the-way place. He might go further and cut the brand from the hide and the earmarks off so that its possible discovery would leave the finder at loss as to the owner. A hide found with altered earmarks or with the brand cut out showed that a thief had killed the animal, but proving identity was something else.

The final episode in twenty-eight years of fighting for law

[40] *Ibid.*

was the only one in which an XIT cowboy was killed. After the Yellow Houses and Spring Lake were sold, the Bovina and Escarbada divisions were placed under one foreman, John Armstrong, who had succeeded Ira Aten. The near-by JJ Ranch was under the management of Gene Ellison, an old friend of Armstrong. A JJ cow had been burned into SHS connected.[41] Ellison drove her to the Bovina Ranch where he and Armstrong killed and skinned her.

Ellison satisfied himself as to the original brand, and swore out papers for the arrest of J. W. Williams. Williams claimed to have bought the cow, or at least he claimed that he held a bill of sale to her. He, in turn, swore out papers for Ellison and Armstrong for killing the cow. Bad blood was aroused. Armstrong and Williams met at the depot at Bovina, November 18, 1908; the latter opened fire with a .30–30 Winchester and shot Armstrong off his horse. A trial at Canyon resulted in a hung jury. At Amarillo a six-year sentence was returned, the case reversed, tried again, and nine years were given.[42]

The trial was typical of early-day judicial proceedings. It has long been the practice of cattle rustlers to rely on the evidence of perjurers. The defense went down to Fort Sill, Oklahoma, to get a man as witness who was in jail at the time Armstrong was killed. He testified that he saw Armstrong rope Williams and drag him along the ground by the horn of the saddle just before the shooting took place. Armstrong's horse was not caught until the morning following the shooting, but the rope was still done up on the saddle. The rope would have been dragging from the horn had the story been true.[43] A stretching rope has undone more than one rustler, but here one loosely coiled silently proved one man a perjurer and sent another to the pen.

When the last cow was sold, when the last beef was tallied

---

[41] ʄʄ

[42] J. P. McDonald to J. E. H., June 25, 1927.
[43] *Ibid.*

over to the buyers in 1912,[44] the vigilance of the Syndicate cowboys against rustlers of XIT cattle came to an end. For more than a quarter of a century this institution, often represented by 150 bow-legged, dust-begrimed riders of the plains, fought for law and order. What the Panhandle Stock Association had meant to the eastern Panhandle, the XIT alone meant to the far western portion. From the time when Matlock and Boyce expelled practically the entire range force because of its lawless character, through the fights with organized thieves along the Canadian, over in New Mexico, and even along the eastern fence lines, from 1885 to 1912, the XIT Ranch was an institution of law. It did for the western tier of Panhandle counties what county organization had failed to do.[45] It gave of its money, its men, and its time in a long fight for law—a sometimes seemingly thankless venture, but an incalculable, because an indispensable, asset to any civilized society.

[44] R. L. Duke to J. E. H., March 21, 1928.
[45] C. Goodnight to J. E. H., September 2, 1927.

CHAPTER IX

The Montana Trail

For twenty years that wildly imaginative venture that pushed millions of cattle throughout the virgin range of the West along the Texas Trail had been at its height. Then Dodge City was closed to the trail drivers from Texas in 1885, when the quarantine line was extended to include southwestern Kansas.[1] Thereafter, the great trail movement entered upon its declining decade. With the exception of a little driving to Kiowa and Liberal, Kansas, and to Trail City, Lamar, and other Colorado rail points, most of the herds trailed to northern ranges by a course that left Kansas to the east. This route was often called the Northern Trail,[2] and, more specifically, by the name of the state or territory to which it led, as the Wyoming or Montana Trail.[3]

In 1886 fifteen thousand head of XIT steers were sold and trailed north. These first XIT steers, divided into several herds, skirted Kansas, passed through Colorado, and to Spearfish on the Little Missouri.[4] The total drive from Texas over the Northern Trail that year was estimated at 225,000 head.[5]

It was common knowledge to the cow country that steers matured in the north spread in loin and frame and grew to greater size, and the LS, Milliron, Matador, N–N, 7D, and the XIT were some of the Panhandle outfits that maintained breed-

[1] Wright, *Dodge City, the Cowboy Capital*, 260.
[2] *Bureau of Animal Industry Report*, 1885, p. 297.
[3] *Prose and Poetry of the Live Stock Industry*, I, 529.
[4] J. E. May to J. E. H., June 29, 1926.
[5] *The Tascosa Pioneer*, September 29, 1886.

ing ranges in Texas and finishing ranges in the northern terri-tories.[6]

The first of the XIT trail herds were driven to grass near Spearfish, and kept on pasture by the famous firm of Day and Driscoll, before the Syndicate secured a northern range of its own. Yet the Texas Trail, born in trouble and nurtured on danger, could not escape conflict and controversy. Dispatches from Denver erroneously announced that the trail was closed in 1887.[7]

In 1889 six herds of XIT steers, totaling some 15,000 head, followed the first into the Black Hills. In 1890 the Ranch drove 10,000 more to place on its newly acquired open range "be-tween the rivers"—the Yellowstone and the Missouri—in Mon-tana. There the company adopted the policy of "double-wintering" before shipping them as aged steers, fat off grass, to the heavy-beef market at Chicago. Thus the company, like many other outfits, tied its production into its finishing busi-ness by a trail that stretched for more than a thousand miles, from its best cow range on the Yellow Houses to where their steers grew to heavy maturity around the headquarters on Cedar Creek, sixty miles above Miles City.

Here, in the words of George Findlay, their "cattle . . . scattered over a territory of about 200 miles east and west and about 75 miles north and south. It was," he continued, "a very broken country, largely made up of what is known as bad lands and in which were a great many other ranchmen." Each of these exercised at least "nominal control over a certain portion" of the range, where the work—the roundup—was carried on in keeping with his wishes. Sometimes the general work required two or three wagons for the Syndicate alone, as the roundup on this wide range was, at times, divided into as many different operations.[8]

[6] J. E. May to J. E. H., June 29, 1926; G. N. Jowell to J. E. H., Janu-ary 17, 1927; see *The Tascosa Pioneer,* August 13, 1887.

[7] *The Tascosa Pioneer,* July 30, 1887.

[8] *Abstract of Record,* Charles D. Babcock *vs.* John V. Farwell and others, Appellate Court of Illinois, 1st District, October, 1913, p. 486.

This ranch was placed under the management of O. C. Cato, an old-timer of the open-range school. Cattle were driven annually to replace those shipped to market. The usual drives were 10,000 to 12,500 head, though 20,000 head were driven one year. This movement continued until the trail closed. After that, but at more than double the cost, cattle were shipped by rail from the Buffalo Springs Division and carried on the Montana range to maturity.

In keeping with the Texas style, the XIT's went to Cedar Creek and began working the range with a "pot rack" outfit, provoking the derision of the old-established ranches there that were used to well-equipped wagons supplied with tents. The Texans, too, found the climate severe, and soon Cato was authorized to buy big wall tents for the tail-end of his wagons. Many of the cowboys from the south decided to stay. Among these was a Syndicate hand named P. E. Long, who recalled that:

Any cowpuncher who has worked in Montana likes the country "between the rivers"—the Yellowstone and the Missouri. That was a country of big ranches. The XIT headquarters was on Cedar Creek, sixty miles north of Miles City. Almost due north sixty-five miles on the Missouri, at the mouth of Prairie Elk Creek, was the CK Ranch. It had bought out the old N–Ns about 1900. Almost due west of the XIT was a ranch owned by an eastern syndicate, the LU Bar, on the Little Dry. About forty miles to our southwest was the Bow and Arrow outfit on Custer Creek. About 150 miles north, between the Musselshell and the Missouri River, was the N–. The country was rolling with no timber until you got up above the Bull Mountains, northeast of Billings. This was the extreme western line of the territory that we worked over.

About April 15th of every year the managers of the different ranches went to Miles City and held what was called the "stock meeting." There they mapped out the line of work. In that territory between the rivers we had two general roundups, "the east work," and "the west work." These works began about the first of May and ran until about the 10th of July. Both works started together.

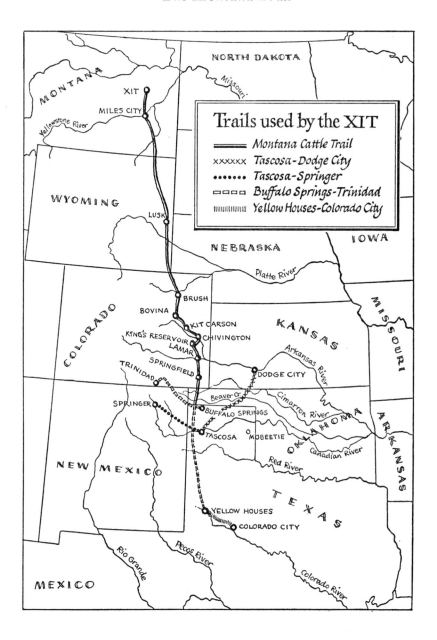

The LU Bar, CK, and XIT had two wagons out at the same time, one with the "west" and one with the "east work." The Bow and Arrows had a wagon for the "east," but just sent a "rep" with the "west work." These outfits, with the L7, on the Big Dry, and "reps" and wagons from other ranches, started the two "works" together on the head of Red Water. They worked down it to its mouth, and the "west work" turned west to work up the Missouri and over to the Bull Mountains. The "east work" went down the rivers and then turned back to meet the other. The "west work" dropped in and loaded its wagons at Forsythe, west of Miles City. The boys got on a drunk, and then, when they got down to Miles City, they pulled a good one. The XIT usually loaded out at Terry, a little place just at the mouth of Cedar Creek.

A man named Fry ran what we called the "band wagon." He loaded this up with clothing, cinches, straps, stirrup leathers, and other cowboy supplies and came out to meet the work about the head of the Little Dry.

The beef work started about the 10th of August and lasted until snow flew. We would still be at it in December. The LU Bar shipped from Miles City and the XIT shipped from Fallon. The Syndicate shipped 22,000 head to Montana in 1902. We began unloading them at Fallon, but we could not get them across the Yellowstone. We tried to ferry them across, but it would have taken us forever, as we could ferry only a carload at a time. So we shipped them on east to Glendive, where there was a five-span bridge across the river. The city commission decided it would not be safe to put more across the bridge than a half carload at a time. The bridge swayed a lot, but, when the commission left, we shoved them over in a stream.

The roundup outfits were made up of ten riders, two horse wranglers—a day wrangler and a "night hawk," and a cook. We used a big bed wagon in addition to the chuck wagon, as the Montana beds were not like these Texas beds. The tent and beds would be stacked up so high you couldn't throw a rock over them. It was a sight to see those outfits breaking camp. The first wagon to the next water got the best location on the water, and it was a regular wagon race from one camp to another. I have seen the lines handed up to the cook fifteen minutes after breakfast was over. Those outfits used stoves to cook with, and they were strong on light bread.

The Montana Trail

Rufe Morris, an old Dutch boy from Del Rio County, Texas, ran the outfit on Cedar Creek when I went there. The old Hatchet Ranch, six miles north of Fallon, on Cabin Creek, was bought by the Syndicate, was used as a subdivision, and was run by Bob Fudge.[9]

Tex Willis, another old-timer on the same outfit, vividly recalled a few of the old ranch hands:

Bob Fudge was the most typical cowpuncher the Xs (XIT) ever had. He weighed 325 pounds, was a fine roper, and could ride a small pony further and easier than any man I ever saw.

Ed and Bill Harrison, ex-Confederate soldiers, were the greatest wagon bosses or trail herd bosses that ever pointed a herd or swum a mess wagon. They were diplomats; Ed Harrison was with . . . Quantrell's Band.

Osie Cato was a great man.

Al Boyce stayed on my Alberta ranch on Belly River; Al had a good heart.

Stanley Miller, the greatest dude, looked like Tom Mix but was a better man. Stanley died in Deer Lodge penitentiary for that Harlem Mountain Bank robbery.

Well, the old days of Levi Strauss overalls, California salmon-colored trousers, flannel shirts, J. O. Bass and McKinney spurs, and Myers and Walker's saddles . . . are gone forever.[10]

In Texas, the yearling steers were driven from the various breeding divisions and concentrated in the Buffalo Springs pastures. As two-year-olds they were taken on to Montana. No yearlings were driven, but after the close of the trail a few were shipped by rail. George Findlay usually traveled to Texas to see them started, receiving them from A. G. Boyce, the general manager there. He returned to Chicago by rail, and at the proper time proceeded to Miles City, and to Cedar Creek by hack to meet the drivers to check the cattle in to Manager Cato, there. For three months in between, the herds were in complete control of the bosses of the individual trail outfits—

[9] P. E. Long to J. E. H., July 15, 1928.
[10] Tex Willis to J. E. H., December 4, 1928.

131

men seasoned in the psychology of cows and their kind, constantly pointing their way by the polar stars as each, in effect, patiently juggled a fortune with his hands.

When Boyce parted from the trail bosses at Buffalo Springs, usually prematurely bowlegged but responsible youngsters with a streak of hell in their hearts as they faced the hazards and rigors of the drive, his directions were simple. "Keep your eye on the north star," he told them, "and drive straight ahead until you can wet your feet in the waters of the Yellowstone." [11] Brief indeed for ten men with 2,500 steers setting forth on an 850-mile drive, when troubles beset that drive from end to end.

No Man's Land, or the Oklahoma Panhandle, where law seldom reached, was a refuge for hard characters. Nothing disturbed the passage of the XIT herds until 1892, but in the spring of that year a tax was imposed on all trail herds that passed through the Strip. Before the herds were placed upon the trail, Boyce and Findlay heard of the scheme.

Ab Owings, experienced in the ways of the trail and no apprentice in those of the world, was sent with the first herd. Ab was a big, long, freckled-faced Texan, a great storyteller in the days when a story meant an anecdote of the soil, not waves of ether free from static. Off the trail he was downright "ornery" when he was put to freighting. When at the ranch he never passed through a gate without "hubbing" and tearing down a post. When riding fence, he forgot his pliers, rode and saw, but repaired not. On the trail, he could forget more than most men knew and still be a better boss.[12]

We can imagine Ab throwing the herd off the grassy slopes of the bed ground in the early morning light. As the cattle stretched from the night's rest and moved off to the north, the pointers—those men who directed the herd along its course—moved up to where the lead cattle were stepping out, the swing men dropped into place behind them, the flankers pushed in the

[11] Forest Crissey, "The Vanishing Range," 4; J. E. Moore to J. E. H., February 26, 1927.

[12] J. E. Moore to J. E. H., February 26, 1927; B. P. Abbott to J. E. H., June 25, 1927; J. Frank Mitchell to J. E. H., June 10, 1927.

cattle along the outer edges, and the drag men behind eased the stragglers off the bed ground. Meanwhile, with loaded wagon, the cook moved ahead to prepare the noon-day meal, and as the sun warmed stiffened muscles, the cattle began to graze. But when a drag hand pushed them forward, Ab's voice boomed clear to the farthest pointer: "By God, let 'em graze. They'll walk as soon as they get dry."

After filling with grass, the cattle began to want water, threw up their heads, and began to walk. The herd strung out, and Ab and the outfit trailed along with it, often riding for miles without having to turn a cow or sweat a horse, in the artful and finished way of real hands with cattle.[13] In 1892, Ab led the way into No Man's Land, prepared to let the trail boss immediately behind know if he should be held up for the tax and warn him of any danger.

He was met by armed men, representing themselves as United States marshals, on the Cimarron, and when he refused to pay the tax, they placed him and his herd under arrest. Ab sent a cowboy back to notify Boyce and Findlay. On his way the cowboy passed the second herd to take the trail, which was being driven by Ealy Moore, and told him that Ab's outfit was being held.

When I got to Cold Springs two days . . . after leaving [Moore wrote], an officer, at least he called himself one, came to my herd and told me that they had Owings and his herd under arrest down on the Cimarron river and were going to hold him until they collected the tax and if I wouldn't try to pass on thru but would stay where I was they wouldn't put a man with me. . . . I had been instructed by Mr. Boyce not to try to pass the other herd in case it was held up. . . . I very readily promised to stay where I was . . . until they said for me to go. . . . Messrs. Boyce and Findlay came up and paid them by check, under protest, and we were allowed to pass on thru. . . . But the XITs together with other ranches who were driving herds North and had to pass thru No Man's Land . . . took this tax graft into Federal Court and

[13] *Ibid.*

133

finally beat it, so, by 1894 we could drive thru without being molested.

The tax totaled eight cents on each steer. A charge of five cents was made upon entering, and then, being in, the drivers paid three cents to get out. The very method pursued proclaimed the tax a fraud, which, had it been collected upon the twelve thousand XIT cattle alone, would have netted these "officers" a convenient sum.[14]

Trail wagons were loaded with provisions and the necessary equipment at Channing, Texas. The first outfitting point along the trail was Lamar, Colorado, a shipping point on the Santa Fe Railroad. Brush was the next supply point, next Lusk, and next Miles City, just before the Montana range was reached.[15] The company made arrangements with mercantile houses in these towns, and the cooks swung their four-mule teams in to secure bacon, flour, coffee, chewing tobacco, and other necessities of trail life. At these points the bosses might draw needed money to pay for watering their herds or to bail out cowboys who "celebrated" too boisterously at the end of a long thirst. No provision for bail or fines was included in the legitimate budget of the XIT bosses, but this trouble was an oft-recurring one on the old Texas or Northern Trail. The trail stores were a distinct advantage to the drivers, as supplementary camp equipage could be bought, alleviating the necessity of loading the chuck wagon so heavily at the beginning of the drive.[16]

Nesters, then the bane of the open-range men, had settled near the trail towns, built irrigation ditches, which the drivers paid to cross, and fenced the waterings, which the drivers paid to use.[17] Stretching for a hundred yards along the South Platte, where the trail crossed just below the town of Brush, Colorado, was a vacant strip of land—obviously vacant because it lay in the course of the trail, where thousands and thousands of hoofs

[14] J. E. Moore to J. E. H., November 12, 1925.
[15] J. E. Moore, Ms., "Diary of a Trail Trip to Montana, 1892," copy, Panhandle-Plains Historical Society.
[16] J. E. Moore to J. E. H., February 26, 1927.
[17] Moore, "Diary," 5.

beat down the soil during the summer months. Then two men with keener inclinations of graft than moral scruples came and built a fence across the land and charged a toll of five cents upon every animal driven over the trail.

In 1884, J. E. May, driving for the LS, was forced to pay these grafters; but the next year, May, driving the lead herd on the trail, struck a road that led to a bridge above the ford, refused to be turned back, and blazed a detour that broke the swindlers' game. As he trailed on toward the North Platte, he met a man who told him that those holding the land had made a barrel of money the year before.[18]

Between the men who followed the plow and those who rode herd over the cattle from Texas no very cordial feeling ever existed. The nesters of western Kansas plowed furrows around their farms and raised "old billy" if the drivers allowed their cattle to pass over these "fences." The Texas cowboys, likewise "ornery" individualists, had decided ideas that they and their steers might go where they pleased, and their traditions of many years supported such views.

Practical jokes added to their troubles. When a man rode up to a herd with a complaint, he could never find the boss. Perhaps he came to him at first, and inquired where he might find that responsible person. The boss pointed the aggrieved to some cowboy on the far side of the herd, who took more delight in tall tales than in veracity. When accosted as the boss, he disclaimed the honor and directed him around the herd to another.[19] And so he circled the herd until he was fighting mad.

At times the cowboys indulged in more than pranks, as when Chris Gish, driving for the Syndicate in 1894, threw his herd into a small pasture near Sterling, Colorado, where a German was reserving some grass. Chris was obdurate to *Deutsch* invective, and the pasture owner hurried to Sterling and recourse to law, and the entire outfit was placed under arrest. With Chris out of circulation, John McCanless, or

[18] J. E. May to J. E. H., June 29, 1926.
[19] J. E. Moore to J. E. H., July 6, 1927.

"Scandlous John," had to take charge and the company paid the bill.[20]

Four XIT herds of 2,500 each and two X herds, owned by the Reynolds brothers of Albany, Texas, were camped within a few miles of one another along the trail near Bovina, Colorado. On the evening of May 30, 1892, a snowstorm struck and drifted them together. These, held in charge by riders night and day, were turned loose early in the morning to drift with the storm. The cowboys stood night guard in summer clothes. Ealy Moore held his herd until two o'clock in the morning before releasing it and leading his near-frozen cowboys to the wagon and their "suggans." Twenty-three of his steers and several of his horses froze to death, while the boys with the X herds lost all the horses they had ridden in the afternoon and evening, twenty-eight head.

At daylight the cowboys crawled from their beds into six or eight inches of snow, found their surviving horses, drove them about to warm them up, and secured corn for feed from a near-by farmer. The corn was shelled into tarps spread upon the snow. Breakfast over, the riders began gathering their cattle, throwing the six herds together to have a roundup of about 14,000 head, one much too large to work. It was separated into four herds, and the cattle that did not belong in one were cut and thrown into their original herd.[21] With plenty of profanity about any such country "where it snowed and blowed in the summer-time," and with numerous resolutions to quit cow-punching for the girls and the potential domestic troubles they had left behind them, the shivering cowboys again headed north behind their gaunt and shivering steers.

From the Yellow Houses, on the southern end of the XIT, to its ranges on Cedar Creek, Montana, the Northern Trail was over 1,000 miles long. The steers were moved as yearlings to the north end, and kept until they were twos. After loading their wagons at the railroad at Channing, the trail bosses set out for Buffalo Springs, where they received their herds. With

[20] *Ibid.*   [21] J. E. Moore to J. E. H., February 26, 1927.

fresh horses the trail herds swung out from Buffalo Springs across into No Man's Land, now the Panhandle of Oklahoma, averaging twelve to fifteen miles a day. To the Corrumpa, where the herds watered first, was a good day's drive, and another of brisk trailing to the Carrizo. Another day upon the trail with good luck placed them on the Cimarron above the 101 Ranch. From there the drivers pointed their herds a little west of north and trailed by Carrizo Springs, Freeze Out, Butte, and Clay Creeks to cross the railroad near Lamar.

From the Arkansas, near Lamar, the trail led up the Sandy to be joined by the eastern drive that came by Trail City, thence to Kit Carson, and north up Wild Horse to the Republican. The next water was at Hell Springs, then at Walker Camp, after which a good two days' drive placed the herds on the Beaver, and two more on the South Platte. The trail followed down Horse Creek twenty-five miles and crossed the divide to the North Platte. Cattle swam it at the mouth of Rawhide, but the wagons crossed on the government bridge at Fort Laramie sixteen miles above.

The outfits trailed by Lusk to replenish their chuck, struck Hat Creek at the store that bore that name, followed its course to the Old Woman, kept on to Lance Creek, and to Lodge Pole. Down the Buffalo they trailed to the Belle Fourche River, across to Cottonwood, and down it to the Little Powder. A fifty-mile stretch intervened before they struck the Big Powder; thence to the Mizpah and to Pumpkin Creek. Down it they struck the Yellowstone. They crossed the river to follow its course northeast for sixty miles, then turned their herds loose on Cedar Creek to fatten on the Montana grasses for two years before going to the slaughtering pens of Chicago.[22]

The Yellowstone was too swift to swim by horse. The saddle horses, driven in ahead of the herd, swam across a short neck of water to a little island, and the cattle followed. From this island they plunged into the main current, treacherous because of an undertow, and swam for the opposite shore. A ferryman

[22] Moore, "Diary," 8–9; see appendix for complete log.

of three-score years deftly handled a canoe, battled the current, and, if necessary, paddled alongside the lead cattle to keep them from swimming into a mill—a circle in which they became helplessly confused and floundered until drowned. After the herd was crossed, the boatman came back for the cowboys and their saddles. One or two cowboys always crossed ahead of the herd, took their lariats, and roped a horse as the remuda came out, to use in catching mounts for the others. The herds crossed five or six miles above Miles City, and the chuck wagons were ferried over at the town.[23]

Crossing the North Platte and the Yellowstone was never a matter without concern to the drivers. One little bobble with the herd and everything seemed to go wrong. If the sun shone in the eyes of the cattle, they had difficulty in seeing the opposite bank and would not swim. If a herd once balked, several days might be required to put it across. Moore had trouble on the North Platte in 1892, and helped six herds to cross before his would take the water. Among these were an N–N herd, an X herd, and the XIT herds driven by Dan Cole and Chris Gish. Moore recalled that in 1893, "when Milt Whipple, who had the lead herd, got to the Yellowstone River, his cattle balked on him and wouldn't take the water. I brought my herd up the next day and put them in and while they were crossing Milt put his herd in with mine and we got about one thousand head of his across and he had to do that way with the next two herds before he could get all his cattle to take the water." That year both the North Platte and the Yellowstone were brimming full and swam the cattle from bank to bank.[24]

But the job of swimming the Platte was all in the day's work. The owners paid trail hands $35 a month to work eighteen to twenty hours a day driving "dogies" to the North, and the troubles of swollen rivers were one reason for the high wages. More than one rider on the Northern Trail drowned in the waters of the Platte and the Yellowstone, and many others,

[23] J. E. Moore to J. E. H., July 6, 1927.
[24] *Ibid.,* November 12, 1925.

with tears streaking their dirty faces, watched their horses go under.

The trail hands set out from the Texas range with most of their wardrobes upon their backs, and from the day they left Buffalo Springs until they reached Montana they were with the herd night and day, often pulling off nothing but their boots and hats to sleep, and with no change of clothes unless they stripped to bathe in the turgid Platte or Yellowstone. When the spirit moved, they bathed in the creeks and dried in the wind. They ate XIT beef for the first two weeks on the trail, but when the cattle they were driving became too tough to eat, they borrowed from the ranchmen along the way with scant compunction. They told the time by the sun and stars and pointed more than one greenhorn, as unversed in astronomy as in the pranks of the range, to the north star and told him to call the next guard when it "went down." When stormy nights brought on stampedes amid snows and rains, cowboys on guard made sincere vows never to drive again, and as they turned back down the trail they sang to themselves:

Oh, I am a Texas cowboy
Far away from home,
If ever I get back to Texas
I never more will roam.

Montana is too cold for me
And the winters are too long;
Before the roundups do begin
Our money is all gone.

All along the Yellowstone
'Tis cold the year around;
You will surely get consumption
By sleeping on the ground.

Come all you Texas cowboys
And warning take from me,
And do not go to Montana
To spend your money free.

139

But stay at home in Texas,
Where work lasts the year around,
And you'll never catch consumption
By sleeping on the ground.

But the lotus was in their blood. When green spears of the buffalo-grass pushed up through the old, when, as the wrangler drove them in of a morning, the horses pitched and kicked and ran and rubbed off their dead winter hair against the "snubbing" post in the center of the corral, when "coosie" scrubbed up his chuck-box with soap and hot water, when saddle riggings were being looked over and new stake ropes bought, the lure of the open trail was upon them. Again they drove, and as they headed north they sang again, but to a different tune:

I am a Texas cowboy and I do ride the range;
My trade is cinches and saddles and ropes and bridle reins;
With Stetson hat and jingling spurs and leather up to the
*   knees,*
Graybacks as big as chili beans and fighting like hell with fleas.
If I had a little stake, I soon would married be,
But another week and I must go, the boss said so today.
My girl must cheer up courage and choose some other one,
For I am bound to follow the Lone Star Trail until my race is
*   run.*
            Ci yi yip yip yip pe ya.

Each trail outfit was usually made up of eight cowboys, the boss, the cook, and the horse wrangler. All supplies, pots, Dutch ovens, other cooking equipment, and rolls of bedding were carried in the chuck wagon. Trail hands were paid $35 a month, ranch hands but $25. Most of the trail hands were laid off when the herds reached Montana. Some began work for the beef outfit there, in which way Texas range methods passed over the trail to all the Great Plains cow country. Not wishing to secure work in the North, or unable to secure it, they might lie around the ranch a month or two, ride the caboose with a shipment of cattle to Chicago, and secure a pass back to Texas. Enough men were retained to bring the wagons and combined remudas back down the trail. When five outfits were on the trail, the teams from two wagons were turned into the remuda and these wagons were trailed behind two others. The fifth wagon was driven by the cook, who fed the outfit on the way back. Three months were required for the trip north and two back to Texas "empty."

Two kinds of horses were used on the trail, day horses and night horses. Good night horses were ridden only on night guard. In the evening the remuda was driven into a rope corral, and all the cowboys caught and saddled their night horses. These were staked near the wagon with ropes about thirty feet long. On the trail the stake rope was not tied fast around the horse's neck, but was looped over it in a slip noose. When called for his guard, the rider slipped the rope off without delay, dropped it to the ground, and rode to the herd. With his bridle by the head of his bed and his boots and hat stuck under his head for a pillow, the cowboy slept with most of his clothes on. Ealy Moore always drove his stake pin so near his bed that his horse might graze within four or five feet. Thus he was never over sixty-five feet from his horse. If he heard the cattle stampede, he jumped out of his bed roll, pulled on his hat and boots, and was on his horse and away in two minutes.[25]

During the first few days upon the trail, four men stood guard, holding the cattle about two hundred yards from the wagon. Within a week the high-grade cattle, rarely so bad to stampede as the Longhorns, were becoming "trail broke" and the number of men on guard were reduced to two. Within two weeks the cattle were being held nearer the wagon, with the night horses staked on the opposite side, and four men were standing guard in relays one night, and the other four the next. Thus each man had unbroken rest every other night. After a month on the trail the cattle came right up to the wagon, making it necessary for the cowboys to push them back before going

[25] J. E. Moore to J. E. H., July 6, 1927.

to bed. At night, as well as during the day, certain steers were always in the same relative position in the herd.

Continual standing of guard for five or six months became monotonous. As they came back down the trail one time, Ealy Moore left the outfit at the Belle Fourche and turned east to pick up some horses. When the boys camped that evening, they threw the remuda into someone's little horse pasture to escape herd. Upon hearing the bells a few of the horses wore, the owner of the pasture came down during the night, rounded the remuda up, and refused to turn it over to the boys next day except upon the payment of twenty-five dollars. That was easy. Milt Whipple gave a check, signing the name "A. Owings." It seemed like a good joke, but old Ab had traveled too many trails to be induced to pay it, and the matter fell back upon the company for settlement.

Chuck for the Syndicate outfits was always considered above the average. The fare consisted of sourdough biscuits, potatoes, beans, coffee, beef, dried fruits, and a small amount of canned goods.[26] Jim McLaren, trail boss and one time foreman of the Escarbada, bought ham, eggs, and butter along the trail. His chuck, compared with that of the average outfit, was what Delmonico's was to a hamburger stand. These delicacies were not allowed by the company, but Jim bought them at each opportunity and placed them on his account as "potatoes."

Old-timers tell that George Findlay met Jim after he had delivered his herd and asked him how much it cost to feed an outfit. Jim's accounts had already been submitted, unknown to him, and Findlay held the figures. He professed ignorance, and, upon being pressed for particulars, said that among other items it would take two and a half pounds of potatoes a day for each man. Findlay thumbed the leaves of his little notebook. Jim, they say, was soon looking for another job, for each of his cowboys, by his own figures, had eaten over twenty pounds of potatoes a day.[27]

26 Moore, "Diary," 3–6.
27 B. P. Abbott to J. E. H., June 24, 1927.

The Montana Trail

The XIT and other outfits trailing to the North could have sent their herds by rail after 1887. Apparently, with the risks of the trail—stampedes, blizzards, swollen rivers—and the troubles incident to passing through a country rapidly filling with settlers and being criss-crossed by wire fences, there were advantages in shipping. But driving was cheaper than shipping, and cattle driven well—handled by such men as Dan Cole, Ab Owings, and Ealy Moore—reached the end of the trail in better condition than when they were started. One year in which the XIT shipped to Wendover, Wyoming, and trailed on from there, it cost almost as much to drive that far as it would have cost to drive from the ranges of Texas.[28] Railroad rates upon steers to Montana were about $1.50 a head in 1892, but that year Moore drove a herd of 2,500 head at an expense of $1,801.80, or at a cost of a fraction over $0.72 a head.[29] The cattlemen of Texas continued to follow the Long Trail after the railroads were built simply because it saved them money.

Opposition of the Kansas settlers, expressed legislatively through the quarantine laws, finally closed the Kansas Trail. The difficulty of driving the Montana Trail without trouble increased in direct proportion with the settlement of the country. The coming of the nester, his control of the waterings, and his network of barbed wire fences finally closed the last segment of the great Texas Trail. But it will not be forgotten in American history, for it was the greatest and most spectacular pastoral institution of all time.

A few herds, among them 12,500 steers that bore the XIT brand, went over the trail in 1896,[30] and one stubbornly pushed north in 1897.[31] Driven by "Scandlous John" McCanless, it had difficulty in getting through. After that, the Texas Trail became a matter of memory. Well-bred, aristocratic steers were

[28] J. E. May to J. E. H., June 29, 1926.
[29] Moore, "Diary," 8.
[30] J. G. K. McClure, Ms., "Among the Cowboys of Texas," 8.
[31] H. W. Eubank to J. E. H., July 1, 1926; J. E. Moore to J. E. H., July 6, 1927; G. N. Jowell to J. E. H., January 17, 1927; John McCanless to J. E. H., March 21, 1928.

CHAPTER X

When the Grass Began to Grow

F RESH LIFE came to the cow country when the grass began to grow. The "spring roundup," or the "general work," as it was often called, began when the grass came in the spring. Herds took the Texas Trail beneath balmy skies to follow the green grass north upon the heels of retreating winter. The oldest cows cut awkward capers as their strength returned, bulls bellered and got on the prod, and horses, putting on flesh after the rigors of winter, bucked and played as the wrangler drove them into the corral. Thus the time of year in a cow camp was measured, not by calendar dates, but by the coming of grass, for these men of saddle leather lived exceedingly close to the soil. Always ready riders, they never plied a quirt more willingly or patted a cow pony's neck more affectionately than when the range began to "green up."

Green grass came early or late in keeping with the arrival of spring and the season's rains. About the middle of May thin streaks of dust shimmered upward with the heat waves along the horizon, danced through the mirages across the plains, and drew to a common focus at Tascosa. The jingling of silver over the bars brought the tinkling of glasses in answer as thirsty cowboys from the Turkey Track, LX, LIT, T Anchor, 101, Cross L, LE, LS, and XIT outfits lined up to pay their respects to rye and Bourbon as their horses rubbed off winter hair against the hitching racks.

A dozen cooks cracked their whips over their four- and six-mule teams as they drove up to Howard and McMaster's or Rinehart's store for a two months' supply of chuck. As each finished his loading, he rushed over to push his way through the earlier arrivals and "belly-up" to the Equity or the Cattle Exchange Bar. Eventually, with the help of Providence and the good sense of their mules, most of them managed to get their wagons out of town and camp above Tascosa. Hard by, horse wranglers lolled in their saddles while their remudas grazed quietly. Then there was hilarious mixing of sourdough, frying of great beef steaks, and making of coffee as an occasional yell and the report of a six-shooter sounded from the direction of the town.

The next day the outfits strung out up the river to begin the spring roundup in New Mexico. Back down the river they worked, half across the Panhandle of Texas and more, to meet the lower Canadian roundup. Each day these riders rounded up a range from ten to fifteen miles square, branded the cattle they gathered, rounded up the range immediately below the next day, and so until all the country along the Canadian had been "worked." [1] By fall the work was done. But this was before the days of wire.

After the country was fenced, each outfit worked only its own range, aided by "stray," or "outside," men who came in with mounts of horses, but no chuck wagon of their own, and stayed until the work was done. At the end of the work they drifted their stray cattle back home.

With a range as large as that covered by some of the old general roundups under fence, the XIT still faced the problem of substituting methods by which its cattle could be handled rapidly and efficiently. The ranch stretched nearly two hundred miles from north to south and varied widely in topographical features. After taking charge in the summer of 1887, Boyce

[1] *The Tascosa Pioneer,* June 12, 1886; *ibid.,* March 30, 1887; James East to J. E. H., February 22, 1928; Frank Irwin to J. E. H., September 24, 1927; Harry Ingerton to J. E. H., April 8, 1927. L. Gough, "Sketch of the XIT Ranch," 4.

decided to cross-fence this range into a number of separate ranches.[2]

His system of organization called for seven divisions, each division to be under the direction of a foreman, who was in turn responsible to General Manager Boyce. Boyce was responsible to the owners. Each division was named and numbered. Beginning at the north end of the ranch and progressing south they were: (1) Buffalo Springs; (2) Middle Water; (3) Ojo Bravo (Bold Spring); (4) Rito Blanco (Little White River); (5) Escarbada (The Scraping); (6) Spring Lake; (7) Las Casas Amarillas, or The Yellow Houses.[3]

Because of the varying range conditions, some of these divisions were better adapted for beef than breeding purposes, and their use varied accordingly. Buffalo Springs was set aside for a steer ranch. All steers raised upon the other divisions were trailed to Buffalo Springs as yearlings. An excellent ranch, but lacking the protection of the Canadian country, this North Plains range helped to acclimatize the Texas cattle during the year they remained there for the more rigorous winters they would spend after passing over the Northern Trail to Montana.

Middle Water Division, besides being used for breeding purposes, was the "cut-back," or cull ranch. Undesirable cattle, such as off-colors and defective animals, were "cut out" from other divisions and thrown into the Middle Water, where they were left until ready for shipment. Ojo Bravo, with headquarters on a tributary creek of the Canadian, the Agua Caballo, near the New Mexico line, was a breeding range. Rito Blanco was used in part as a beef ranch. Old, barren, and dry cows fattened upon its fine grama, and when the grass came, raced to its bog holes to escape the heel flies.

When the northern drive was stopped, the beeves were grazed on this division until ready to be shipped to market. Besides the range adjacent to Rito Blanco Canyon north of the

2 J. E. Moore to J. E. H., February 26, 1927.
3 J. E. Moore to J. E. H., November 8, 1927.

Canadian, this division included the Alamocitos country to the south, where at first the general headquarters of the entire ranch was located. Farther south, the Escarbada, Spring Lake, and Yellow Houses were strictly breeding ranges.[4]

Each division was cut into a number of pastures. The Buffalo Springs ranch of 470,000 acres, which in the late nineties grazed 35,000 steers, was divided into four large and five small pastures. The Yellow Houses Division, which was at the same time ranging 20,000 Hereford cattle, was divided into five large and twelve small pastures. Forty-seven windmills and a large number of surface tanks furnished water for its herds, and the range was cared for from the divisional headquarters and two line camps.[5]

In the fall of 1898, J. J. Hagerman was building what is now the Pecos Valley branch of the Santa Fe Railway. This line crossed the ranch in a southwesterly direction from Amarillo. Hereford, Farwell, Texico, and other towns sprang up along the new trail of steel. About midway across the ranch a switch was put in and a little town started up. Cowmen shipped in cotton seed to be used for feed, and in unloading it a little was invariably spilled along the track. The XIT had a bunch of high-grade Hereford bulls just arrived from Missouri. The right of way was unfenced, and the bulls gathered at the switch to eat their fill of spilled cottonseed. Then, lazily content, they often lay down upon the track to chew their cuds, and when the train came by, they bull-headedly held their ground with aristocratic mien. To avoid a wreck the engineer was forced to stop while the brakeman climbed off with a prod pole and chased the bulls away.

The switch had not been named, and the conductor reported his shipments at the division point as so many cars to or from "Bull Town." However appropriate the name, it was too vulgar

[4] J. E. Moore to J. E. H., February 26, 1927; R. L. Duke to J. E. H., July 6, 1927; H. W. Eubank to J. E. H., July 1, 1926.

[5] L. Gough, "Sketch," 2–3; J. G. K. McClure, Ms., "Among the Cowboys of Texas," 16.

for railroad men, and upon their maps they wrote "Bovina."[6] Bovina became known for a short while as a New Mexico and West Texas cow town and was reputed to be the largest inland shipping point for cattle in the world.[7] It likewise became the headquarters of division number eight of the XIT Ranch, formed, ten years after the other divisions, by cutting off land from Spring Lake.

Each division operated as a separate ranch. Every calf was branded with the XIT upon its side, the last numeral of the year upon its shoulder, and the number of the division upon its jaw. A cowboy, looking at an animal branded with a figure 3 upon the jaw and 4 upon the shoulder, knew immediately that it was from the Ojo Bravo Division and that it was a calf in 1894. No particular attempt was made to keep each division's branding upon its own range, as the cattle were shifted about. But the advantage of the year brand lay in the fact that the age of every animal could be thus told at a glance. When the general manager ordered a number of cattle of a certain age gathered for sale, he knew that the order would be carried out without a mistake.[8]

The foreman of each division made a monthly report to the general manager. The report included a statement of range conditions, the condition of the cattle, the number that had been branded, the number lost, weather reports, the number of men working, and the wages that were being paid. One copy of this statement was filed at the headquarters; the other was sent to the Chicago office, where it was tabulated. Then the foreman made an annual report, giving a digest of his monthly reports and summarizing the conditions of his ranch. All business affairs, such as the paying of accounts and wages and the purchase of supplies, were handled at the general headquarters.[9] Each foreman had his own wagons, horses, and camp equipment. He hired and "fired" his own men. When one became

[6] B. P. Abbott to J. E. H., March, 1928.
[7] James D. Hamlin to J. E. H., September 22, 1927.
[8] Ira Aten to J. E. H., February 27, 1928; Gough, "Sketch," 5.
[9] *Ibid.;* Gough, "Sketch."

perverse and could not be "fired," Boyce showed up and sent him on his way.

Once a cowboy, discharged at Spring Lake, refused to leave. Boyce happened by on one of his periodical trips about the ranch and asked the foreman why he did not tell the puncher to saddle his horse and move on. The foreman replied that such an order would mean that one of them would be killed. Early next morning Boyce was at the breakfast table ahead of the cowboys with his six-shooter lying in his lap. When the cowboy entered, Boyce said: "This ranch is not big enough for both of us. Immediately after breakfast one of us is going to leave, and it's not going to be me." It was not.[10]

With such an organization each division worked independently of the other. No foreman was bound to wait upon another, but went about his own work in keeping with his own ideas and upon his own initiative.

The beginning of the spring work depended upon the growth of grass. On the southern divisions early grass enabled the wagons to start late in April or by the middle of May. The regular crew of ten or twelve cowboys upon a division like the Escarbada was then increased to twenty-five or thirty. Except for a few line-riders, windmill hands, and freighters, all of these men lived with the chuck wagon from the breaking of spring until the northers of December. Wherever they spread their bed rolls and stuffed their hats and boots under their heads for pillows, wherever the chuck wagon camped and the cook yelled "chuck-away," "chuck," or "come and get it," there was home for the cowboys.

Bolted into the rear end of the wagon was the chuck box. The hinged "lid" or cover opened from the top and was supported horizontally by a single prop to form a table. Convenient drawers held tin plates, cups, and cutlery. Other drawers and shelves were stored with coffee, cans of sugar, salt, soda, molasses or "lick," lard, and other articles of frequent demand. In the bed of the wagon the cook carried a large amount of

[10] B. P. Abbott to J. E. H., June 24, 1927.

flour, bacon, sugar, beans, dried fruit, some cases of canned goods, and a reserve supply of "lick."

There too the beef was kept. A fresh beef was killed when needed, usually in the late afternoon, quartered, and hung alongside the wagon or between the spokes of the wagon wheel. The cool night of the High Plains chilled the meat, and immediately the next morning it was wrapped in a tarp or in slickers and placed at the bottom of the wagon. Bed rolls were thrown in upon it to help shut out the noonday heat, and the meat would usually keep fresh for several days. Each night the operation was repeated, and usually by the third day the beef, a sucking calf, had been eaten and another was killed.[11]

Beneath the chuck box, attached to the bottom of the wagon bed, was another large box with a hinged door, in which "coosie" stored his pots, pans, and skillets while moving camp. Upon the side of the wagon, stake ropes were carried for use in picketing "night horses." A keg of water was attached to one side; to the other, often a tool box. Usually grain for the teams was stored in the front end of the wagon beneath the spring seat.

Camp was moved almost every day, sometimes twice daily. After a breakfast ready before daylight, the cook might break camp, drive ten or twelve miles, and prepare dinner for the roundup to be thrown together at that point. Then he often had to make another move before camping for the night. Some cooks swung a beef hide under the wagon and in this *cuña* (cradle), as it was called, carried the wood the horse wrangler helped gather as they moved from one camp to another. Upon the plains ranges where no timber grew, a two-wheeled wagon was added to the camp equipment. It occupied a menial social position among camp equipment, and was politely known as the "chip wagon." Nevertheless, it was essential to the preparation of the meals, as it held half a wagon load of cow chips, enough, with proper economy, to cook at least three meals. Properly fanned by a good stiff wind, they made a very hot

[11] Gough, "Sketch," 9–10.

fire, but it did take quite a pile of cow chips to cook a skillet of biscuits.[12]

In the chuck box, or in the bed of the wagon, the cook carried a keg or large earthenware jar, streaked and bespattered with white. This held the sourdough for his biscuits. Tenderfeet are always astonished that an outfit with 100,000 cows should not have enough milk for drinking and cooking purposes. They will always be astonished. That is why they continue to be tenderfeet. Drawing from his supply of sourdough at mealtime, the cook made biscuits which rose like hot rolls by their own yeast, replenished his sourdough with water and flour, and returned the keg to the wagon. Besides hot biscuits baked in his "skillets," or Dutch ovens, he prepared beef, potatoes, beans, and often some dish from canned tomatoes or corn. "Lick" and stewed dried fruit, peaches, apples, or prunes were the only desserts, unless the cook happened to be particularly good humored and cooked a cobbler of canned or dried fruit. The skillets and pots of food reposed by the fire, the coffeepot upon some coals. When "coosie" yelled, "chuck," and squatted upon his heel in the shade of the wagon to rub the few remaining particles of sourdough from his hands, the cowboys made a rush to the chuck box for plates, cups, knives and forks, heaped their plates, and drew back out of the way to sit upon the ground or upon rolls of bedding and eat their meal in comparative silence. A lot of talk at mealtime may bring on ulcers in a cow camp.

Lord of his realm in every case, the cook, if communicative, sat against a rear wheel and directed remarks upon cattle, the weather, or the general perversity of "horse rustlers," to the group as a whole. Few, if any, "paid him any mind." But next to those of the wagon boss, his wishes about the camp were respected, and even the boss was not beyond his jurisdiction. For a cowboy to leave the wagon with his bed not rolled when camp was to be broken that morning constituted an almost unpar-

[12] C. F. Vincent to J. E. H., June 26, 1927; R. J. Frye, to J. E. H., June 26, 1927; B. P. Abbott to J. E. H., June 24, 1927.

donable breach of cow-camp etiquette. For anyone to ride his horse so near as to raise a cloud of dust to blow over the wagon while a meal was in preparation was nearly sufficient cause for murder, certainly for unrestrained profanity.

An ill-tempered cook would often ruin the morale of a cow camp. A good-humored one who did his work well always improved it. If the cook became lost in passing through unknown country and night came on, it was never his worry. He simply camped his wagon and made himself at home. He knew the cowpunchers would hunt him up. He could be independent, as he had their beds and all the "chuck." When Indian dangers became a thing of the past, trail bosses always kept their wagons ahead of the herd, not behind it, if they wanted to get efficient work from their cowboys. In the rigorous life they lived, the wagon, after breakfast at 4:00 in the morning, always looked good by 12:00 to them.[13]

Each cowboy's bed was rolled in a tarp and secured with a double rope or with two straps. Usually it was made up of blankets and a few "suggans" or quilts. When rain or snow came, the cowboy covered his head with the tarp, tucked it under around the sides of his bed, and was fairly secure from water. Sometimes two cowboys combined their "hot rolls" to sleep together. The act of dividing it was called "cutting the bed."[14]

Out around the remuda rode the horse wrangler, the "rustler," or the "horse pestler," as he was variously called. Usually his was considered the most menial position in cow work. Many tenderfeet received bitter initiation to the life of the cow camp by wrangling horses. The wranglers helped the cook gather wood and harness his team. His most important duty was to "loose herd" the remuda where the grass grew best until it was needed at the roundup grounds for a change of mounts, which was often three, and sometimes four, times daily.[15]

13 M. Huffman to J. E. H., November 30, 1927; Gough, "Sketch"; C. F. Vincent to J. E. H., June 26, 1927.
14 Gough, "Sketch," 10.
15 Ira Aten to J. E. H., March 1, 1928.

In the broad expanse of the plains country, cowboys often rode one hundred miles a day over all manner of country, and such riding took much horse flesh.[16] In spite of its unpopularity with real cowhands, the position of the horse wrangler was an important one, and really good wranglers were scarce.

At evening "night horses" were roped out of the remuda and kept at hand for the night's riding. In the usual absence of corrals, the remuda was driven into a "rope corral" formed by three or four cowboys holding lariats among them to form an obtuse U. After the horses were inside the U, the opening was closed by a line of cowboys whose horses were to be caught, or by another rope. A trained cow pony would not break from this corral. Ropes were dropped after the horses were caught, and the remuda resumed grazing, now under the care of the wrangler.

The night horses were staked out by driving iron pins or wooden stakes into the ground and tying the horses to them. Though the rope might drag along the ground thirty-five feet between the pin and his neck, the rope-wise pony never became entangled in it. If a herd was being held, horses for all the cowboys who were to stand guard or "night herd" were caught and staked. Otherwise, only those horses to be used by the cowboys who happened to be on "horse guard" were caught. Each night the remuda was herded so as to be ready for the start on the next day's "drive" as soon as breakfast was over. Night horses were for night use only. A cowboy looked for a quiet "clear-footed" horse, of good eyesight, to reduce the danger of falling while running with a stampede, and for a horse that could find his way back to the wagon on the darkest night.

Many night guards were ridden by dozing cowboys, who, nodding the hours through, sat in the saddle upon a horse that needed no touch of bridle rein but jogged the circle around the herd with faithful regularity, and put back every cow that attempted to escape from it. Good night horses, along with "cutting" and "roping" horses, were prized beyond price and

16 *Ibid.*

genuinely loved by the men who rode them. A little buckskin mustang called "Dunnie," that stirred the dust along the thousand-mile Montana Trail for several seasons, never placed his foot over a stake rope in all that time. "Night LS," carrying Yellow Houses cowboys upon many night herds, never failed to find the wagon when the guard expired, and even walked to the end of his stake rope, dropped where the rider first mounted, when it was so dark the night herder would have to get down and feel for it in the dark. Upon breaking camp next morning, the boys "pulled up their stakes" and dropped them in the wagon—thus the origin of the expressive synonym for moving camp or location.

Good "cutting" horses were the talk and the darlings of the cattle world. Davis Roan died under the saddle while cutting a cow at a Yellow Houses roundup. Whiskey, Cheyenne, Old Nig, and Sorrel were fast and faithful horses in a herd. But night horses, too, were in a class to themselves, for in reckless rides on the darkest nights, the cowboys "gave their souls to God" while life and limb depended solely on their horses.

A spirited, four-footed phantom host impatiently stamps at the hitching racks of the past, pricking up their ears as cowboy voices echo from dusty corrals calling Midnight Alice, Jake Kilrain, Vinegaroon, Sam Bass, King James, Bill Nye, Leatherlip, Governor Hogg, Knot-Belly, Milk Shake, and many another name.[17] The dust from their hoofs long since "mingled with the dust of the stars," but to ageing riders memories of such horses spring afresh with the first grass of every spring.

The first work after the wagon started was to gather the yearling steers and trail them from all the breeding divisions to Buffalo Springs. When a foreman delivered his steers to the boss there, he received a receipt for them as though they had been sold. While the steers were being gathered, only the big

[17] R. J. Frye to J. E. H., June 26, 1927; B. P. Abbott to J. E. H., June 24, 1927; Ms., S. K. Bynum, Panhandle-Plains Historical Society; C. F. Vincent to J. E. H., June 26, 1927; Gough, "Sketch"; McClure, "Among the Cowboys of Texas."

maverick calves were branded to safeguard them from the rustler. Back from Buffalo Springs and the delivery of the steers by the middle of June, the division outfits usually began branding immediately. Day after day through late June, hot July, and into August, the work went on. Seven days a week these cowboys rode hard, rounding up, roping, "cutting," and branding calves.

Breakfast over, they were in the saddle and by daylight were on the drive, often miles away. Sometimes the entire crew rode together for ten or fifteen miles before the wagon boss checked the cavalcade and "told off his men," or scattered his riders. Two who rode good horses and who knew the country were designated "lead drive men," one of whom might be the wagon boss himself. As some of "the drives" demanded harder riding than others, the boss usually "told off" his men with respect to their ability and freshness.

As each designated man dropped out, he was expected to start and move towards the roundup grounds all the cattle between him and the two riders immediately on either side. The intervals between riders varied with the topography of the range, but on the great circles made upon the open plains, one cowboy often worked back and forth across a strip of country two to four miles wide. The lead drive man rushed on his longer round at a high lope, generally riding much farther than the others, for he had to complete the circle and "head" those cattle on the farthest edges of the "drive" into the roundup, and have them there at the same time the others arrived. The cowboys were thus on "the drive" or "out on circle," and as "the drive" came in, the roundup was thrown together. Thus, by spreading in a great fan or circle, the cowboys often rounded up 150 square miles of country on one drive.

After the drive was in, the cowboys changed mounts, began "working the roundup," cutting out the strays and "dry stuff." Then they began branding, sometimes simply by dragging the calves out of the roundup on the open range. Instead of throwing the roundup into a corral, they held it under herd on the range while cowboys roped and dragged the calves out thirty or forty steps from the herd to a branding fire. Cowboys on foot "went down the rope" to meet the jumping and bawling calf as the roper dragged him up, to flank or "lay him on the sod and take him off the line." Usually they "flanked" the calf by catching with left hand the rope just against the calf's neck, or the ear on the side opposite him and by slapping the right hand into the flank on the corresponding side. By a jerk upward and a pressure of the knees against the calf's side when it made its next jump, the cowboy sent the calf's feet outward and it came down upon its side. The "flanker" slipped the rope from over its head and the roper went back after another calf.

"Flankers" worked in pairs. As the calf fell, the flanker's partner grabbed the upper hind leg, sat upon the ground behind, pulled back upon the leg and forced the under leg forward by pushing against it with his boot heel, while the flanker dropped down on the calf and held it by propping a knee on its neck and pulling back on its upper foreleg. Thus the calf was unable to kick or escape while being branded, cut, and marked. The operation over, it was allowed to scamper back to the herd and maternal consolation. Most of the ranch branding was done in corrals, as this made available for other uses the cowboys required to hold the herd while in the open.

If the morning drive was a short one and yielded only from two to three hundred calves, these were branded out, another drive was made early in the afternoon, and the calves were branded before night. Sometimes 500 head were branded during the day. If as many as 350 were brought in on the morning drive, another drive was not made that day.[18] The outfit moved from one part of the range to another each day and continued branding until the entire range was "worked." One division might begin work before the others. But before it was through, branding would be under way on all the divisions. The work took about two months upon a ranch like the Escarbada.[19]

[18] Ira Aten to J. E. H., March 1, 1928; C. R. Smith to J. E. H., March 20, 1928; J. P. McDonald to J. E. H., June 25, 1927.
[19] Ira Aten to J. E. H., March 1, 1928.

When branding was done, cow work was dropped for two weeks or a month. All the cowboys were kept at lighter work, often loathsome to them, such as riding and repairing fences and cutting hay from the natural meadows in the dry lake bottoms or the valleys of the "draws." [20] When September came, the cooks replenished their supplies of grub to go upon the beef work.

Toward the first of the month the outfits were again upon the range with horses fresh from their rest, their "set-fasts" haired over and backs sound. From 500 to 1,000 beef cows were gathered on each division from among the old, off-color, and dry cows. All the heifers were retained upon the ranch, but the steers were sent to Montana to be fattened. If an off-colored cow had a calf, she was kept upon the range. Then if she had no calf the next year and became fat, she was thrown into the beef herd and shipped. This culling out of undesirable colors and defective animals, together with the use of "blooded" bulls meant a rapid improvement in the quality of the herd.

The fall branding, which was light, was done while the beef herds were being gathered and was made up only of late calves or those missed during the summer. The fall roundups were conducted in the same way as were the spring roundups, except that the beef cows were thrown into a separate herd called the "cut." This "cut" was not released, but was herded by the cowboys night and day, and finally put upon the trail to the railroad at Channing. There, about the first of October, the cows were shipped to Kansas City or Chicago. Cows not fat enough in September were gathered about the first of November, along with old bulls no longer wanted upon the range.

After delivering the second beef herd late in November, each outfit trailed back to its division. The cowboys who wished to be home for the Christmas holidays were "given time off." Six or seven were kept with the wagon to help gather the bulls. Instead of rounding up the entire herd, the cowboys just rode through the range drifting the bulls out before them. The

[20] *Ibid.,* J. W. Stevens to J. E. H., November 24, 1927.

wagon continued its itinerary, and every two or three days a few cowboys were sent to the bull pasture with the animals that had been gathered. This pasture had been reserved during the spring and summer so that the grass would be good, and was chosen for the protection it would afford during the winter.

Upon the range, bulls have a tendency to bunch up in the fall, and this made the task of gathering an easy one. Old bulls, accustomed to being segregated, would sometimes be found "walking the fence" of the bull pasture in the fall, and it was necessary only to open the gate to get them inside. All the bulls were gathered by Christmas and from then until the first of June, they grazed free from the disconcerting combats sexual business seems inclined to engender. However desirable this peace and tranquility may have been, it was not for the bull's sake that he was kept apart, but to insure a uniform calf crop during the spring and early summer months. Uniform calf crops meant better prices, fewer winter losses in both cows and calves, and fewer opportunities for the rustlers to pick up mavericks.[21] No calves were wanted until the grass had started in April and the cows had become strong and had begun "to put on flesh."

When the last bull trailed through the gate into the pasture set aside for him, the chuck wagon drew into headquarters after more than eight months out in the weather. The remnant of cowboys on hand then usually took "off" and went to the nearest town, sometimes to paint it a little red. Often overpainted themselves, they indulged, as many other men of lonely, trying, outdoor lives, in the attractions of cards, drink, and dance hall. Yet many cowboys indulged in none of these attractions, but they never found themselves recorded in song and story.

The cowboy added life, happiness, and good-will wherever his pony's hoofbeats rang upon the crisp morning air. Many a child who had never known more homely comforts than a dugout offered, while listening expectantly for the tinkle of Santa's

[21] Ira Aten to J. E. H., March 1, 1928; M. Huffman to J. E. H., November 30, 1927.

CHAPTER XI

Bog Camps, Lobos, and Prairie Fires

With the first heavy frosts of fall the last hints of green gave way to gold, russet, and yellow. Cured into good, substantial forage, dry grass sustained the cattle until spring rains brought it to life again. The chuck wagon stood idle at headquarters, the remuda enjoyed quiet days in the horse pasture, and the "regular" cowboys were "holed up" in winter camps. In keeping with nature's season, work on the range was least active when the grass had turned brown.

Where but two line camps were necessary upon such a division as the Escarbada during the summer, five were kept up during the winter and spring.[1] To describe the camp men as being "holed up" is true but in part. The worse the weather became, the more they had to ride. When storms were raging, drifting cattle had to be thrown back from the plains into the breaks, and weak cattle demanded closer attention. Then the waterings froze over, and the cowboy chopped ice so his cows might drink. His work was easiest when the weather was balmiest.

Two cowboys were given a wagon, camp equipment, and saddle horses about the first of January and put to "wolfing" upon those divisions where lobos, the great predatory wolves of the plains, were most numerous. They were paid no salary from

[1] Tombstone and Trujillo were year-around camps. Tierra Blanca, Salt Well, and Toro were winter camps.

then until the cow work started in April or May, but they capitalized on a bounty of five to ten dollars paid by the company upon every lobo caught. Some counties paid an additional ten. With good fortune the "wolfers" made more money during these few months than they did during all the rest of the year as cowpunchers.[2]

These lobos, or "loafers," were about the size of a Newfoundland dog, very cunning, and difficult to trap. The principal ways of killing them were by running them down horseback and by finding their dens. Cowmen estimated the annual depredations of a lobo at seventy-five head of cattle. The wily fellows preferred fresh meat, rarely returning to a carcass, which made poisoning practically impossible.[3] Several, banding together, rounded up a small bunch of cattle, and choosing a weak cow or steer, ran at its hind legs every time it came to the outer edge of the bunch, slashing at the great tendons in its hind legs. When they had cut its hamstrings and disabled it, the killing was easy.[4] Big calves and yearlings were common prey, and losses amounted to thousands of dollars annually.

The lobo took shelter along the caprock and in the breaks, and at night ventured out upon the plains for several miles in search of meat, and after gorging on his fresh kill, returned to shelter in the roughs. Early of a morning the two "wolfers" saddled their horses and rode along the edge of the plains just above the caprock to cut off any late-returning lobo as he lazily trotted back to the shelter of the broken country. Upon intercepting a wolf, they turned him back across the level plain and gave chase. The wolf was usually so full of beef that he could run but poorly, and after a chase of from two to four miles the "wolfers" were usually able to ride upon and shoot or rope him.

In March the lobo pups began to arrive. Then a she wolf, jumped by hunters or dogs, headed for her den in all haste. During this season the wolfer used a pack of hounds in trailing

---

[2] Ira Aten to J. E. H., March 1, 1928.
[3] Gough, "Sketch," 6.
[4] McClure, "Among the Cowboys of Texas," 21: R. J. Frye to J. E. H., June 26, 1927.

XIT hands at the "Fourth of July" Corral, 1896
(Panhandle-Plains Historical Society)

Early herd of registered Herefords on the XIT

Hotel Rivers, at Channing, where XIT visitors stopped

Aberdeen-Angus bulls at an **XIT** windmill

Cowboys riding in to Tascosa
(Erwin Smith photograph)

Sheriff Tobe Robinson

The bull pasture at Escarbada

James H. East in 1884

and locating dens.[5] When he arrived at the cave or den, the hunter took a short candle in one hand, his six-shooter in the other, wiggled into the den, and shot the wolf by the reflection of the light in her eyes. Rarely did he have to crawl inside more than ten or twelve feet, though sometimes the holes were deeper. The dens were often so narrow that he could worm his way in only by keeping both arms extended ahead of him. The explosion from his gun always put out his candle. He backed out of the hole to re-light it and went in again before he could be sure of the effect of his shot.[6]

Charlie Orr and Frank Fuller were "wolfing" one spring on the Escarbada. Obviously, it was an eerie sort of business, and a question of propriety as to who should go first led to a delay at the entrance to a lobo's den. Being men of sporting blood, they settled the argument by drawing straws. Orr drew the long straw and had to go first. With six-shooter in hand he crawled until he could see the wolf's eyes gleaming at him. Up came the six-shooter and the reverberation shook dust from the walls and dinned in the cowboy's ears. Unfortunately he missed his aim, and the lobo, seeing a gleam of light over Orr's back, made a break for the outside. The space was not enough for her to pass through and she wedged over Orr's back. Frantic with fear she began scratching furiously in an attempt to dig out, and every scratch carried away some of the cowboy's clothes. Finally she dug through and Fuller shot her as she came out. Nine pups were found in the den, but Orr's back was bare and showed marks of the powerful claws.[7] This mattered little, for it was a profitable day's work since a cowboy's back is tough and work shirts were cheap.

A lobo disturbed at her den leaves at the first opportunity and does not come back. Thus to leave a den meant to lose the wolf. Dumas Hall, an eighteen-year-old boy keeping camp at Toro in 1906, crawled into a lobo's den, and, while feeling

[5] Ira Aten to J. E. H., March 1, 1928.
[6] Allen Stagg to J. E. H., June 29, 1926.
[7] Ira Aten to J. E. H., March 1, 1928.

around in the dark, was bitten through the hand by the old bitch. After backing out to survey the damage, he armed himself with his lariat and skinning knife and went into the den again. When he came to a narrow place through which he could barely squeeze, he thought he heard his horse running away. For a cowboy far from camp this was genuinely disconcerting, but when he stopped to listen to the rhythmic beat of his horse's hoofs, he heard instead the pounding of his own heart. Squeezing through the narrow place, he crawled on. By striking ahead of him with his knife, he crowded the wolf into a small hole, tied his lariat around her hind legs, pulled her out, and killed her with rocks. He went back and got ten pups from the hole, one of the largest litters found upon the ranch.[8]

Allen Stagg, another XIT cowboy well versed in lobo lore, hunted along the Canadian for several seasons. He killed eighty-four lobos in 1896 alone, and upon one or two occasions was wedged into their dens in narrow places. After crawling into the den and killing the mother lobo, he fished the pups out by means of a long pole to which was attached a metal hook.[9]

Lobos, when not gorged, were fleet and hard to run down. Few horses could equal their speed for the first four or five miles. Therefore the cowboy who undertook to catch one held his horse down to a "long lope." When the wolf began to tire, he let out his horse a little, and after a long chase, often of ten to fifteen miles, he was able to ride upon and rope the animal.[10] J. Walling, one of the camp men on the Yellow Houses, once ran a lobo twenty-five miles. He got the wolf, but "just the same as killed the horse," breaking his wind and leaving him unfit for further use. Yet experienced hunters claim that Walling could have saved his horse if he had known how to run a lobo.[11] There was more than one way to handle a wolf.

During the late nineties, the company paid annual bounties upon approximately 200 lobos, and its cowboys did much to

[8] J. P. McDonald to J. E. H., June 25, 1927.
[9] Allen Stagg to J. E. H., June 29, 1926.
[10] Gough, "Sketch," 6.
[11] H. K. Baughn to J. E. H., June 25, 1927.

clear the plains of this predatory animal,[12] the last of which was killed in this section in 1916.

Toward the first of March, heel-fly time came, and the cowboys began "riding bog." Attacked by a heel fly, the weakest old cow sets forth at full speed toward the nearest mud or water hole, and she will splatter into a miry spot with complete abandon of her usual discretion, intent only upon escaping the winged terror at her heels. In order to watch these boggy spots adequately, line men were placed in special camps called "bog camps." [13]

The Canadian was very boggy at times, and during the spring many cows were caught in its quicksands. Consequently bog camps were set up at intervals of every twenty or twenty-five miles. Four men in each camp rode in pairs, two up the stream to meet the cowboys from the camp above, and two down the river to a point halfway between their camp and the next below. They so timed their rides that when they turned to "back-trail" to their camp in the late afternoon, all cattle along the river were to be headed from, not toward, the water. For every cow to be headed away from the river meant that she had watered and would not return, get into the bog that evening, and spend the night there. There was little hope of saving a weak cow that struggled in the water and mud throughout the night.[14]

When an animal was found in a bog, one of the cowboys pitched his rope around her neck and dragged her out by the horn of his saddle. If he could not get his horse near enough for this, he might lengthen his rope by tying another to it. Quicksands of the Canadian, however shallow, packed around the legs and sides of a mired animal and held it so tightly that it could not move. The cowboys scratched or shoveled or tramped the sand from around the animal. When the sand was loosened, the water rose through it. Then the animal was pulled out by the neck, as to pull one by the horns would sometimes break the

[12] Gough, "Sketch," 6.
[13] Ira Aten to J. E. H., March 1, 1928.
[14] S. K. Bynum to J. E. H., November 5, 1927.

neck. From day to day until the "spring work" started, or until rain came and raised the water level above the boggy places, these line men rode in the wake of the vicious heel fly, pulling bogs and cursing this little insect that caused so much trouble. Cattle became strong enough to pull out of the bogs and these camps were abandoned for another year when grass came in the spring.[15]

Many other phases of ranch work demanded the attention of the foreman and cowboys. Line-riders watched for needed repairs along 1,500 miles of fence. Much work was necessary to keep it in repair, and many camp men "rode fence" with nippers and a bootleg of staples upon their saddles.

Each division kept one or two "windmillers," whose only duty was the care of the mills. These "windmillers" lived upon a never-ending journey that carried them in a circle from one mill to another. They lived in the open the year around. A personal chuck wagon supplied with tools was their only home. They camped where night overtook them as they moved from mill to mill, repairing where attention was needed and passing on where it was not. About once a month they swung in by headquarters, replenished their store of provisions, repaired their tools, and reported to the foreman any neglect in greasing the mills on the part of the line-riders. Then they were off again in summer heat or winter blizzard.[16] One of the ranch "windmillers" in Castro County always had to help hold the elections, since there were only five men in his precinct, and he was forced to serve as one of the election judges.

Lamb and Bailey counties were attached to Castro for judicial purposes before they were organized. During the election of 1896 a box was held at Spring Lake. The boys from the Yellow Houses, the S Ranch, the Spade Ranch, and two "windmillers" and a cowboy from Red Tower came there to vote. Harry Baughn, foreman at the Yellow Houses, was presiding officer. Other cowboys and a "windmiller" were judges. When

---

[15] *Ibid.,* Ira Aten to J. E. H., March 1, 1928.

[16] Ira Aten to J. E. H., March 1, 1928; B. P. Abbott to J. E. H., June 24, 1927.

the polls were closed at 6:00 o'clock, the five judges began counting the votes. Only twenty-one had been cast, but the cowboys worked from then until five o'clock the next morning before all the votes were counted and the results announced.[17]

Many interesting experiments marked and marred the evolution of this pastoral institution. At the Yellow Houses the tallest windmill tower in the world lifted its wheel 130 feet above the canyon's floor to catch the wind sweeping across the Plains and raise the water from a bare forty-foot level.[18]

Some of the XIT men in 1885 discovered a coal lode in New Mexico. The Capitol Company bought the mineral right from the government, and by November, 1886, over two hundred tons of coal had been mined from it, mainly for use upon the ranch.[19]

Barbed wire held first place among fencing materials until D. H. Wilson, president of the United States Electric Fence Company, appeared in Tascosa early in 1888 direct from Chicago.[20] He was armed with a Pinkerton detective commission, two six-shooters, and numerous affidavits concerning the success of the electric fence he had invented. With the typical assurance of a tenderfoot he expected to "revolutionize" fencing and "supplant . . . barbed wire." To prove the effectiveness of his fence, he contracted with the XIT Ranch to fence a pasture and construct a telephone line to the Alamocitos. The phone line was to be thirty miles long.

An "overshot" wheel at Alamocitos furnished water power for a generator. The electricity thus supplied was to be used in charging the second and top wires of a four-wire fence. The editor of *The Tascosa Pioneer* was enthusiastic over the innovation.

The electricity in these two upper wires is what gives them virtue as a fence [he wrote]. Stock touches them, and the shock is more effective and less injurious than the snagging by deadly

[17] B. P. Abbott to J. E. H., June 24, 1927.
[18] *The Sudan News* (Texas), July, 1926, p. 19.
[19] John V. Farwell, *Report* of 1886, p. 7.
[20] *The Tascosa Pioneer*, January 14, 1888.

barbs. . . . Many posts are dispensed with, fifty feet being easily sufficient between any two with this system. . . . The electricity may become as powerful as to literally knock cattle off their feet, in case they keep endeavoring to break over. Stampedes are the only things that can accomplish a break. As to the telephone feature, the cowboys will all carry hand-phones, and by grounding and fastening to the electrified wire at any point of the fence they can ring the bell at the ranch office. Then changing to the telephone wire they can talk over it. Should this electrified wire break at any time the bell is started ringing, and by that the accident is made known.

With the successful conclusion of the experiment it was generally understood that the system would be substituted for the fourteen hundred miles of fence that had already been built upon the XIT Ranch. Amazed at such evidences of progress the editor exclaimed, "Where will science lead next?" [21]

No doubt old ranch hands asked the same question, and what fluent, sarcastic comment must have poured from the bunkhouses and cow camps as they thought of carrying telephones upon their saddles and calling in to headquarters that an LX bull had torn down the east fence, or that Old Dynamite had been bitten by a rattlesnake! That dream, as even a tenderfoot should have predicted, was not to come to realization. Yet fifty years later electric fences would be common.

The cowboys were all skeptical of the electric fence, but none more so than "Little Jack" Luckett, range rider on the Alamocitos. Repeatedly warned by the electrician of the danger of touching the second and fourth wires, "Little Jack" jogged along the newfangled fence line eyeing it in mistrust. At length he could not resist an experiment. He picked up a piece of wire some six feet long and by means of a stick looped one end over the charged fence. His horse, with dangling bridle reins, stood basking in the sun and perhaps dreaming of the luscious pasturage along the Alamocitos. Man's thirst for scientific knowledge always takes precedence over regard for simple animal

[21] *Ibid.,* March 17, 1888.

feelings, and "Little Jack" raised the end of the wire upon the stick until it made contact with the bridle bits. No more tender spot could have been touched than the pony's mouth. The little horse thought lightning had struck him. He reared up, pawing at his head, and fell over backwards upon the saddle. Scrambling to his feet, he set out for the ranch as hard as he could run, and "Little Jack" walked in, cursing the eminent success of his experiment.[22]

The LX Ranch also tried out the electric fence, but it was an impractical venture for large enclosures, though it is widely used as an expedient.[23]

Nothing caused as much dire alarm in the cow country as a widespread prairie fire. Loss of grass often meant—still means —loss of the reserve essential to existence, and posed immediate bankruptcy for the owner. Thus it was an unwritten law of the range that upon the outbreak of a grass fire everybody instantly dropped whatever he was doing and rode or drove at full speed to fight it. In the early days chuck wagons were loaded and left with the ranch cook unmercifully plying his whip to pitch quick camp alongside the path of the fire and stir up a quick meal to feed the fighters, who worked at the job night and day until the catastrophe was checked or put out.

The human dangers of fires in the short-grass country were often exaggerated. They rarely resulted in loss of life, though such a veteran range hand as Phelps White, who eventually acquired much of the Yellow Houses, barely escaped, and only after terrible burns. In the same region a freighter named Doug Elkins, while hauling corn from Amarillo across the XIT to the 7D Ranch, had his own close call. In the warmth of the day he lay back on his sacks of grain for a nap as his six-horse team walked down the familiar road. A grass fire blew into his horses as he slept. Naturally, they swung in tandem to run with it, but the fire caught and enveloped them. One horse dropped dead in the harness and the others were singed to the skin, but

[22] J. Frank Mitchell to J. E. H., June 10, 1927.
[23] E. C. G. Austen to J. E. H., July 7, 1927.

Doug escaped to the burnt-over ground from his blazing sacks of grain.[24]

Charles Goodnight, the great authority on the range, could recall no case in which a plainsman lost his life from such fires, though other old-timers refer to Jim Clark, once range manager of the JA Ranch, who moved to Old Mexico. While fighting a fire there in 1907 he was caught in the flames—though probably in the back-fires set by his own Mexican hands—and burned to death.[25]

Grass fires were set in many ways. In Indian times the savages often set them deliberately to harass their enemies or to concentrate game for their hunts. With the white men, carelessness was more often than not the cause—carelessness with campfires, with cigarettes, and eventually with matches. Nature too had a part, as the violent lightning of the High Plains thunderstorms set many fires, though frequently the rains that accompanied them in turn put them out. Even matches dropped in the grass, pecked at inquisitively by birds, were suspected of starting others. At last, malicious setting of the range accounted for many.

When barbed wire was enclosing most of the ranges of Texas in the early eighties and the struggle for free grass was at its bitter height, grass was burned in retaliation for alleged grievances held against the fence men. In 1884 Texas passed a law making the burning of grass a felony.[26] But most grass-burning offenses upon Texas ranges were matters for settlement outside court.

When Ira Aten, former Texas Ranger, was brought to the Escarbada Division to fight the cattle rustlers of eastern New Mexico and the western Panhandle, he put into effect a vigorous system of frontier law. Men rode the western XIT fence line, which followed the New Mexico boundary, with Winchesters upon their saddles and six-shooters in their belts, taking a shot at anyone seen upon the fence without evident good busi-

[24] B. P. Abbott to J. E. H., June 24, 1927.
[25] Jim P. Wilson to J. E. H., February 4, 1929.
[26] Gammel's *Laws of Texas*, IX, 598.

ness. Neighbors told Aten that the thieves would burn him out if he did not quit fighting them so viciously.

I told them I could not help it if they did [said Aten], but if I caught one doing it, I was going to kill him if it was the last thing I did.

One time in the winter of '96 I saw a fire start about the center of the ranch, and I made for it. It was about thirty miles from the Escarbada. The instructions were for everybody to leave what he was doing when a fire started and go to it. We fought this fire all that night. We rested at the Trujillo camp and then went across to Endee ten miles from there, kind of looking for whoever set the fire. As we came back between sundown and night, I saw two men ride off into a little draw. I did not pay much attention to them, as I thought they were riders looking for cattle. I rode on a little ways, and then saw the fire boil up from the Trujillo Bull Pasture, where these two men had gone. We fought that fire all that night and got in to the ranch about morning. Some of the boys had seen and recognized two men in the pasture.

I strapped on my gun and said to myself, "Right here is where Brown gets killed." The rustlers knew that the company would fire me if they could keep me burned out, and I knew that I had to stop the devilment if I held my job, and I made up my mind to kill this man. He went armed all the time and I knew there was a chance of him getting me. But that is the way you want a man if you are going to kill him—you want him armed. I set out after him. His friends suspected what I was going to do, so Brown left and did not come back for several years.[27]

Aten had moved to California, a thousand miles away, before Brown returned to the Panhandle. "That," said Aten, "was the last time my range was set a-fire maliciously." [28]

The XIT Ranch lost so much grass that some of its foremen ordered their cowboys to smoke only when they were around mills or other waterings, where all the grass had been eaten and tramped away. Cowboys did not observe this rule faithfully, but it caused them to be more careful. Ira Aten, working upon

[27] Ira Aten to J. E. H., February 26, 1928.   [28] *Ibid.*

the theory that for every fire there was a cause, said that nine times out of ten he could trail a fire to the man who set it.[29]

When drought came and dried the grass prematurely, there was danger during the spring and summer, or until the country began to "green up." The most dangerous period was during the fall and winter, but what is said to have been the most destructive prairie fire to have swept the South Plains came in the month of June, 1879. It originated on the Z-L Ranch in Crosby County, where there was considerable "shinnery." Hundreds of wild hogs ranged this dwarf-oak country, prolific and hardy upon the acorns that grew there. Hank Smith, the first settler in the South Plains region, described this fire and the hogs.

One day a cowboy decided he would set fire to the shinneries and run them out. The fire got away and started on a wild rampage in a northeasterly direction. No one ever learned for certain which way the hogs went. The fire swept the Plains country, and, spreading as it went, sped across the Blanco Canyon, moving before a terrific wind from the southwest. There was practically no cattle in the country, and few people to care where the fire went or what it did. It crossed the Blanco into the Quitaque, Boggy Creek, North and South Pease River and Tule Canyon country, while before it fled thousands of antelope and turkeys, hundreds of deer and a sprinkling of cattle and horses. The fire swept thousands of square miles of country to the south and southwest, north and northeast of Mount Blanco. All through the country at that time, especially along the streams, were hundreds of magnificent groves of fine timber, particularly cottonwood and hackberry. . . . This fire killed the timber and in effect literally wiped it out.[30]

The XIT losses were severe for years. Notice has already been taken of the complications caused by the first fire that struck the northern end of the ranch during the winter of 1884–85—the first year of operations with cattle. While the LE Ranch people, who suffered seriously from the fire that

[29] Ira Aten to J. E. H., February 26, 1928.
[30] *The Crosbyton Review*, February 29, 1912.

swept out of the XIT range to devastate them, bitterly accused Metcalf's fencing crew of starting it, other old-timers insisted that it originated in the Arkansas River country of western Kansas.

Billy Dixon, the buffalo hunter, told how it burned south through the Oklahoma Strip, jumped the Cimarron River near the 101 Ranch as cowboys from that section fought it from either side, and how it then raced south for nearly a hundred miles farther to play out in the breaks of the Canadian.

Whatever its origin, it struck the XIT to the northwest of Buffalo Springs, and put everybody at that headquarters into an old fashioned "swivet." Mac Huffman, punching cows there at the time, described the outfit's efforts to save some portion of the Syndicate's grass.

George Collins was the range boss. He was badly excited when he saw the fire coming and sent riders out to bring in men. We left the ranch and went eighteen or twenty miles to a point a little south of where Texline is now. We rode up to the fire at night. It was burning through the bluestem grass, three feet or more high in the Perico Draw. The flames looked like they were going sixty feet high. Collins told us to look out for cow paths or some other advantage to fight the fire along. We fought the fire along its east side all that night and went in to Buffalo Springs about ten o'clock next day. After dinner we hooked up a wagon and Hugh Perry drove it full of men farther north to the Corrumpa and we fought the remainder of the day and all that night. But all the grass we saved was about two miles square in the Dallam County Pasture. We lost all of the Middlewater country as the fire did not stop until it got into the Canadian breaks.[31]

The XIT lost nearly a million acres of grass in this fire. Collins threw 4,000 head of his cattle across the line into New Mexico to drift far and wide before the severe blizzards of the winter that followed. He threw the remaining 18,000 head south to the unburned country along the Canadian. By the

[31] M. Huffman to J. E. H., November 30, 1927.

next summer losses had depleted the original herd of 22,000 to 16,813 head.

Fires resulted in loss of cattle in a country of high grass, but since cattle naturally dropped into any trail they struck after being placed upon the move, and since most trails eventually led to water, tanks, creeks, or lakes, where the grass was tramped and eaten away, they usually escaped by stopping at these places.

The LE Ranch, along the Canadian in the high-grass country, lost a number of steers in the fire of 1885.[32] About the same time grass fires were stampeding the mustangs and cattle of the North Plains of Texas over the big drift fence that was built from the eastern Panhandle into New Mexico on the west. Wherever bunches of horse or cattle hit this fence with a fire behind them, they flattened it out and left work for the fence builders.[33] The XIT's lost few cattle in the big fire of 1894, but a fire to the north of the Canadian in the high sagegrass of the Middle Water Division took a toll of 200 head of cattle.[34] More small calves were lost in fires than cattle of any other age, as calves, left by their mothers while they go to water, remain lying in the grass until their mothers return, and hence may easily be caught by fast fires.

Frank Yearwood and his Spring Lake cowboys fought a bad fire upon that division in 1887 until a snowstorm put it out. Lightning weirdly played over the plains during the storm. A "sort of preacher" in the crowd prayed and sang during the intervals of rest, while the boys "cussed" and swore loudly that "they would rather be anybody's yellow dog in an ash hopper" than a waddie out working for the Syndicate at $30 a month. This fire traveled sixteen and one-half miles in about two hours. When it struck the sagegrass in the sand country of the western Panhandle, flames shot high into the air, where the wind caught their tips and hurled them back to the ground to set fire to the grass as much as sixteen feet ahead of the burning portions.

[32] *Ibid.*
[33] John Arnot to J. E. H., April 8, 1929.
[34] B. P. Abbott to J. E. H., June 19, 1927.

Finally the snow smothered the fire. The weather was bitter cold and the cowboys, completely lost, attempted to reset the fire to keep from freezing to death, but the snowstorm was too heavy.[35]

One of the worst prairie fires of the western Panhandle broke out in the LFD country of New Mexico late in November, 1894. A west wind sent it racing toward the Spring Lake ranges. For a week before it reached the state line, as diverse winds slowed its progress, smoke hung over the Texas plains like the heavy haze of Indian summer. Every night Syndicate cowboys saw its red glow rise and fall like the distant aurora of the northern lights. Checked here and there by fighting cowboys, it broke forth afresh and crossed into the Syndicate range where the Running Water Draw is cut by the New Mexico line to the south of Farwell, Texas.

Pres Abbott, a Spring Lake cowboy, was hauling a load of pipe to a well-driller's camp on Frio Draw when the advance tongues of flame came through, striking the Syndicate on a twenty-mile front. He turned one of the mules he was driving loose, jumped upon the other bareback, and rode into the Running Water Camp. He met Fred Finnicum, the camp man, coming in from his ride, and together they fought the fire all night. About daylight they met the riders from Blackwater and Red Tower camps. After getting a bite to eat, they rode down Running Water Draw and fought fire along the Blackwater Pasture fence in an attempt to save the grass there. Cattle, in passing back and forth along along the fence, had beaten out "cow trails" running east and west. The fire was burning from west to east, but fires spread to either side, ever widening the path of flame. Using these cow trails as fire guards, the cowboys fought to prevent the fire from spreading south.

Mac Huffman, then foreman at Spring Lake, with two of his "windmillers" joined the original four about the middle of the afternoon. By evening they had worked eastward almost to Red Tower, and the camp man went in, cooked, and brought

[35] J. Frank Yearwood to J. E. H., December 9, 1927.

out to the others some very bad biscuits and bacon. A brisk wind blew up and for a time no attempt was made to fight the advancing flames. Eleven men were fighting the fire along its southern edge when it crossed the east line of the Syndicate's range. They turned and rode back to Red Tower, where Jack Bradford had one "hot roll" made up of a tarp and three "suggans." At one o'clock in the morning the eleven men spread these "suggans" and their saddle blankets upon the floor of the camp, and had their first sleep in forty-two hours. But even that was not to last long.

About three o'clock someone got up and looked out to the west. The wind had changed to the north and the fire had broken across into the Blackwater pasture behind them and was burning south. After a little coffee, bacon, and bread they set out again. They fought for the remainder of the night, all day, and until two o'clock the next morning. Three of the boys dropped into Spring Lake for a little sleep and the others stayed with the fire. At daylight these three returned to the blistering work. The fire reached the sand hill country in southern Lamb County that day, and about four o'clock in the afternoon they at last succeeded in putting it out. The first two cowboys had been working almost continuously for three nights and almost four days. The first night they did not lie down, the second they slept two hours, and the third, three. Rawhide could not have been tougher.

All rode to Spring Lake on the fourth night and went to bed to sleep until early daylight. Mac Huffman "rustled" them out and sent cowboys in every direction to scout out the country for dead cattle and to see if there was any unburned grass. Along Blackwater Draw smoking ash heaps showed where haystacks had been, and mile after mile of blackened land stretched to the north and to the south, with not a spear of grass left. Cattle had drifted to the waterings, where the grass was tramped away, and few had been burned to death.

That afternoon sweating horses brought riders into Spring Lake from every direction at a "long lope." Their reports showed that Syndicate land almost twenty by sixty miles—from the Canadian breaks to the sand hills—had been burned clean of grass. The next morning Joe Anderson, mounted upon a gray horse called Dash, rode out of the corral and, before the short fall day was done, rode into Amarillo, a distance of eighty-five miles, to report to Manager Boyce. Boyce had been in Fort Worth when the fire started. His son, Al Boyce, had seen it and wired him. He came in on the train soon after Anderson reached Amarillo. Anderson met the train, reported, and Boyce went on to Channing that night. When he got there, he found Montgomery, foreman of the Ojo Bravo, and some of his cowboys giving all their attention to the mazes of the old Virginia reel at a town dance. Boyce went to the dance and told Montgomery to forget the Old Dominion, take his outfit, and strike south to meet the cattle which would be heading north from Spring Lake. As the evening stars swung past the meridian, the outfit, with unfulfilled social obligations, were riding south toward Torrey's Peak on the Canadian. There was no time to lose.

Boyce sent instructions back to Spring Lake by Anderson advising Huffman to place all cattle on the trail for the Canadian. Already they had been without feed for several days and there was dire necessity for hurry. With every available man in the saddle and the "windmiller" as cook, the wagon left Spring Lake upon the first morning of December. The first roundup was thrown together on Frio Draw, seven miles east of the site of Friona town. Not counting calves, 4,300 head of cattle were counted out to Montgomery. He swung his wagon around and without loss of time was upon the trail for the unburned breaks, declaring he would not stop his outfit night or day until he had the herd upon grass and water.

Huffman rounded up the west half of the Capitol pasture the next day and placed 4,500 head "above calves" upon the trail. In spite of "played out" horses and a snowstorm to face, he placed this big herd, far too big for easy driving, upon the Canadian at the mouth of Skunk Arroyo with the loss of but fifteen calves, which broke back from the herd and which the horses were too weak to "head off." [36]

The speed of prairie fires varied with the speed of the wind, the dryness and the length of the grass, and its thickness upon the ground. There are cases of fires traveling as fast as a man on a running horse. When the wind was high, fires rarely advanced on a solid front miles in width, but pushed forward as wedges of flame driven fiercely and swiftly through the range. These wedges represented the fastest-moving portions of the front, and were more dangerous than the sides—the spreading lines along the flanks. If the wind was blowing strong, little attempt was made to fight the lead fires, as the heat was so intense that it would kill a man.

Thus, upon reaching a fire, the cowboys advanced as close as possible toward its lead point and fought along the sides where its advance was slower and its heat less intense as it widened its span against the force of the wind. They fought with the wind to their backs, advancing with the fire and putting out every particle of flame and smouldering cow chip. While the dew of early morning was falling or the wind had abated, men thus beat out the fire on either side of the wedge, with the objective of finally squeezing it down to a point and putting it out. But when the wind was blowing a gale, as it has been known to do in West Texas, fires were rarely put out until they reached some natural obstacle such as the caprock, a creek bed, or relatively barren hills.

Back-firing as a means of control was sometimes tried, but when there was nothing to protect except grass, any attempt to start a wide back-fire to cover the path of the advancing wedge, without means of controlling it, simply amplified the trouble already at hand. Successful back-fires usually depended upon some advantage along which to set them such as a cattle trail, a furrow, a fire-guard, a creek, or a road. Such an advantage, of necessity, had to intersect the course of the advancing fire.

[36] M. Huffman to J. E. H., November 30, 1927.

When such a feature was available, some cowboy would quickly soak the end of his rope in kerosene, if the oil was at hand, set it on fire and trail it at a trot behind his horse, thus firing the grass just to windward of the natural guard. Meanwhile fighters on the ground with saddle blankets, slickers, and wet tow sacks watched to see that the flames did not jump the guard and get away. The back-fire was thus forced to burn slowly into the wind until the main fire met it and both burned out. But not until the settlement of the country, when roads were cutting the sod into convenient fire-guards and plowed fields were turning the range into checker-boards, could back-fires be used to real advantage. And then, when the remedy was available, the ill was almost gone.[37]

The most effective method of fighting fires was by the use of drags followed up by men on foot with brooms, chaps, saddle blankets, slickers, or any old thing convenient for beating out the scattered embers. The most effective drag was that most conveniently at a cowboy's hand—the nearest beef he could rope and kill. When men reached the scene of a fire, their ropes came down and they snared the first calf, yearling, or small steer they could "dab it on." Somebody immediately shot the animal in the head or cut its throat if a gun was not handy. They cut off its head with their pocket knives, so that it would not flop around, skinned one side of the animal from belly to back, and left the hide in place. Then, tying to the lower fore and hind legs, two men took off, dragging the beef by the horns of their saddle. One took the grassy side, the other the side of the fire, and by straddling the path of the flame, they dragged the beef directly along it with the loose, wet hide flopping out behind and men on foot to finish the job. Often they rode at a trot while the men on the ground worked in reliefs. It was necessary, too, to change the horse on the burnt side at least every twenty or thirty minutes, on account of the heat on his feet. Once failure to change a strong-pulling, dependable XIT horse

[37] The author has discussed this subject in some detail in "Grass Fires of Southern Plains," West Texas Historical Association *Year Book,* 1929, Vol. V, 23–42, a portion of which account is reproduced here.

in time—one especially good in the fire—resulted in ruining his feet. They got so hot that his hoofs sloughed off. Other horses were lost from losing one or more feet.[38]

Many modifications of this "beef drag" were used. Sometimes a heavy beef or cow was cut half in two, down the back, and the carcass made into two drags. These, after being used for hours, were fairly "barbecued" by the heat, and at times furnished a meal for weary fighters far from camp with nothing else to eat. Sometimes an old cow was skinned, with hunks of flesh left on the hide, and the hide alone was used as a drag.

When beef became more valuable and a measure of system reached the range to cope with more frequent fires following the advent of the farming settlers, some ranches kept drags at every camp. The XIT made them of heavy chains, interlaced to resemble huge fish nets, but still to be pulled by the horn of the saddle. These cut the fire away from the grass but did not smother it out. So again the fighters turned to unlucky yearlings caught near by, and dispatched them for hides to pitch over the chains.[39]

Lacking these, a couple of posts thrown into a wagon sheet or a heavy cotton suggan left in a bed tarp into which several buckets of water were thrown, with the folded tarp gathered at the ends with two catch ropes, made excellent drags. The durable tarps held water, the soaked suggan gave weight, and such a drag would stay wet and effective for several miles.[40]

The value of fire-guards was obvious at once, and the XIT's turned to them from the first—after their "costly experience" of 1885. They were made by plowing two or three furrows, "on both sides of the fence," about one hundred feet apart. On a still day, after the grass had matured, a cowboy dragged an oil-soaked rope behind his horse and burned the space out. Within a year after the first bad fire, 1,000 miles of furrows had been plowed. More than 700 miles were again plowed in

[38] Ira Aten to J. E. H., February 26, 1928; C. F. Vincent to J. E. H., June 26, 1927.

[39] C. F. Vincent to J. E. H., June 26, 1927.

[40] Fred Scott to J. E. H., April 7, 1929.

1887, at a cost of $1,077.66, as reflected on the ranch books. The JA's were already using them, and neighboring outfits— the LX's on the Canadian, and the IOA, the 2 Buckles, and others on the South Plains—were making it a regular practice in the nineties.[41]

And yet the losses continued as vagrant cow chips and, with the coming of the farming settler, drifting tumbleweed added to the hazards. After frost has hit the Russian thistle or tumbleweed, it snaps loose from its brittle tap root and, light and round as it is, tumbles along with every wind that blows. It burns with explosive vigor, and when caught in the suction caused by grass burning in a brisk wind, has been seen to shoot into the air fifty feet high and sail as a ball of fire for a hundred yards before hitting the ground again to start a fresh fire and speed the devastation.

Thin, dry cow chips, too, while conveniently stoking many a pioneer settler's stove, added to the fire-fighter's troubles. When they were caught in fifty- to seventy-mile winds, the dainty, wafer-like chips were rolled along with the fire like tin plates, crossing roads and guards and starting other fires beyond the reach of the parent flames, and even destroying barns and pioneer homes.

Such was the case in Crosby County in the nineties when a grass fire burned within a mile of the town. The settlers poured out to guard it, but the chips rolled and filtered through their lines to lodge beneath floors of buildings and even to catch in the shingles and set fire to roofs, burning several buildings to the ground.[42]

Even yet grass fires are a continual threat to the men whose fortunes are built on grass. But for the most of the old XIT ranges, the problem has been effectively settled by turning under sod despite the cowboy's warning that "the best side's up." The boiling white smoke of burning grass chokes nobody now, but as for dust—"Well, that's another thing."

[41] West Texas Historical Association *Year Book,* 1929, Vol. V, 40–41.

[42] R. B. Smith to J. E. H., February 17, 1929; John D. McDermett to J. E. H., April 28, 1929.

CHAPTER XII

From Longhorn to Thoroughbred

THE FOUNDATION HERD of the XIT Ranch was Longhorn "stuff." With favorable climate the breed was prolific. But Longhorn stock did not produce the quality of beef the market of the eighties was coming to demand. However, when bred to good sires, the cows produced stock of better beef qualities than the average Longhorn steer. Through the use of high-grade bulls, a generous cut-back of undesirable stock, and the retention of heifer calves from year to year, what was originally a "cold blooded" herd might rapidly grow into good beef stock. This method of "grading up" was practiced on most Texas ranges. The XIT adopted it.

During the decade and a half following the Civil War, Longhorn cattle were the economic salvation of Texas. They were gaunt and wiry, independent and perverse. As a product of the wilderness they did well where blooded cattle would have perished of drought, travel, and thirst. They were more easily handled than blooded stock, both in the roundup and upon the trail. Because of breadth of horn they spaced themselves better under herd—keeping plenty of room—thus traveling with greater ease, less heat, and less loss of flesh. Their hoofs were tougher, their legs longer, and their endurance greater than high-grade "stuff." They ranged a much wider scope of country, went longer without water, suffered more hardships, and took better care of themselves upon the range or in stampedes than any other breed. Old age did not find them toothless as it often finds improved cattle, and in breeding usefulness they lived nearly double the span of their successors. In every Longhorn herd there trailed steers with personalities as clear cut as the men who drove them. Those steers will live in story.

One named Old Blue led JA herds up the trail to Dodge City. During eight seasons he walked at the "point," his lank, blue form and the clatter of the bell he wore directing the beeves that trailed behind. He was never shipped to market, but was always brought back with the remuda. He was a pet that saved the Palo Duro cowboys much work in crossing rivers, in holding a course, and in corralling at Dodge. The names of many Palo Duro cowpunchers are forgotten. That of Old Blue is not.

Longhorns always cared for their young with the solicitude and ferocity of a wild animal. Rarely could a Longhorn calf be jumped from the bed in which its mother had left it and chased so far away but that it would return to that very spot to meet its mother again. With sensitive nose, ears, and eyes as aids to protection, these cattle had lived in the wild state in Texas for more than two centuries: ever since 1693 when Father Massanet deserted his East Texas mission. They identified their calves more by smell than by sight, and some trailed by scent like a "hound dog."

One spring the Canadian roundup had worked down the river to the neighborhood of Adobe Walls. Two or three hundred head of cattle were being held under herd. Each day they were driven on to the scene of the next day's work. In the herd was a large, black, line-backed cow weighing close to twelve hundred pounds. She was a descendant of the wild herds that once roamed the Texas prairie lands, but had been bought in New Mexico by the JA outfit.

One morning as daylight came and relieved the last riders on night herd, the cowboys discovered that the line-backed cow had given birth to a calf. The cook was supposed to load the newborn calves of his own brand upon his wagon and haul them to the next camp. The JA cook pulled out, followed the roundup by a circular route twelve miles down the river. But he forgot the black cow's calf, which was left upon the bed ground. As soon as the outfit made camp, J. E. Farrington, the foreman, missed the calf. He was a sensitive, sympathetic man, and took the back track in search of it. He found the calf upon the bed ground, placed it across the saddle in front of him, and struck straight across country to the camp.

In the meantime the day herders allowed the cow to escape. Farrington, apprised of this, knew that she would return to the bed ground in search of the calf, and turned back to get her. He took the direct route by which he had just come in. Within a mile or two of the bed ground he saw the cow coming to meet him along the trail he had made while carrying the calf. His curiosity was aroused and he dropped behind to watch her. Like a fox hound upon a warm track, she followed along Farrington's trail by the scent of the calf he had carried to camp. By sundown she reached the herd, and after the trip of twenty miles, soon found her calf. Farrington rode to the chuck wagon, wiser in the ways of cows. The observant Goodnight, who owned the outfit, said that it was "the most remarkable example of cow sense I have ever known."[1]

Next to maternal affection the Longhorns' attachment to their native soil was a predominant trait. Texas steers that grazed the ranges of Montana hankered to return to the sunny Nueces country, while others, upon escaping along the trails, sometimes back-tracked to their original stamping grounds like a lost kitten.

At Horsehead Crossing, in the late sixties, Goodnight lost a Longhorn cow from his herd that was being trailed west from Palo Pinto County to the northwestern territories. Upon his return to Palo Pinto from the trail, Goodnight found the cow on her home range. She had made the return trip of about four hundred miles alone.

Some years later, in 1875, Goodnight took three herds from

[1] C. Goodnight to J. E. H., February 25, 1927.

the John Chisum range on the Pecos, in southern New Mexico, and sold them to Hunter and Evans at Granada, Colorado. These big dealers sent them into the Indian nation, to Eagle Chief, to be wintered. The following year Goodnight located the Palo Duro Ranch in the Panhandle. Two of these steers crossed the wilderness of western Oklahoma, pushed through the thousands of buffalo upon the range of the eastern Panhandle, and drifted into the Palo Duro in an attempt to return, by a direct route, to their home range on the Pecos. Their instinct of direction was as canny as an Indian's, for the trail by which they reached Indian Territory looped to the north and west through Kansas and Colorado for more than a thousand miles. They were taking the short cut home by a course about half as long.

Before the XIT and other ranches fenced the Panhandle country, the "northern drift" gave much trouble. Severe blizzards drove the cattle from the Beaver, the Cimarron, the Arkansas, and even the Platte rivers down into Texas. As far south as the Pease, the roundups "cut" cattle belonging on the Platte in Nebraska. For all that world was open, and those Texas steers, placed on northern ranges, drifted before blizzards with the stride of a horse.

Among famous walkers a worthy companion to Old Blue was a steer of similar color called Old Slate. Like Andy Adams' poker steer, "he was born in a chaparral thicket south of the Nueces River in Texas." The Civil War could not have been over when he arrived and began to do a little fighting of his own. He grew to maturity in the Santa Gertrudes country, and came to love the mesquite and chaparral as only a Longhorn can. Jim East, veteran of the Texas range, met Old Slate while preparing for the trail.

In 1876 I was driving for King and Kennedy [East recalled]. A good many of our cattle were sold in Colorado. Bates and Beal, who started the LX Ranch on the Canadian, bought some of them. In the herd that we delivered to them on the Arkansas, near Granada, loomed Old Slate, the biggest steer I ever saw. He wore

King and Kennedy's Laurel Leaf brand and was what we call a "moss-head," a worthless old thing, as he must have been fifteen years old then. His color was a blue-slate, and he looked like he was seven feet tall. We delivered the herd and turned back for South Texas. From the banks of the Arkansas, Old Slate, towering above all the other steers, watched us go.

Then one day during the winter a rider on the Santa Gertrudes found Old Slate grazing in the brush. Through southern Colorado, across the Panhandle, and down through Texas, Old Slate had trudged the miles away, and now contentedly rubbed his neck against a mesquite, a thousand miles by trail from where the South Texas cowboys had left him.

Again in the spring of 1877 [East continued], we had Old Slate in another herd headed for the same ranch on the Arkansas. We delivered him with the other steers. For three seasons the riders managed to keep him there, and he grew larger than ever. But he was always thinking of the chaparral of South Texas. In 1880, John Ray brought a bunch of LIT cattle down to the LX's, and Old Slate was among them. I had left South Texas and was working for the LX outfit. We had crossed the Panhandle on our second trip north with Old Slate and I thought it was the prettiest cow country I ever saw. But Old Slate did not. He still had South Texas on his mind.

We kept him on the ranch until we started a herd to Caldwell, Kansas, for shipment to market at St. Louis. Old Slate was thrown in. In the herd was a six-year-old red white-faced steer called Baldy, and a spotted one that the boys called Christ. Both kept wanting to head for South Texas. But Old Slate was the worst. We "necked" Baldy and Christ together and kept them in the herd. Old Slate was turned over to me. I put a bell on him and roped and hobbled him every night, and we finally got him to Caldwell. His horns were so wide that two men had to twist his head to one side to get him through the car door.

The train pulled out for Kansas City, and Harry Derrick went with it to care for the shipment. At Pierce City, Missouri, the cattle were unloaded to be watered and fed. Old Slate, tired of captivity and as mad as he could be, jumped over the high railroad corral fence and went tearing down through a cornfield, scaring the farmers out of their wits. They pulled down their old squirrel rifles and shot and killed him.

Rebellious Old Slate never reached the butcher's block, but died in a cornfield of Missouri, still yearning for the chaparral of South Texas.

Cattle of such traits stocked the West and formed the foundation herd for the XIT Ranch. By the close of the eighties approximately 130,000 head were inside XIT fences.

Colonel Babcock, in recommending the establishment of the ranch in his report of 1882, had the use of thoroughbred bulls in mind.[2] In 1876, Goodnight brought about 150 head of high-grade Shorthorn cows into the Panhandle with his first herd. These did not prove satisfactory. Polled Angus were scarce and high of price, and Panhandle cowmen turned to the Hereford.[3] In 1882, O. H. Nelson brought the first registered Hereford bulls to the Panhandle. During the next eight years he placed over 10,000 high-grade Hereford bulls upon Panhandle ranges.

The demand for Herefords in England in 1883 was said to have been "phenomenal," [4] and breeders were being taxed to supply the American demand. By the late eighties this demand had so depleted the supply and so increased the price upon high-grade males that the XIT was unable to use them in large numbers.[5] Many low-grade bulls were placed upon the ranch in the late eighties, but better ones were bought each year until 1892, after which date only purebred bulls were bought. With low-grade cows and no more good bulls than the ranch had at first, improvement of the herd was slow.[6]

In 1889 systematic work of herd improvement began. Such work, slow under favorable conditions, was more difficult because of the size of the ranch. Not all of the cows upon the ranch were of the same grade. Different grades occupied differ-

[2] Babcock, *Prospectus*, 22.
[3] C. Goodnight to J. E. H., June 1, 1928.
[4] *The Dallas Herald*, August 23, 1883.
[5] Ms., "The Capitol Syndicate or XIT Ranch," 2.
[6] *Ibid.*

ent pastures. Males of three different breeds had been brought in: Hereford, Durham, and Polled Angus. Certain grades of cows early seemed to lend themselves to improvement better with the Herefords, others with the Angus, and still others with the Shorthorns. Gradually the selection and sorting, which seemed most in keeping with this improvement, was done. Since the ranch was about two hundred miles long, and, on the average, twenty-five miles wide, fenced and cross-fenced,

it offered good opportunities to test these three breeds under practically similar conditions and after a few years the pastures in which the Shorthorn bulls were kept and those in which the Hereford bulls were kept and those in which the Angus bulls were kept began to show the respective breed characteristics and every year, by careful selection of animals—undesirable because of color or quality—the herds rapidly assumed to all appearances the quality and character of the pure breds.[7]

The XIT definitely set itself the task of determining, so far as it could by such an experiment, what breed was best adapted to the plains country. The results are interesting, particularly since the conclusion in regard to Polled Angus cattle differs from that reached by most pioneer cowmen of the Panhandle, though it finds support in later years.

Buffalo Springs was early set aside as a steer division, Middle Water was used for culls, and the Rito Blanco and Alamocitos country along the Canadian were set aside for Polled Angus. Ojo Bravo and the divisions to the south of the river—Escarbada, Spring Lake, and the Yellow Houses—were set aside as Hereford breeding ranges, but Durhams were placed in a few pastures.[8] Early cowmen from Colorado had brought some Shorthorn stock with them. Thus they were not new to the Panhandle when the Syndicate introduced its grade and registered males. However, already some cowmen had decided that they were not hardy enough for this climate. The breed did

[7] George Findlay to Chas. Gray, May 20, 1910.
[8] R. L. Duke to J. E. H., July 6, 1927.

From Longhorn to Thoroughbred

well, but, lacking the rustling qualities of the other two, was not long retained.[9]

The use of Herefords in the Panhandle was widespread. Herefords were among the first grade bulls to be bought by the XIT, and soon four divisions were devoted to them. George Findlay, who was general manager of the ranch from the Chicago office at that time, favored the Angus. He gave as one reason for the spread of the Herefords the fact that they "were being pushed by a coterie of breeders exultant over the conflicts they had gone through with the Shorthorn sponsors"—breeders who were aggressive in the advertisement of their stock and who were able to supply the demand with reasonably priced bulls. Therefore "the Herefords soon became the dominant breed in the Panhandle." [10]

The Syndicate bought Herefords from some of the most prominent breeders of the country. Early purchases were made from the noted pioneer breeders, William Powell and T. L. Miller of Beecher, Illinois. In the early nineties a string of good bulls was bought from Goodnight and placed upon the Yellow Houses. In 1892 a registered herd of 44 bulls and 111 cows were bought from T. L. Miller, which, with a few registered cows from the Farwell brothers of Montezuma, Iowa, formed the basis for a registered herd of Herefords for the ranch. From time to time fresh blood was introduced, and eventually this herd practically supplied the ranch with bulls. By 1894 registered bulls had been placed in the Sod House pasture on the Yellow Houses, and soon T. F. B. Sotham was coming there to purchase the grade calves for eastern feeders.[11] The Herefords were pre-eminently good rustlers, hardy, prolific, and possessed of fine beef qualities. They continue to be by far the most popular breed of range cattle in the Southwest.

In spite of Findlay's keen interest in the Polled Angus, Boyce became discouraged and was about to ship them all to

[9] George Findlay to Chas. Gray, May 20, 1910.
[10] *Ibid.*
[11] Ms., "The Capitol Syndicate"; H. K. Baughn to J. E. H., June 25, 1927; *The Tascosa Pioneer,* May 10, 1890.

market. Goodnight suggested that he place the bulls in a pasture where there were none of any other breed, and place all his off-color cows with them. He tried this plan and was well pleased with the results. But the Angus never gained the favor its supporters thought it deserved.

While the Herefords were being brought to the attention of everyone in search of good stock through the enthusiastic advertising of their breeders, and were obtainable in good numbers and at reasonable prices, the Angus were hard to obtain, high in price, new to the section, and handicapped by the color prejudice many held against them. Breeders of other stock, anxious to push sales of their own, disparaged the Angus, claiming that the bulls bunched together on the range causing a short calf crop, that improvement did not take place so rapidly as with Hereford and Shorthorn, that they were not hardy enough to stand the hot summers or the cold winters, that, in short, they were unsuitable for range purposes. "Therefore," wrote Findlay, "the Angus came into . . . [the Panhandle] at a rather unpropitious time and had to fight against ignorance, prejudice, and jealousy for its foothold there. These sentiments were not wanting on the XIT Ranch." [12]

The Alamocitos pasture was the first to be set aside for Polled Angus stock. In 1891 actual work of "trimming up" the herd began, and soon the entire Rito Blanco Division, of which the Alamocitos was a part, was set aside for the breed. From year to year all the old cows with horns were cut out, and the blacks, the "muleys," and others showing the Angus strain were kept upon the range. In time all the horned "stuff" was disposed of, and a black, polled herd, predominantly Angus, was achieved. [13] In 1892, following the same plan as with the Herefords, fifty-five registered cows and a number of bulls were bought from Arnold brothers, of Hansford County, Texas, and from the Farwell brothers, of Montezuma, Iowa, for the beginning of a bull herd. Anderson and Findlay, of Lake Forest, and

[12] George Findlay to Chas. Gray, May 20, 1910.
[13] R. L. Duke to J. E. H., July 6, 1927.

From Longhorn to Thoroughbred

George Farwell, of Mt. Morris, Illinois, furnished the ranch with Angus sires.[14] In 1892 the ranch owned 1,000 head of thoroughbred Hereford and Angus cattle. Nothwithstanding the maintenance of herds for raising bulls, during 1898 some $87,000 was spent for Hereford, Durham, and Angus sires.[15]

No breed of cattle ever "handled" so well upon the range as the Longhorn, and probably none so poorly as the Angus. In herd, the Angus are inclined to become excited and pay little attention to their calves. "Muley stuff" jams together more closely, suffers more from the heat, and loses more weight from handling than "horned stuff," unless cowboys exercise the greatest patience.[16] But Findlay was enthusiastic over the results that the Angus showed.

After the adoption of the three breeds [Findlay wrote], each was given a very fair trial and the result . . . demonstrated that there was no breed better adapted for the range than the Angus. They were prolific, hardy, good rustlers, early maturers and good sellers. The steers of this breed are very generally the first to be sold off the range and have usually commanded a premium over the others.[17]

In 1889 there were practically the same number of cows in the Alamocitos pasture in which Angus bulls were placed as in the Minneosa pasture where Hereford bulls were placed. In 1890 the calves branded in the Alamocitos pasture numbered 3,064, in the Minneosa pasture 2,698 and there were branded in the pasture in which the black bulls were a larger number of calves for the years immediately following than in the other. The actual results on this ranch satisfied the owners and those connected with it that there is nothing at all in the claim that the Angus are poor breeders on the range.[18]

The Company came to regard the Angus, Findlay continued,

14 Ms., "The Capitol Syndicate or XIT Ranch," 2.
15 Gough, "Sketch of the XIT Ranch," 7.
16 J. E. Moore to J. E. H., July 6, 1927.
17 George Findlay to Chas. Gray, May 20, 1910.
18 George Findlay to the *Gazette*.

both as feeders and beeves—the quickest and best sellers, and when time and conditions permit we have always found it to our advantage to ship the Angus beeves by themselves as there seemed to be a wider market for them in the stockyards and they have almost invariably brought better prices than the others.[19]

When the sales of land began, making it necessary to dispose of most of the cattle, the Durhams and Herefords were sold first. By 1910 the Angus was the only breeding stock upon the ranch. "This decision," to quote Findlay again, "arrived at after probably better facilities for testing the breeds than have ever been afforded anywhere else, speaks more for the breed as a range breed than columns of query and argument." [20] The Angus herd, when the Rito Blanco was stocked at its heaviest, numbered close to 35,000 head; and even when the Alamocitos country was sold to Murdo MacKenzie and the Matadors in 1901, there were still over 20,000 head. At the sale of the last cattle in 1912, this "was, for all practical beef purposes, a purebred herd." [21] From the Longhorn stock, in twenty-four years, the Syndicate built up what was undoubtedly the largest herd of high-grade Polled Angus cattle in Texas.[22]

Boyce took much pride in building, from a nondescript herd, one which commanded the attention of all feeders wherever good cattle were in demand. XIT cattle came to rank with the JA herds, the best in the country. Car-lots representing the different breeds were taken to leading livestock shows.[23] The champion yearling Aberdeen Angus steers off grass at the Fort Worth show in 1900 were from the XIT. During the same year, at the Chicago International Live Stock Exposition for the Southwest district, the first, second, and third prizes for yearling steers off grass were awarded to the Angus, Hereford, and Shorthorn lots respectively. All awards went to cattle from this ranch. Steer calves from the ranch took the same awards in

19 *Ibid.*
20 George Findlay to Chas. Gray, May 20, 1910.
21 Ms., "The Capitol Syndicate or XIT Ranch," 2.
22 H. F. Mitchell to J. E. H., June 10, 1927.
23 Wm. Boyce to J. E. H., June 28, 1927.

the order of the breeds named, while two-year-old fed steers, bred upon the ranch, took the first three awards in their class for the Southwest. J. F. Kiester, of Emery, Illinois, fed the Herefords which took first place in this class. The car-lot of two-year-olds weighed 1,431 pounds and sold at $9.30 a hundredweight, which was claimed, at that time, "the highest price ever brought by branded range-raised steers." [24]

In 1905 the Syndicate sent a lot of Angus steers to Denver, thence to Kansas City and to Chicago. They took first prize in their class at every place. One steer was bought by a Chicago hotel for $2,100. Everyone who ate there for the next three or four years had the opportunity of ordering at a fancy price, if the menus were to be believed, a choice steak from this prize Angus, and the cynical suspected that that "muley" steer paid his cost many times over. [25]

The experiments of the XIT Ranch with the Hereford, Shorthorn, and Angus breeds was of much value to the Panhandle-Plains country. The quality of these three herds emphasized the stock-raising advantages of the region. Much profit accrued to the Panhandle through the reputation for good cattle which the XIT helped establish. The cattle of this part of Texas came to be known "as a class by themselves in outstanding excellence." [26]

[24] *Land Booklet,* 16–17.
[25] R. L. Duke to J. E. H., July 6, 1927.
[26] Ms., "The Capitol Syndicate or XIT Ranch," 2.

CHAPTER XIII

Old Tascosa

Among the tributaries of the Canadian in the western Panhandle is one named Atascosa. It is a stream of no great length, heading among the sand hills and wandering in uncertain course for a few miles along its bed to lose its clear current either in the thirsty sands or the turgid waters of the river, depending on the seasons. The stream widens near its mouth to form a beautiful little valley, which is bounded by the Canadian to the south and the rambling caprock to the north. Legend relates that a Mexican bogged his ox train in crossing the stream many years ago. Therefore he named it *Atascosa*, which means boggy or quicksandy.

Tradition further tells that in this little valley the traders of New Mexico used to meet the Indians of the plains, and that here they bartered items dear to the Indian's eye and palate for stolen horses and cattle. When the Plains Indians were placed upon reservations, the sheltered nook by the Canadian was deserted for a few years.

In the spring of 1877, the village of Tascosa, sired by the frontier and nurtured from the breast of a vast and virgin pastoral country, sprang to life, not full blown, but, withal, a lusty and vigorous infant. With something of poetic completeness she died with the frontier. After a decline of years the life span of "Old" Tascosa closed in the middle nineties.

Her life history was short, varied, and tempestuous. Her citizenry, representative of the frontier, was cosmopolitan. From

194

East, North, and South came adventurous spirits; some seeking land and homes, some the business opportunities of a new country, many ranching enterprises, and more, with no definite purpose, found their way thither impelled by that urge which has ever set the face of the pioneer toward the setting sun. Horsemen all, they rode with ease; hardy, self-reliant, and individualistic, they moved with confidence. Southern Europe had her bronzed sons who observed the Mexican national holiday, *El Cinco de Mayo*,[1] as zealously as their ancestors ever celebrated the national holidays of old Castile. Representative of the Nordic strain were aggressive men who recalled with pride that the sun never set upon the crosses of St. Andrew and St. George. Into this melting pot of the frontier poured Anglo-American elements to produce a new culture that was distinctly Southwestern and altogether American.

Buffalo hunters came at first. After them bull whackers and mule skinners, whose reputation for scorching, as well as charming, profanity has never been equalled, handled the long freight trains that brought the necessities of life—flour, beans, bacon, and chewing tobacco—from Dodge City. Across the southern Kansas plains, through the Neutral Strip, and on to Tascosa along a two-hundred-mile trail, they handled their "strings" of oxen, bringing food and news from the outside world.

But most prominent among the Tascosa types was the cowboy. From long months upon the range and trail he came to drink and "celebrate," to dance and gamble, to be sort of human and sociable. Scattered among them, as bowlegged as any, a "mustanger" was sometimes seen—a type long since passed. There were adventurous Englishmen, shrewd Scotchmen, and, as always, belligerent and happy representatives of the Emerald Isle. Men with Eastern culture and college educations lent dignity to the group.

Horses of unknown brands and of doubtful, though unquestioned, ownership, stamped many an hour away before hitching racks as their riders, of equally uncertain pasts, drank

[1] "The fifth of May" is the Mexican national holiday.

and gambled. A few professional gamblers regularly plied their trades. During the roundup seasons the stages from Dodge supplemented the local riff-raff with additional sporting men and women, the saloons did a fine trade, and the earnings of many cowboys changed pockets on the turn of a card at monte and poker. A little woman called "Frenchy," whose past rested safely among the unwritten biographies of Creole New Orleans, sat before a table and dealt the Mexican game with graceful efficiency.[2]

Considering the love of the frontier folk for exciting sport, it is not surprising that horse racing was a popular diversion. Frequent races were run with a corresponding frequency of exchange of money.[3]

Rooster fighting was sometimes popular during the winter.[4] Rivaling this pastime was the Mexican sport known as "pulling the chicken." A description of one of these events is to be found in *The Tascosa Pioneer*, the newspaper of the town, of July 31, 1886. The sport celebrated San Diego's Day, July 25.

A lusty young rooster was procured, and three hundred yards below town the fun opened. The rooster was buried in the earth, his head only being left above ground, and the young men and boys who wished to participate in this part of the programme were mounted and gathered about. . . . Then they dash by, one after another, and as they pass the rooster each man swings himself down from the saddle and reaches for its head. The chicken naturally dodges more or less and renders it no easy matter to catch him. Finally secured, however, by the lucky grab, the body is brought out by a jerk which generally breaks the neck, and the horseman, chicken in hand, dashes away at his best speed, all the rest giving chase for the possession of the rooster. If another overtakes him and wrests it from him, then he leads the race until someone else can take it.[5]

[2] Sources of this description: James H. East to J. E. H., September 27, 1927; E. C. G. Austen to J. E. H., July 7, 1927; John Snyder to J. E. H., June 30, 1926; Charles Goodnight to J. E. H., January 12, 1927.

[3] *The Tascosa Pioneer*, September 15, 1888.   [4] *Ibid.*, January 12, 1889.

[5] See also the issue of June 23, 1888. For a good description of this game see R. B. Townshend, *Last Memories of a Tenderfoot*, 147–61.

A dramatic club for the entertainment of the community was formed in 1888.[6] Young men of the town organized the "Tascosa Social Club," one purpose being that of minstrel entertainment.[7] For Washington's birthday it announced a program "to eclipse everything heretofore offered. The club is in shape," wrote Editor Rudolph, of *The Tascosa Pioneer*, "to do just what it threatens."[8] A reading and lounging room was provided just next door to a saloon.[9] The "Tascosa Choir" gave an occasional card party,[10] while the good old conservative game of chess found a few devotees who spent their evenings "in a brown study over the absorbing perplexities" of it.[11] An oyster supper marked the superlative in a changing order—a benefit for the Sunday school, which needed an organ.[12]

Not content with an organ, "common talk" declared that "the acquisition of a cornet band is the one thing needful, the achievement of all achievements that will render life worth living and write for us the brightest pages in Tascosa's history."[13] Tascosa soon had "the only cornet hand in the country."

In this land of necessary ingenuity and adaptability, the village blacksmith became the coroner.[14] One wonders what grimly humorous twist of fate made him so, or was the work so strenuous?

The weekly and then semi-weekly arrival of the mails, with the coming of mule and oxen trains, always caused a flutter among the Tascosans, but the session days of district court, July the Fourth, and Christmas always caused considerable stir. All the cowboys came in at Christmas. The fiddler resined his bow and, with head thrown back and foot a-patting, played "Turkey in the Straw," "Arkansas Traveler," "Goodby, Old Paint," "Cotton-eyed Joe," and other such favorites. At frequent intermissions the dancers left the ballroom of the Russell

---

[6] *The Tascosa Pioneer*, December 15, 1888.   [7] *Ibid.*, January 21, 1888.
[8] *Ibid.*, February 11, 1888.   [9] *Ibid.*, January 12, 1889.
[10] *Ibid.*, August 11, 1888.   [11] *Ibid.*, January 7, 1888.
[12] *Ibid.*, September 22, 1888.   [13] *Ibid.*, March 24, 1888.
[14] Oldham County Commissioner Court *Records* 1, December 26, 1882.

Hotel while the dirt floors were sprinkled down and the fog of dust settled.[15]

Into Tascosa came the XIT cowboys to enjoy a little diversion. Here came Matlock, Boyce, and Findlay to look after Syndicate business. Here they built a warehouse and stored supplies for the entire north half of the ranch.

Here to Tascosa came Murdo MacKenzie, manager of the extensive Matador Ranch interests, to secure a room at the little hotel. During the night, as the story goes, he heard several six-shooter shots. He jumped from bed, ran to the saloon in the same building, where a man lay upon the floor badly wounded while two men knelt in a corner before a whiskey barrel, from which gurgled the contents through the hole made by a stray bullet. MacKenzie called to them to know if the man was badly wounded and in need of help. "Hell, yes," replied one in the corner, "but if we leave this barrel all the whiskey will waste." [16]

Here, too, Sam Dunn presided over his bar and filled the glasses for thirsty riders. Sam became involved in an argument which waxed with uncertainty until he set down his schooners with emphasis, referred warmly to a proverbially warm place, and drew from beneath the bar a copy of the *Christian Standard* to prove his contention.[17]

Itinerant preachers are said to have discoursed "scriptural logic," [18] and though Tascosa never claimed the spiritual distinction of a church, preaching was sometimes heard in the courthouse. Announcing one such service, the editor wrote: "It is among the probabilities that those who attend will be well entertained, and not unlikely even learn something. Sinners, it's us they're after." [19] However, Amarillo, growing from the open prairie to the southeast to claim the commercial prestige of which Tascosa had dreamed, soon started a church with a steeple, and even a bell.

[15] E. C. G. Austen to J. E. H., July 7, 1927; Mrs. Dan Cole to J. E. H., July 7, 1927.

[16] Walter Farwell to J. E. H., September 21, 1927.

[17] James D. Hamlin to J. E. H., September 21, 1927.

[18] *Ibid.*, January 12, 1889.   [19] *The Tascosa Pioneer,* March 10, 1888.

The paper of June 12, 1886, announced that a Reverend Bloodworth had been in Tascosa "and preached . . . to small but respectful congregations." That night the boys of the city played a joke upon him. They sent a little chap to the hotel with a note for the preacher. "It contained the information that the boys had gotten up a dance and needed money to furnish liquor for the occasion. Would the gentleman donate a small sum to such a worthy cause?"

The editor, touched by a feeling of loyalty to the community and a fear that the wrong impression might go out, wrote in the same issue:

Society is not half so rough as many have been led to believe. It is true that there is probably more personal liberty to the square inch in the western Panhandle than in sections that boast an older settlement, and it is true that our social regulations have been guiltless of church or Sunday School. But in general the people of Tascosa and Oldham are wholehearted, social, and exceptionally civil. Law-breaking is the exception and not the rule.

One may wonder if his assertions were true. Much has been told of the big fight in Tascosa in which four men were killed. That event gave great notoriety to the little cow town and made a substantial addition to her "Boot Hill Grave Yard." Only twenty-six men were killed there during the first six years after the county was organized,[20] though a few did not wait upon that judicial preliminary. The assertion that two or three score men met their end without the consolation of clean sheets, but came to a sanguine death with their boots on, has been denounced as a baseless fabrication. When rumor reported the killing of a man in June of 1888, *The Pioneer* declared: "As a libel on a good moral town it was a success, for there hasn't been anybody even hurt here." [21]

An old trail driver once said of this little village:

I have been in the frontier towns from the Pecos to the Canadian line, and Tascosa was the best I have ever seen. In all the time

[20] James H. East to J. E. H., September 27, 1927.   [21] June 16, 1888.

that it was a frontier town a man was never robbed. . . . You could go into town, get as drunk as you pleased, have all your pockets full of money, and never be touched. Of course it was wide open but not mean." [22]

Hence the belief that Tascosa was at least as good as the average frontier town and that the boast of the editor more than forty years ago was sound.

Moralists may find a strange ethic in the code whereby a man might brand a neighbor's calf or shoot a horse thief, but could not touch another's money. Yet it was so. When, in the early days, the dinner bell rang at the Russell Hotel, the gamblers left their money piled upon the table, the judge, lawyers, and jury filed down from the courthouse, if court happened to be in session, and the dance hall girls came in from their quarters, all to be seated and to eat at the same table.[23]

No history of Tascosa could be complete without a mention of her suburb. Most of the town lots were owned by Jule Howard and Jim McMasters, owners of a large general merchandise store. John Cone came in 1883 expecting to put in a store. Not caring for more competition, Howard and McMasters refused to sell a lot. Cone moved down the river less than half a mile and bought land from Casimero Romero, the original settler there. There Jess Jenkins came to put in a saloon and dance hall. His nickname was "Hoggie" and the place was called Hogtown in his honor. Soon the subdivision became a "restricted" one, limited to dance halls, saloons, and red lights. The sporting fraternity was kept below the hill, where Hogtown reveled by night and slept by day.[24]

In time Tascosa began to assume urban airs. As the county seat of Oldham County, the second to be organized in the Panhandle, she boasted in 1886 of her annual cash trade of $200,-000 to $250,000. She claimed a doctor among her professional

[22] J. E. May to J. E. H., June 29, 1926.
[23] Harry Ingerton to J. E. H., April 13, 1927.
[24] James H. East to J. E. H., September 27, 1927; J. E. McAllister to J. E. H., July 1, 1926; Harry Ingerton to J. E. H., April 13, 1927.

men, and among her business establishments were a millinery shop, a drugstore, mercantile houses, and a book and news stand. Mickey McCormick, adept that he was with cards, ran a livery stable. A saddle and boot shop was a prominent business. Besides these marks of advancement, Tascosa had a sign painter, a dairy, a hotel, a "bread establishment," a wagon yard, and "three barber chairs." Following this list the editor announced: "We will have one more saloon here shortly." [25] Greater prosperity loomed with the coming of the railroad, and in November of 1887 the significant caption appeared: "Seven Saloons, We Boom." [26] Such, in brief, was the economic status of Old Tascosa.

As a trade center she supplied the ranches as far west as New Mexico, north toward the North Palo Duro, east along the Canadian, and south toward Red River. Within this territory grazed in 1886 nearly a million head of cattle over ranges controlled principally by six outfits: the Capitol Freehold Land and Investment, the Reynolds Land and Cattle, the Lee-Scott, the Prairie, the American Pastoral, and the Cedar Valley Land and Cattle companies. [27]

In the simplicity of that life there was not a great amount of business to attend to; but attending to one's own was conducive to personal security as well as profit. Witness a notice published in a western newspaper in the middle eighties:

Any person caught monkeying with any of my cattle without permission will catch h——l!

Yours in Christ,
GRIZZLEY CALLEEN. [28]

Tascosa grew and prospered for several years, but died with the coming of the railroads. The Fort Worth and Denver reached the vicinity of Tascosa, November 1, 1887, but instead of crossing the Canadian at the site of the town, it crossed a mile or more to the west. That spelled her end.

To speed the process, Henry B. Sanborn was giving away

[25] *The Tascosa Pioneer,* June 12, 1886. [26] *Ibid.,* June 12, 1886.
[27] *Ibid.,* June 12, 1886, and March 30, 1887. [28] *Ibid.,* September 29, 1886.

lots to draw Amarillo upon his land;[29] a settlement named "Beer City" was springing up near the northern border,[30] and Sam Wise, the first sheriff of Randall County, was stimulating business by carrying the county's funds to Amarillo to deposit, only to lose them in a poker game before he found a banking establishment.[31]

It was a time when John Haines, late LX cook, rented a horse at Boren and Turner's livery stable in Tascosa, rode over to Amarillo, sold it to Sheriff James Gober, and "skipped down the road";[32] a time when to see an electric light, to talk over a telephone, or to get water from a system of water works, the citizens of Northwest Texas were forced to go to Tascosa, because "no other Panhandle town had them."[33]

Here Scotty (Alexander) Wilson, justice of the peace, once elected, held the office as long as he wished, regardless of elective choice, because no one had the nerve to try to evict him. An offender was fined $200 for disturbing Tascosa's peace by this same Scotty, and when the outraged defendent arose and said, "I'll take this case to a higher court," Scotty crushed him without mercy: "Sit down!" he shouted with an oath that reflected discredit upon the offender's ancestry, "Sit down: *There is no higher court.*"[34] And yet the weekly *Pioneer* reported that "Judge Scotty presided with his usual grace and dignity, and weighed out even justice in a case or two."[35]

As the only town in the western Panhandle when the XIT development started, Tascosa became the focal point for the ranch business. As the seat of the only organized county, all legal papers were filed there, complaints lodged, and laws enforced. It was headquarters for all affairs, public and private, honorable and unmentionable. When the railroad built through, the XIT's shifted headquarters to Channing, which sprang up to the north.

[29] *Ibid.*, September 8, 1888.   [30] *Ibid.*, May 26, 1888.
[31] Harry Ingerton to J. E. H., April 13, 1927.
[32] *The Tascosa Pioneer*, October 15, 1887.
[33] *Ibid.*, December 15, 1888.
[34] Harry Ingerton to J. E. H., April 13, 1927.
[35] *The Tascosa Pioneer*, October 13, 1888.

CHAPTER XIV

Then Came the Nester

UPON THE CREST of the restless Western surge, far on the outer edge of settlement, the trader and trapper came first. After them, moving just before the fringe of settlements, then leaping far beyond following grass and water, the cowmen scattered their herds. Then from the east and north spread a mechanical frontier, and far-reaching rails betokened a changing day. Marching with tread more firm and determined than any other, moving in almost solid phalanxes across plain land and forging along fertile river courses and railway lines, the agricultural frontier pushed into the West. In the eighties the granger, or nester, began claiming the West that hunter and cowboy had wrested from the wilderness. Many weed-grown fields and many shanties in ruin marked their first unsuccessful assaults upon the soil. "The phrase written on one disheartened farmer's wagon top, 'Going back to my wife's folks,' became historic." [1]

But still the nesters came afresh; they experimented with crops; they tried new methods; they combined stock raising with farming; they reclaimed the desert; they transformed the West. "The man with the hoe" was satisfying his hunger for land, and the Panhandle felt the force of that avidity. His coming had been anticipated.

One of the owners of the Capitol Lands gazed with pride

[1] See Emerson Hough, *The Passing of the Frontier*, 154.

203

upon their far-reaching swells soon after acquiring them, and enthusiastically exclaimed: "What a clean stretch of land! Why I could start a plowpoint into the soil at the south line and turn a furrow 200 miles long without a break—and I'll live to see the day when the plow will push the cattle off this range and grain crops will be fed to dairy cows!" [2]

That was prophecy!

At that time not a railroad touched the Panhandle of Texas. But the frontier of steel was pushing southwest from Kansas and northwest from "down in the skillet." Significant for this country are the dates of January 1 and March 14, 1888. Upon the first date the first scheduled train of the Southern Kansas Railway (the Santa Fe) pulled into Panhandle City. Windy March was in full blast when the Fort Worth and Denver joined its two lines to span the Panhandle from southeast to northwest. [3]

Tascosa, left high if not dry, looked with confidence for the extension of the Rock Island into the Panhandle at this time. The road reached Liberal, Kansas, in May, and, in a month, from the "barren prairie" a town of two thousand inhabitants, of four newspapers, of fifty hotels and restaurants, and of thirty real estate offices came into being. "When the Rock Island hits the Panhandle," observed *The Pioneer*, "when Greek meets Greek, then look out all about you," [4] for then "Tascosa will land there with both feet and her cotton hat and will take the name of Eli and will be the lion of the tribe of Judah—when the Rock Island comes. . . . Tascosa will sell more whiskey than for any previous two years in her history—when the Rock Island comes." [5]

The Rock Island came—but in spite of the inducements offered by Tascosa, just forty years later.

The great land boom which raged in Kansas in 1886 was "deliberately devised" by the railroads, partly because of the

[2] Crissey, "The Vanishing Ranges," 4.
[3] J. C. Paul to J. E. H., September 12, 1927; *The Tascosa Pioneer*, March 17, 1888.
[4] *Ibid.*, June 23, 1888.   [5] *Ibid.*, November 17, 1888.

lands they owned, but mainly because of the prospective traffic of a granger population. They "preached steadily the doctrine of diversified farming" and did everything they could to promote prosperous settlement of the West.[6] In 1887 this boom reached Texas.

After the Capitol Lands had been set aside, A. W. Terrell had introduced a bill into the legislature in 1876 to provide for their sale to small purchasers "so that the humblest man might obtain an interest."[7] For a state whose need for a capitol was urgent, nothing could have been more impractical. At the rate the Panhandle was settled, enough land might have been sold to have erected some sort of a building by 1910, but even that is doubtful. However, as has been said, the original plans of the Capitol Company pointed to immediate colonization. But the remoteness of the XIT lands and widespread skepticism as to their agricultural worth made immediate colonization impossible.[8] The advent of the railroads seemed to bring about the conditions toward which the owners had looked in the early eighties. But in spite of the favorable agencies, settlement moved slowly.

Contrary to belief, Panhandle cattlemen offered little opposition to settlement. In 1887 *The Pioneer* said:

Nobody is better aware than they that they must eventually give way for a multitude of smaller cattlemen and actual settlers. . . . The men who have large landed possessions . . . will vie with the state in disposing of them in small tracts and giving liberal terms to the purchasers.

Cowmen realized that immigration enhanced land values.

The utilization of the Panhandle's wide domain . . . by the cattle interests for these past ten years [*The Pioneer* continued] has been properly matter for congratulation and praise. . . . [The cowmen] have redeemed the country from the Indians,

[6] Hough, *The Passing of the Frontier*, 154–55.
[7] *The Dallas Weekly Herald*, January 31, 1884.
[8] Gough, "Sketch of the History of the XIT Ranch," 1–2.

thinned out wild beasts, paid the state an immense revenue, furnished employment to a large number of hands, and when the time comes to give place to the actual settlers . . . they will be found surrendering their little kingdoms with a good grace. May the next phase of Panhandle life be as successfully and as wisely conducted.[9]

W. M. D. Lee, of the LS Ranch, urged his cowboys to file upon school land for their own use, "as he recognized that the grangers would soon be crowding in upon it, and he preferred to see the boys get in a chance at it, too." [10] The Panhandle Stock Association, under the guidance of such men as O. H. Nelson, Dick McAnulty, Hank Cresswell, and Charles Goodnight, did much to prevent that traditional animosity between the nester and the cowman in the Panhandle.

"As an association we favored the settler or nester," said O. H. Nelson. If he was an honest "law and order man," he was made welcome. "We extended the same protection to good citizen nesters that we did to stockmen, realizing that we needed them for the development of the country. This is the principal reason why we had no fence cutting or other lawless or mob acts." [11] The association member with one cow was entitled to the same protection given the big cowman, the inspectors served his interests with equal care, and the association attorneys fought his legal battles.[12] Only a few instances of opposition to settlement marred this general friendliness to granger infiltration.[13]

In connection with the unjust charges of intimidation of settlers by the big companies, it is interesting to note that the largest of them all began agricultural experimentation when the nearest railroad was still roughly 150 miles away. From the first the owners of the Capitol Lands dreamed of the days of settlement. Even as A. C. Babcock made his pioneer inspection

[9] *The Tascosa Pioneer,* March 30, 1887.
[10] *Ibid.,* November 3, 1886.
[11] *The Southwest Plainsman* (Amarillo), February 20, 1926.
[12] Charles Goodnight to J. E. H., June 25, 1925.
[13] *The Tascosa Pioneer,* October 15 and November 12, 1887.

of the area in 1882, he observed with interest that some squatter had broken out an unfenced tract of twenty acres on the Sod House Draw on the southern end of the range, though to what good end history does not disclose.[14]

Much to the disgust of the old-time cowpunchers, the owners were plowing up good buffalograss sod around Buffalo Springs while they were trailing in the first cattle. But the weathered cowhand, seasoned in nature's ways, is an inveterate reactionary when it comes to disturbing her ancient balance. This widespread range, devoid of timbers, stumps, rocks, and weeds, looked like the promised land to the average granger, a natural boon to the high-powered promoter. No wonder they spurned the cowboy's solid if sometimes sentimental advice— "the best side's up; don't plow it under."

A small tract was broken out and planted in 1885 while the cowboys snorted in disdain at the unimaginative wretches *walking* at their work, and " 'lowed" to all and sundry that the drouths and winds would take care of the farmers and turn the soil back to cattle. Eventually, in widespread dust and distress, they did. But nature is never in a hurry, and man is slow to learn. The plowing and planting went on, and though the seed did not get in the ground until late, a fair crop of corn and millet came to maturity before the first frosts fell.

Two hundred lovely acres of grass were devastated by the plow next spring. Thirty-five were put in alfalfa and the others devoted to oats, millet, sorghum, and Indian corn. During the same year thirty acres were broken out in Middle Water and seventy were turned to cultivation at the Yellow Houses while an unusually dry spring dragged into July. But it is a land quickly responsive to any beneficence of moisture, and though the sowing on sod land was not done until early in August, the Yellow Houses gathered a fine crop of millet, sorghum, and corn fodder in the fall, by which time the rainfall had jumped to a phenomenal 23.19 inches.

The north end turned in a crop of alfalfa and oats in addi-

[14] A. C. Babcock to A. C. McDonald, June 27, 1882.

tion, and John V. Farwell, in his annual report to the Capitol Freehold officials in England, saw abundant promise of successful stock farming in the future.[15]

The foreman at each divisional headquarters was required to keep careful weather records. Reports of the rainfall and average temperature were relayed to the general headquarters at Channing on the first of every month. In 1886, the owners jumped into the nursery business on a big scale by planting 5,000 trees—catalpa, box elder, white ash, and soft maple—at Buffalo Springs, of which catalpa and ash did the best.[16]

In 1887 the Syndicate sent an exhibit of truck and farm products to the Dallas State Fair. From a two-acre patch at Buffalo Springs, 4,500 cabbages, thirty bushels of onions, fifty of beets, three barrels of pickles, and much other garden truck was produced. "Such a crop as this," a writer claimed, "from so limited an area is proof sufficient of the fertility of the plains soil." [17]

The next spring R. A. Cameron, commissioner of immigration for the Fort Worth and Denver road, announced: "We propose to advertise [the Panhandle] extensively in the east and seek to settle our line by colonization." At the same time an irrigated farm for demonstration was proposed on the Canadian.[18] The Southern Kansas Railway was active, but citizens had to petition that trains carrying prospectors enter the Panhandle by a daylight schedule so that immigrants could see what manner of country they traversed.[19] A. L. Matlock attended an immigration meeting at Fort Worth in December, 1887, where four towns of this section were represented. Within about two months the Panhandle Immigration Convention met at Canadian.[20] Judge W. B. Plemons urged all counties to "send full delegates," and Tascosa's editor, convention-wise as he must have been, wrote that "at least if the delegates are not

---

[15] John V. Farwell, *Report*, 1886, p. 6. [16] *Ibid.*
[17] *The Tascosa Pioneer*, November 12, 1887.
[18] *Ibid.*, April 14, 1888.
[19] *Ibid.*, March 14, 1888.
[20] *Ibid.*, February 11, 1888.

sent full they will proceed to do their whole duty in that direction when they 'get thar.' " [21]

County organizations were being formed, and on April 12, 1888, the Oldham County Immigration Association was organized with James McMasters as president. The association felt that the Panhandle would support one million people. Already, the association claimed, the country had a substantial beginning in its total population of only a "little less than five thousand, when everybody is counted." To increase this number the association advocated co-operation with the Panhandle Association, with large landholders, and with the immigration bureaus of the railroads. Not absolute dependence upon tillage of the soil, but a combination of farming and stock raising was urged. Sound reasoning is found in an editorial addressed to the Panhandle Immigration Convention.

The immigrant we want is the man with . . . from five hundred to five thousand dollars; the man who will roll up his sleeves and produce something; the man who will take his section or his two or four sections and grow stock on them, grasses, feed, sorghum, forage and some grain; who will have his family here, his home here, his interests here; who possesses and will apply real energies. . . . What we want is a development of productive possibilities . . . an attention to those twin industries of farming and live stock raising . . . which would give the Panhandle an unexampled prosperity . . . we want . . . to encourage . . . immigration, not of city people, not of professional men, for they can come afterwards, but our efforts should reach the populous rural districts of the states north and east, and we will get the population that we want.[22]

Indicative of the interest being felt in Northwest Texas were inquiries about land pouring in from different sections—from Missouri, Georgia, Arkansas, Virginia, New Jersey, Massachusetts, Illinois, Indiana, Dakota, and other states.[23] "Men with hoes" were coming. The editor of *The Pioneer*,

[21] *Ibid.,* February 18, 1888. [22] *Ibid.,* February 18, 1888.
[23] *Ibid.,* December 24, 1887; January 14; January 28; February 11, 1888.

Tascosa's newspaper, wrote, June 2, 1888, that "A half dozen immigrant wagons, loaded with women, tow-headed progeny and other plunder, passed through yesterday morning." Another week brought another paragraph: "Wagons and wagons with white tops, rope-bottomed chairs, tow-heads, brindle cows, yellow dogs and a pervading air of restlessness have poured through this week in the direction suggested by Horace Greeley." [24]

Scattered farms were being opened in all portions of the Panhandle,[25] and settlements were growing apace. By March, 1888, "a good settlement" was reported in Randall County, "a nucleus" in Deaf Smith, "a colony was about to be poured into Hartley from Illinois," "many people" were locating in Potter, while Hansford and Sherman counties were receiving a few new settlers.[26] Two Farwell cities existed at one time. One was in Hansford County, but that on the Fort Worth and Denver secured a post office as Farwell Park.[27] The name was really in demand. When J. J. Hagerman built his railroad south and west from Amarillo to tap the Pecos Valley of New Mexico, Farwell, the capital of Parmer County, arose by the state line to contest the supremacy of its sister village, Texico. Amarillo made an unpretentious beginning in July, 1887, to be the competitor of Tascosa, to be the bone of contention between rival townsite companies, and to be shot up by the cowboys to the delight of Tascosa.[28]

Texline, in the northwestern portion of the XIT, came to life and notice in the fall of 1888 when it was chosen as a division point of the Denver railroad. Rapid growth was expected also because the Syndicate was fostering it, and because it was located near New Mexico, the Neutral Strip, and Colorado. Its rising sun gave promise, and in the roseate hues, crimson was not lacking, as a description of 1888 shows. "Some predict," said the *Tascosa Pioneer*, "that it will be the biggest and the best and the fastest and the hardest and the busiest and the

24 *Ibid.,* June 9, 1888.   25 *Ibid.,* December 24, 1887.
26 *Ibid.,* March 17, 1888.   27 *Ibid.,* September 29, 1888.
28 *Ibid.,* July 16, 1887.

XIT chuck wagon with chip wagon on the side

Roundup on the Rito Blanco

Charles Goodnight, Henry Stephens, A. G. Boyce, and John V. Farwell (far right) at Spring Lake

The Escarbada outfit
Ira Aten, foreman, is at the extreme left
(Panhandle-Plains Historical Society)

Windmill and early conveyances
on the lower Rito Blanco

Corralling a herd on the XIT

James D. Hamlin

The valley of the Canadian

wildest and the roughest and the toughest town in this section. They've already had to station the Texas rangers there—and when that's said enough's said."[29]

More than eighty thousand acres of land near by were cut into farming tracts by the owners in the spring of 1890. Matlock began communicating with an outside immigration agency looking toward the establishment of a colony of farmers upon the land, and indicated that the Syndicate had plans of selling its entire range in such wise as soon as the demand developed.[30]

Counties were being organized, and no longer could Tascosa claim to be "the Capital of the western Panhandle." Land boomers and promoters were swarming all over the country, spreading afar the superior advantages of the spots they settled upon, all "future metropolises." Newspapers, usually of few days and abundant trouble, flared forth with and for each new town. Unique among them was the first Panhandle daily. Upon the staff head of the *Amarillo Northwest* was this statement: "Published every day and Sunday." In the second issue the editor wrote: "It's probable that *The Northwest* is here to stay." It stayed one week.[31] Scarcely less novel was the *Rivers Hummer*, published at the little town of Rivers upon the northern breaks of the Canadian, which town soon became known as Channing, the general headquarters of the XIT. Upon the front page was the salutatory, upon the back, the valedictory.[32] With one printing it died a natural death. At the home of the *Hummer*, Syndicate land was placed on sale through R. W. Priest.[33] Foreign capital, not altogether discouraged by the losses of the middle eighties, was still interested in this part of the Southwest. With its usual bombast, *The Pioneer* of May 12, 1888, declared: "A whole half-dozen . . . blarsted Britishers . . . have . . . been looking over the Panhandle with a view to purchasing the rest of it."[34]

Thus extensive efforts were being made to attract the

[29] *Ibid.,* October 20, 1888. [30] *Ibid.,* March 15, 1890.
[31] *The Amarillo Northwest,* December 25, 1889 to January 1, 1890.
[32] *The Tascosa Pioneer,* January 3, 1891.
[33] *Ibid.,* January 24, 1891. [34] *Ibid.,* May 12, 1888.

granger from beyond the state's lines. But the editors of that delightfully intimate period of journalism did not overlook home potentialities. A pre-nursery editor wrote in a special column of his paper:

It Is Common Talk

That the laying in of a line of baby carriages by our merchants is a pointer as to the gradually changing order of our population and indicates that it is generally understood whither we are drifting.[35]

Such observations indicated that the Panhandle was changing from a land of men to one of men and women; that it was gradually laying aside the predominant masculinity of pioneering. This meant the growth of settlement.

Many of the first settlers were forced to move out because of crop failures. Some eked out a living by gathering the scattered buffalo bones, hauling them to the railroads, and selling them for fertilizer. Some were able to supplement the returns from scanty crops by freighting for the large ranches.[36]

With the early nineties came a season of extreme drouth, and many of the nesters turned their wagon tongues to the east, cursing the West and the man who painted it "golden." What terrible parody was this upon *The Tascosa Pioneer's* sanguine but prophetic editorial of January 28, 1888.

Come to the Panhandle for cheap lands; come for rich and productive soil; come for health; come for seasonable summers and balmy winters; come and raise cereals, fruits, vegetables, sorghum, grains, grasses and forage; come and raise cattle, horses, mules, sheep, hogs, goats or poultry; come and manufacture cheese, butter and tallow; come and open factories, banks, colleges, mills, stores, agencies, and the like; come prepared to make your home with us and lands, openings and opportunities of one kind and another will not be wanting. For there is no longer such another country as the Panhandle awaiting development, and no such

[35] *Ibid.*, March 31, 1888.   [36] Mabry, "Recollection," 7–8.

country destined to the same degree and rapidity of development. Come, and come now.

Skeptics of such visions felt sure of their point of view now. Marcy and the cowpunchers must have been right. Never would the plains of Texas be fit for anything but open range, they said. Yet with the opening decade of the new century the Capitol Reservation Lands became the sites of farms and towns, prosperous in a small measure, vigorous and proud beyond compare, hopeful and optimistic for the unforeseeable future. Perennial aridity works some marvelous and mystical power upon the spirits of men. It certainly is not the bounty of nature; it must be the climate. For as we west of the 100th meridian rather mysteriously say—"there's just *something* about it." Even the unimaginative man walking behind a plow could feel it, for, as surely and as poignantly as the eternal hope of rain, it is eternally there.

CHAPTER XV

Law Suits, Land Sales, Colonization

N<small>OT ALL</small> troubles relating to the management of a ranch grow out of blizzards, predatory animals, bad men, and cattle rustlers. The Syndicate engaged in two law suits of considerable significance.

Amos C. Babcock, a member of the company when the contract for building the capitol was assumed, continued to be a minor shareholder until his death. For the owners of the properties the years had been lean, and Babcock's wife, executrix of the estate, and one Morris K. Brown brought suit against the Farwells and the Capitol Freehold Land and Investment Company, Limited, on behalf of all the minor stockholders.[1] On July 23, 1901, the suit was filed, charging that the Farwells were using the ranch for the promotion of their personal interests to the detriment of the minority stockholders.

Through the District Judge, H. H. Wallace, of Amarillo, sitting in Hartley County, they secured the appointment of receivers for the ranch property. Judge Wallace, evidently careless of the law governing such cases, made the appointment without notifying the company that was in possession of the ranches under lease from the Syndicate. Immediately upon discovering that a receivership had been granted, the Syndicate took steps to appeal from Judge Wallace's order. The Farwells arranged to make supersedias bond in the amount of

[1] *Southwestern Reporter,* Vol. 65, p. 510.

several million dollars, which they expected would be demanded upon such a valuable piece of property as the XIT Ranch. But Wallace set the bond at $25,000. The receivers joined the fight to maintain the order, and the case was bitterly fought in Amarillo, where partisanship ran riot.[2]

The receivers decided, before the appeal came to trial, that they had the right to take possession of the ranch. Charles F. Harding, a later trustee of the Capitol Reservation Lands, gives this account of their attempt.

One of the receivers met Manager Boyce upon the street at Channing and said that he had come over to take possession. Mr. Boyce told him that the custody of the property had been given him by the Farwells, and that any attempt to take it from him except on their order would result seriously. A little later the receivers went to the ranch offices, to demand and take possession of the books and papers kept there in the safe. Mr. Boyce saw them coming. He closed the safe, locked it, and leaned his Winchester up against the door. Two of his boys were present, and other guns were within reach. The receivers appeared and made their demand. Mr. Boyce answered:

"Don't go near that safe or touch anything else in this office. I do not propose to surrender anything. Any attempts you make will be resisted, and force will be met by force."

The receivers retired. Then Mr. Boyce consulted the Company's counsel in Fort Worth. They advised that his conduct had been correct, as well as in keeping with good old western tradition.[3]

The appeal from Judge Wallace's order was carried to the Court of Civil Appeals at Fort Worth. A mountain of expert testimony was piled up from bookkeepers, cowpunchers, foremen, and general managers of the XIT and other great concerns. At last the receivership was declared void. Thus "the receivership fight" ended to the advantage of the XIT and cleared the management of unjust charges.

[2] William Boyce to J. E. H., June 28, 1927; Charles F. Harding, Ms., "The Receivership Fight" (Chicago office).
[3] *Ibid.*

In 1918 another big suit was forced upon the Capitol Syndicate. It so happens that many of the Texas land surveys, made under difficult frontier conditions, are from 2 to 4 per cent in excess of the stipulated areas. These surveys were made by the state and disposed of by sale, endowment, grant, and otherwise. The state officials knew, in patenting the land to Abner Taylor in 1887, that there were errors in J. T. Munson's survey, making the Capitol Tract in excess of 3,000,000 acres.[4] Other surveys in Texas ran to excesses double the percentage of the Capitol Tract, but such errors did not affect the validity of the survey, nor mar the title in selling. No attempt was made to rectify the errors in the survey of the Capitol Tract, and all the land was patented to the Syndicate.

Rediscovering this error, the state brought suit years later and contended that the contract was for the sale of the land, not by the tract but by the acre, and that the state's officers had no right to convey more than 3,000,000 acres. Therefore it contended that conveyances of land in excess of this amount was not binding upon the state, which was entitled to relief in the amount of excess acreage. The state decided, by its second attempt at survey, that the excess was 57,840.5 acres, not quite 2 per cent, and less than the average excess in other surveys for Texas as a whole. And the surveyor, besides admitting errors in his own figures, could not testify in what particular leagues the excess occurred.[5]

By the time the suit was brought, the Syndicate had disposed of the larger portion of the original three million acres to firms and individuals, who bought, in good faith, land patented directly to the sellers by the state. The Syndicate, by the operation of the statute of limitation, was unable to recover this excess in the land that it had sold. But the state contended that *it* had the right to recover the total excess acreage—which, it admitted, the company had never owned—from the small portion of the original tract which remained unsold, thus affirming

[4] Ms., "The litigation by the State of Texas over the Capitol Grant in the Panhandle," 18 (Chicago office).

[5] *Ibid.*, 5.

titles to all the sales made by the defendants to other parties.[6]

Many minds were baffled to know upon what principle the recovery of 57,840.5 acres from a small portion of the Capitol Grant could rectify the titles to all the other portions already sold. But the District Court of Travis County held that it would, and decreed the recovery of 27,613.6 acres in Dallam County and 30,226.9 acres in Hartley County to cover the excess of land from 3,000,000 acres granted in ten counties.[7] The Capitol Syndicate had held the land recovered by the state for over thirty years, had placed improvements upon the land, and was paying into the state taxes upon property which would otherwise have been yielding little.[8]

In the meantime Colonel A. G. Boyce, who had been the general manager of the XIT for eighteen years, retired from the trying work. In his place came H. S. Boice, who once ran cattle in Montana with Berry-Boice Cattle Company, and was later a partner in the Kansas City Live Stock Commission Company. He came to the ranch with a wide knowledge of the cattle business from almost every angle, and his executive ability proved of value to the company in handling and closing out the last of the great herd entrusted to his care. He was a unique character in the rough and ready life of the cattle range. He did not smoke, drink, or indulge in profanity. He said his prayers every night, no matter who was present. But he was a man of force, and his orders were carried out with dispatch.

On November 1, 1912, the remnant of the XIT herds was sold to Dave Trigg and John Shelton. At the Mojares (*mujeres*, "women"), 3,500 steers were turned over, and the final brandings were done at Romero, Perico, Buffalo Springs, and the Bull Pasture. The total number was 13,560 head, "yearlings and up," and about 8,000 calves which were not counted. The remaining land in that section was leased to the same parties for five and one-half years.

[6] *Ibid.*, 22–23.

[7] *Abstract of Title*, "Capitol Reservation Lands," 37.

[8] In the late nineties the Syndicate was annually paying approximately $37,000 in taxes. Gough, "Sketch," 7.

The redemption of bonds of the Capitol Freehold Land and Investment Company, Limited, when due, to some extent forced the sale of much of the land in large tracts. That remaining was held for farming and stock-farming purposes. In 1901 portions of the tract had been placed on sale. Since there was not sufficient demand for farming land, large tracts were sold to cattlemen, and the money thus received was applied toward the payment of bonds and the development of that property which was left. In July, 1901, George W. Littlefield bought 235,858.5 acres of the Yellow Houses.

From the Bovina Division, a few days later, J. E. and J. W. Rhea bought 49,514 acres, and before the close of the year Charles E. Harding bought 17,730 acres. W. E. Halsell bought 184,155 acres of the Yellow Houses and Spring Lake lands; and north of the Canadian, E. L. Halsell and Thomas S. Hutton bought 150,646 acres. The Matador interests started their operations along the Canadian west of Amarillo with the purchase of 198,732 acres in June of 1902, at the price of $2.40 an acre.[9] During the same year William J. Tod and F. D. Wight bought a total of 136,560 acres in the Buffalo Springs country. These sales were handled by Colonel Boyce, J. Henry Stephens, and William Boyce.

Following these heavy sales to cattlemen, the company directed its interest toward colonization. A number of causes helped to make the time propitious for such work. In other sections of the Panhandle the available school land was being taken up rapidly. Farmlands in the North had so advanced in price as to make their purchase prohibitive for any but men of means, and prospectors were anxious to get cheap lands. The possibility of the enhancement of values, caused by further settlement, was an inducement to some buyers.[10] The company used this legitimate argument to advantage in promoting sales, but buying for speculative reasons alone hurt the sales in later years.

[9] Maps of XIT lands, Dalhart office; H. F. Mitchell to J. E. H., June 10, 1927.

[10] *Land Booklet*, 2.

About this time outside immigration agencies centered their attention upon Texas. Beginning about 1900 the Canadian railroads and government extensively advertised the "free wheat lands" of Alberta and Saskatchewan. In one season this campaign for immigration took away more than 150,000 young farmers from the Middle Western states. "In one year the state of Iowa lost over fifteen million dollars of money withdrawn from bank deposits by farmers moving across the line into Canada." [11]

By 1905, capitalists, railroads, and statesmen of this country began an attempt to check this immigration, and keep these farmers in the United States. "Then was the time when a good many newspapers discovered Texas in general and the Panhandle in particular. The railroads and the newspapers spread the news of the coming-out party of the Panhandle, and it became quite an event in immigration circles." It was enough of an event to enable the company to sell about 800,000 acres in tracts from 160 to 640 acres in extent. Since these averaged about 200 acres, it was plain that the land was being bought for agricultural purposes. [12]

Thus with the approach of another land boom in the Panhandle in the early 1900's the speculators swarmed in. At first the Capitol Company "had too much land . . . to do business on a retail basis, and therefore most of its sales were of a wholesale character to land and other development companies." [13]

In 1904 the company granted to George H. Heafford, of Chicago, Hardy W. Campbell, of Lincoln, and Charles E. Wantland, of Salt Lake City, an option for the purchase of large bodies of land in Parmer and Dallam counties. The organization which these men formed was later known as the Farm Land Development Company. They paid from $2.50 to $6.00 an acre for this land with liberal terms.

The next large contract was made July 5, 1906, with W. W. Ryan, an associate of George G. Wright of Kansas City, who

[11] Hough, *The Passing of the Frontier*, 169–70.
[12] Crissey, "The Vanishing Range," 4.   [13] *Ibid.*

purchased 176,814.35 acres at prices ranging from $5.00 to $6.00. This land, and additional tracts bought by Wright, lay in the Escarbada and Spring Lake country, a long distance from the railroad. About the same time C. E. Tuttle contracted for 34,823.05 acres, title to which was taken by Ben I. Tanner. Late in December of 1906, Milton Rice and Frank W. Gates purchased 26,976.99 acres at $4.50. Minor purchases were made by Lewis Hines, J. F. Edwards, Frank F. Loomis, W. P. Soash Land Company, and the Western Land and Immigration Company.[14]

These development companies began selling to small buyers. They brought in prospectors by the train load, imbued them with the agricultural prospects of the country and a desire to buy. Soash started a town on the Fort Worth and Denver, between Dalhart and Texline, and called it Ware. He built a hotel for the accommodation of his prospectors, went back to Iowa and other of the corn belt states, and brought in special trains loaded with real farmers. But they bought for speculation, and then most of them returned to their homes.[15]

"Big Ed" Connell, of Hereford, former Texas Ranger and Syndicate cowboy, after several years chasing rustlers, got into the real estate business. In 1906 he carried George G. Wright out for an inspection of Syndicate land, and later described his sales.

I never saw anything to equal Wright's organization. He shipped down a lot of automobiles for use in showing his prospectors around. He would unload five and six hundred prospectors at a time, most of whom were from Illinois, Iowa, Indiana, Oklahoma, and Missouri. I don't think he sold any land to men who did not see it, but I don't think he ever tried to sell to one who did not buy. Wright paid five dollars an acre for this first land and paid his agents five and six dollars for selling it. It was sold at twenty-five dollars an acre. Besides additional options from the Syndicate, Wright bought 100,000 acres from Bill Halsell at Spring Lake,

14 J. F. Heissler to Samuel H. Roberts, March 27, 1928.
15 R. L. Duke to J. E. H., November 8, 1927.

four leagues from C. F. Harding, and 80,000 acres from Tom Kelly. He sold every acre of this in a little over two years and must have cleared a million dollars on it.[16]

The results of this land policy were, however, not satisfactory to the company. Most of the purchases were made by non-residents, many of whom were not farmers, but bankers and capitalists, who bought with no intention of settling upon the land. As a consequence, the company created the office of land commissioner.

F. W. Wilsey was the first to hold the place. The land was turned over to him for sale. He began work in 1905 and made a great success in his efforts. He was succeeded by Hoyt King in 1909. King held the place until November, 1910,[17] when his office was taken by Garret A. Dobbin. Dobbin was commissioner until December 31, 1913. The office was discontinued for some time, and on November 16, 1914, F. W. Wilsey, having finished some work he was doing for the railroads, was re-employed as sales manager. Fay W. Clark succeeded him as land commissioner for one year, until March 1, 1917, after which the office remained vacant for several years.

In 1900 the young law firm of William Boyce and James D. Hamlin, of Amarillo, was retained by the Capitol Syndicate as Texas counsel. Upon Wilsey's appointment as land commissioner in 1905, he engaged the colorful Hamlin as resident representative of the owners, with headquarters at the newly established town of Farwell on the Texas–New Mexico line. From that time until his death this cultivated man of towering physique, scintillating conversation, and unsurpassed zest and poise in any company and any situation became symbolic of the XIT and suggestive of its far-flung ramifications.

His zest for convivial people and adventurous learning seemed insatiable. He was as much at home with Caesar and Virgil in the original as in friendly talk with a crew of cowboys. He was as effective in quieting a barroom brawl as in

[16] Ed Connell to J. E. H., October 31, 1927.
[17] J. F. Heissler to Samuel H. Roberts, March 27, 1928.

representing his principals before a committee in Congress. He was, in effect, the consummation of an eager, classically disciplined mind molded in all the colorful and variegated experience of the Texas frontier.

He set up his offices at the village of Farwell, served for twelve years as county judge, and for more than a quarter of a century capably represented the Capitol Company and its successors while finding ample time to cultivate his learning, his individualistic interests, and his aesthetic tastes. Incidentally, as it seemed to those who knew him best, his office sold some 200,000 acres of land, practically settling and developing Parmer County as well as considerable portions of the counties adjoining it.

For a time Samuel H. Roberts, former house attorney for the John V. Farwell Company, in Chicago, joined social and intellectual interests with "the Judge" as he took over the work of the general land commissioner for the company at Amarillo. He took charge of the office in 1926, just as the tremendous oil and gas development of the Panhandle got in full swing. And though the proven lands lay outside the XIT range, he shortly leased some 180,000 acres with a net return of more than a quarter of a million dollars in leases and an equal return in committed explorations. His services continued until his untimely death on a mountain road in New Mexico.

At that time his offices were in Dalhart, the substantial little city that had grown up adjacent to the ranch lands on the north end. Here, for years, the faithful Bob Duke had been riding herd on company interests—from the management of various divisions to the sale and lease of residual pastures. In the middle and late twenties this was an active region, bustling with the boom in cattle and agricultural development that ranged through Mennonite colonization and vast wheat farming to the eventual return of dust-blown fields to native grass. Before that boom burst, 62,000 acres of grazing land in Oldham and Hartley counties were sold to Julian Bivins and the Matador Cattle Company at approximately $475,000.

All these zestful men are gone, and so are the Capitol Lands. As each dropped the reins of this vast enterprise, they were gathered in younger hands, and in Texas finally came to rest in the confident and efficient control of Hamlin Y. Overstreet, of Farwell, Texas. He became resident representative for the Capitol Reservations Lands, a real estate trust that had been formed by the Chicago owners on June 4, 1915, to take over the lands after the cattle had been sold and the English bonds had been paid off.

Hamlin Overstreet, "the Judge's" nephew and namesake, began his rather trying but never monotonous apprenticeship under his expansive uncle at Farwell, October 1, 1925, where there was a staff of experienced land men to help sell to settlers. Roberts' office shortly began pushing their disposition in the Buffalo Springs country, where a demonstration farm, a nursery for free distribution of shrubs and trees, and a company hotel were maintained for the benefit of prospectors and purchasers. Earlier hotels had been built and kept up by the company at Farwell, Texline, and Channing.

Modern farm homes were built on many of the tracts and sold with the land at cost, and the result of the change of policy from block sales to promoters to actual colonization work through their own land commissioner was heartening to the owners. It put a stop to most of the unfortunate speculation, prevalent under the old system, that pushed prices to unhealthy heights and still left the plains unsettled.

One outgrowth of the policy, however, was that of finance, which came to be handled in large part by the company, too. When sales were first being pushed to settlers in 1903, land could be financed with 10 per cent cash payments, and the balance in nine annual notes at 6 per cent interest. The company required a larger margin of one-fifth in cash, and the remainder in eight years at the same interest. It spurred the sales through granting settlers long options on adjoining tracts of equal acreage.

After the down payment, usually the only way for the company to get its money was for the farmer to turn it from the land at the point of a plow. But farming on the plains of Texas is fraught with extreme hazards of intermittent dust and drouth, of violent windstorm and flailing hail. Production is uncertain and harvest even more so. Yet the company gained the reputation of never foreclosing on a settler who was really trying to make his land pay, but "carried" many hard-pressed creditors for years. Others more fortunate hit the rich bounty of heavy yields and high prices and paid off in one year. Money was lent for improvements, too, and another nursery was kept up near Farwell for the hopeful wives of settlers who wished to soften the lines of simple plains homes. Thus at last, as the original owners had dreamed, the Syndicate turned into a genuine colonizer of the grasslands of Texas.

The final paragraph in this outline of its history should at least suggest the strong thread of stability that characterized the development of the Capitol enterprise from the first. Good men turned active minds and ready hands to its problems and stayed until the job was done. Two illustrations suggestive of its opening chapters and its close should, at last, suffice.

The first of these, George Findlay, came out of the rugged environment of Scotland as a youth, in 1872, to join the John V. Farwell Company. He symbolized those twin virtues of that rigorous land—warm affection for cattle and a proper regard for money and economy. Thus, while helping look after the John V. Farwell books in 1878, he joined, with James Anderson of Lake Forest, in importing what he claimed to be the first herd of registered Aberdeen Angus cattle from Scotland. Further importations and careful breeding built their herd at Lake Forest, and later in Allen County, Kansas, into the largest registered herd of its kind in the United States.

But mainly George Findlay devoted his stable talents, his industry, and his disciplined mind to the development of the XIT enterprises. He first came to the ranch on an inspection tour in 1886; he was placed in charge of its finances and improvements in 1887; and in 1889 he returned to the Chicago office to look after its business there. From then until his death half a century later, he "devoted his splendid talents and all his time to the Texas Estate—during the years it was operated as a cattle ranch and subsequently in the management and disposal of the lands. His high character as a man and his loyalty to the interests of his principals entitled him to the confidence and affection which they bestowed upon him." No man was so intimately connected with the development of the Capitol Lands as was he. Thus did the Old World temper and restrain the natural but sometimes excessive optimism of the New.

This tradition of stable character remains after the lands are gone. Hamlin Overstreet still represents the Farwell interests in Texas. When he liquidated the Capitol Reservations Lands, December 31, 1950, a quarter of a century after starting with the company, he had reduced their holdings by sale to settlers to a bare 20,000 acres—the last of the 3,000,000-acre tract that the first Farwells and their associates had gotten in exchange for the capitol at Austin.

The only vestige of this original enterprise—besides the superb granite State House in Austin—is the Capitol Mineral Rights Company, of Chicago. This corporation, in the hands of the builders' descendants, holds mineral rights under portions of the original acreage, still firm in the belief that it is good to own property in Texas.[18]

Not the least notable feature of these men, who, with courage, fortitude, and imagination served this great venture, was their staying quality. They were stubborn in adversity. For decades enterprise and stability instead of profits were written most prominently upon their balance sheets. In the end, enhancement of value, following long periods of capital loss and renewed capital investment in developing the country, pulled their accounts into "the black." But it was only over the long pull.

In between was a lifetime of bold and imaginative enter-

[18] *Abstract of Record,* Charles D. Babcock *vs.* John V. Farwell and others, Appellate Court of Illinois, 1st District, October 1913, p. 241; James D. Hamlin to J. E. H., June 14, 1928.

prise, of false starts and all but cataclysmic failures, of trying experiences and, eventually, seasoned judgment. Back of that were freedom and faith—freedom to dare and faith in the future. Back of it all was the untrammeled nature of the human spirit, conceiving in vast design and carrying through in minute detail.

The historic panorama of which they were a dynamic part is still calculated to stir the imagination of healthy men. To begin with, here was the state of Texas, by special treaty still possessed of her own domain of millions of acres of frontier land untouched by man, 150 miles and more removed from the nearest railroad. Here was an ambitious state in need of a capitol to meet its growing pains, and yet without money with which to provide it. Here on the plains of Texas were 3,000,000 acres for those who would venture—venture to borrow and build; to borrow again and develop; and to borrow millions more in a skeptical market to pour down the thirsty rat holes of inexperience, of fire, depression, blizzard, and drouth.

Here were trails to be blazed, outlawry to be suppressed, fences to be built, ranges to be stocked, water to be provided, and men to be tested and discarded or kept. Here was change to be met, hazard to be overcome, and inexperience to be transmuted into wisdom and profit. Here was a desert empire, begrudgingly but potentially productive, upon which to try it all, and seven decades of vigorous human life in which to do it. Here was the frontier and freedom and challenge.

Back somewhere in the warp and woof, in the fabric of America was the stuff with which to do it. It coursed strong in the veins of men. It flowed out of the then untrammeled markets of enterprise to conquer the obdurate ranges of Texas and change the life of the West. That story which is only suggested here is still not half told.

Appendix

Logs of Early Trails

Selma, Ala.
April 27, 1928

Dear Mr. Haley:

Your letter April 4 inst. reached me at San Antonio. In compliance therewith I am handing you herewith, log of the trail or road from Tascosa to Dodge City and from Tascosa to Springer, New Mexico. And also trail from Colorado City to the Yellow House ranch. Sorry I can not make you a nice map showing these roads—I am trying to get a log of the route from Buffalo Springs to Trinidad, Colorado. El Moro is just on the outskirts of Trinidad. Will also try to get a log of the trail cattle were driven on from Tascosa to Montana. Shall be glad to give you any information I can at any time.

I am

Yours sincerely
W. S. Mabry.

P.S. In my recollections of the XIT ranch I stated I did not remember the name of the man who Col. Campbell brought to Buffalo Springs to look after the Cattle. As I now recall it, his name was Collins.

Yrs. W. S. M.

TASCOSA TO DODGE CITY

Tascosa to Little Blue stage stand	35 miles
Little Blue stage stand to Zulu (Jim Cator's)	30 miles
Zulu (Cator's) to Hardesty's Ranch	40 miles
Hardesty's Ranch to Jim Lanes on the Beaver	35 miles
Jim Lanes to Hines Crossing on Cimarron	40 miles
Cimarron to Hoodu Brown's on Crooked Creek	20 miles
Hoodu Brown's on Crooked Creek to Dodge City	42 miles
Total	242 miles

TASCOSA TO SPRINGER, NEW MEXICO

Tascosa to Reynolds Ranch LE	36 miles
Reynold's Ranch to Punta de Agua	9 miles
Punta de Agua to Mineosa	15 miles
Mineosa to Harris Ranch	20 miles
Harris Ranch to Nells on Texiquite	25 miles
Nell's Ranch to Mesa Seco	40 miles
Mesa Seco to Taylor's ranch	25 miles
Taylor's ranch to Springer, N. M.	6 miles
Total	176 miles

LOG OF THE MONTANA TRAIL AS KEPT BY EALY MOORE

Copy of May's Log Book of trail to Monta.[1]

From Buffalo Springs to Corrumpa 15 miles, from Corrumpa to Carrizzo 15 miles, from Carrizzo to Cimarron above 101 Ranch 15 miles, from Cimarron to Carrizzo Springs via Road Canon 18 miles, from Carrizzo Springs to head of Freeze out 18 miles, from Freeze out to Butte Creek 10 miles, follow down Butte to mouth of Maverick 30 miles, from Maverick to water on Clay Creek 15 miles, 30 miles to Lamar water half way, from Lamar 12 miles to water on Sandy, follow up Sandy to Kit Carson, water twice on

---

[1] This log was kept by J. E. May, of Vega, Texas, who drove for the LS Ranch in 1884, and later for the N–N's. Both outfits had ranches in the Panhandle and finishing ranges in Montana. J. E. May to J. E. H., June 29, 1926.

The original diary is in the Archives of the University of Texas, Austin. It was first printed in part in the original edition of *The XIT Ranch of Texas,* and then in full in *The Panhandle-Plains Historical Review* (Canyon, Texas), 1932.

the way, Cross R. R. at Carson and follow up Wild Horse Creek two waters on Creek, from head of Wild Horse to Republican 18 or 20 miles, from Republican to Hell Springs 18 miles, from Hell Springs to Walker Camp 18 miles, water in Arroyo 1 mile north, from there to water on Beaver 35 miles, from there to South Platte 30 miles, from South Platte to Pawnee 25 miles from Pawnee to Pawnee Buttes 15 miles from Pawnee Buttes to Pine Bluffs 25 miles. from Pine Bluffs to horse creek 30 miles, follow down Horse Creek 35 miles and cross the divide to North Platte 12 or 15 miles. Cross Platte at Mouth of J. M. Creek 30 miles from head water on J. M. Creek to Lusk 25 miles from Lusk to Hat Creek Store 14 miles down the creek to Old women 10 miles from Old women to Lance Creek 16 miles from Lance Creek to Lodge Pole on Cheyenne 25 miles. Up Lodge Pole and down Buffalo to Bellefourche 60 miles from Bellefourche to Cottonwood 20 miles down Cottonwood to Little Powder 12 miles, from where you strike Little Powder to Big Powder 50 miles, from Big Powder to Mizpah 15 miles from Mizpah to pumpkin Creek 18 miles down Pumpkin Creek to Yellow Stone 60 miles, down Yellow Stone to Ranch on Cedar Creek 60 miles.

Channing, April 20, 1892

Left C.[2] at 10 o'clock A.M. and nooned at the tank 3 miles from C. on the Rita Blanco Road, and stayed at the North E. Mill and laid over there on the 21st; got kicked that morning by a horse.

April

22nd   Moved to the LE Camp on the Pounde Agua
23rd   Camped 4 miles north of Middle Water Ranch
24th   Moved to the mill 3 miles East of the twin mills in the Farwell Park pasture
25th   Helped Webb to round up at twin mills in the morning in the eve I moved 3 miles East of Farwell Park.

April

26   I moved to the No. 2 mill 7 miles N. E. of the Park.
27   Laid over at same Place.
28   "   "   "   "   "
29   Moved to the Agua Frio, and helped Webb to round up.
30   Moved to the Buffalo Spring pasture.

[2] Channing, Texas.

May

1st   Received my first cattle
2nd   Moved to Pirico
3rd   Moved to Agua Freo, and received the rest of my cattle.
4   Left for Montana
5th   Stayed on the head of Cold Springs
6   Stayed on Cold Spring
7   "   "   "   "   rained
8   "   "   "   "   rained.[3]

May

9   Moved to Wild Cat Creek
10   "   " Cimarron river
11   "   " four miles from head water on Auberry Canyon
12   Got off the trail, went too far East; stayed about 16 miles S. E. of Springfield.
13   Got to within 3 miles of Springfield, Colo.
14   Moved to Sprg.fd. and Stayed there until the morning of the 15th.
15   Camped 10 miles North of Spngfd.
16   Watered on Butte and camped 2 miles East of Butte Mountains
17   Camped on Clay Creek missed the upper water on Clay.

May

18   Watered at the 10 mile water on Clay from Lamar, and camped four miles from Lamar that night.
19   Passed through Lamar and crossed the Ark. river.
20   Got to the King Resivoir at noon and stayed there until next day at noon cold wind from the N.
21   Pretty cool cold north wind. Left K. R. after noon and went to Big Sandy.

[3] The cause of this delay was an illegal tax upon herds crossing "No Man's Land," the Panhandle of Oklahoma. This strip was a hideout for outlaws, and some of them posing as United States marshals practiced the swindle of charging a tax of five cents upon every animal coming into the strip and three cents for those going out. Hence the tax on trail herds amounted to eight cents a head. Owings was placed in the lead, and when held up for the tax, sent word back to Moore, who delayed until the matter might be settled. Boyce and Findlay came up and finally paid the tax on the first two herds, but under protest. The other three herds turned west into New Mexico to miss the tax. J. Ealy Moore to J. E. H., November 12, 1925, and February 26, 1927.

22	Watered five miles below Chivington on B. S. and Camped at Chiv. that night.
23	Moved 10 miles south to B. S. Cattle Balked that morning
24	Camped 10 miles farther north on B. S. [Big Sandy]
25	Got to Kit Carson
26	Went 10 miles north to wild horse creek
27	Stayed near a sheep camp and layed over until noon next day
28	Stayed in seven miles of the Republican river.
29	Got to Republican An X herd over took me at noon, it rained that eve.

May

30	Got to Bovina, big snow storm that night and lasted until 10 o'clock next day. Cattle all got away. 4 XIT herds and two X herds got together.[4]

May

31	Took my wagon and outfit and pulled South to catch my herd, got about eight hundred that day and located the rest.

June

1st	Began to drift cattle north
2	Got my cattle and camped at Bovina once more.
3	Trimed up and got ready to hit the trail.
4	Camped on dug out 10 miles from Bovina. Came another storm that night, held my herd all O.K.

June

5	Camped about 3 miles South of Walkers Camp.
6	Camped on head of Beaver over took Milt that Eve.

[4] These X herds belonged to Reynolds brothers, of Albany, Texas. The cowboys with the various herds were dressed for summer weather. Moore held his herd until about 2.00 o'clock in the morning, when he took his men to camp to keep them from freezing. At daylight he crawled from his "suggans" into six inches of snow, got his horses, and found six herds of cattle, 15,000 in all, drifted against the railroad. The X cattle were cut out, and the 10,000 XIT steers were then divided equally between the four outfits. Twenty-eight head of the X horses, ridden the afternoon and night of the storm, froze to death. Moore lost three horses and twenty-three head of steers from freezing. Moore to J. E. H., February 26, 1927.

7   Camped 2 miles south of Abbott

8   Watered on Beaver at noon and moved on down the creek about 6 miles

9   Camped 3 miles South of Brush, Colo.

10   Passed Through Brush and crossed the South Platte river Camped six miles north of Brush

11   Camped at the Big Alkali lake 8 miles S. of Pawnee

12   Camped six miles north of Pawnee

13   Camped three miles South of Pawnee Butte

14   Camped fifteen miles of Pine Bluffs, Wyo.

15   Passed by P. B. rained that evening.

16   Camped twenty miles from P. B.

17   Got to Horse Creek

18   Got to Hawk Springs on Horse Creek.

19   Camped three miles North of Horse Creek

20   Camped three miles North Platte, helped a N–N herd and Chris across that day.

June

21   Assisted Jim Vaughn to cross his herd in the forenoon, and tried to cross mine in the afternoon, but failed.

22   Assisted Jack Horn to Cross.

23   Helped to cross Mil's my own and Dan's herds, Camped one mile from river.

24   Camped 8 miles up Raw Hide from the river

25   Made a cut off of about four miles and camped just below Coffee's ranch.

26   Camped 10 miles of Lusk.

27   Passed through Lusk, Wyo. and camped six miles beyond.

28   Watered on Hat Creek, had a race with Milt, Came out ahead. Camped that night 6 miles below water.

30   Passed over divide and camped on Cheyenne, Milt passed me that night.

July

1   Camped about five miles up Lodge Pole from the mouth

2   Camped about 10 miles farther up Lodge Pole.

3   Lay over, so as the four herds that was right with me could get a little ahead. And camped on the head water of Lodge Pole.

July

4   Pulled out soon after dinner and drove 11 miles Camped up close to the divide between L. P. and Buffalo Creek.

5   Camped 8 miles from Bellefouche on Buffalo

6   Camped on Bellefouche river. Dan passed me that evening.

7   Camped on divide between Bellefouche and Cottonwood.

8   Camped 3 miles down on Cottonwood.

9   Camped 10 miles down on Cottonwood.

10   Camped about fifteen miles below where the trail crosses Little Powder.

11   Drove through a rough piece of country and camped on L. P. about 10 miles below.

July

12   Camped about 3 miles below the X ranche

13   Camped two miles above where the trail leaves L. P.

14   Passed over the divide and camped on Big Powder river Cattle stampeded, and milled around until about 11 o'clock.

15   Passed over the divide from B. P. to Mizpah and camped 2 miles from Mizpah Creek.

16   Camped 6 miles from Mizpah

17   Got to Pumpkin Creek. Camped 5 miles below where we struck the Creek.

18   Camped 10 miles farther down the creek, near the Harris Ranche.

19   Camped near Beebee P. O. on Pumpkin Creek

July

20   Camped about 3 miles above where the road crosses Pumpkin.

21   Camped 15 miles from Miles City, Mont.

22   Watered on Tongue river and camped on the breaks of the Yellow Stone.

23   Crossed Yellow Stone and camped about 1 mile from it.[5]

[5] The trail wagons crossed the Yellowstone on the bridge at Fort Laramie, about sixteen miles above the trail crossing. The trail outfits put the horses in first, swam them, and then the herd. An old man with a canoe pointed the cattle across. The Yellowstone was one of the worst rivers trail herds had to cross. It was so swift that a horse with a rider could hardly swim it. Moore to J. E. H., July 6, 1927.

24   Camped opposite Miles City.

25   Camped about 2 miles from where the trail strikes the river the first time.

26   Camped where trail leaves the river and comes back again the second time. Messrs. Findlay Farwell & Cato stayed with us that night.

July

27   Camped on Custer Creek. Bunched the cattle at dark and left them. They were counted that morning.

28   Milt over took me that morning and we began to dehorn. Camped that night on the divide between Custer Creek & Cherry.

29   Got to Cedar Creek and turned loose.

Horses Left

May

18   Left two horses, one black and one grey, both locoed.

22   Had one bay horse to die from drinking too much alkali water.

26   Had a good grey horse to fall and break his neck.[6]

May

30   Had three head of horses to freeze and one to come so near it that I had to leave him.

June

10   Left a couple of crippled horses on the South Platte at Brush, and had one to run off.

Cattle Left on Trail

May

8   Cold Springs   10

12   16 miles N. of Cim.   1

13   Spring Field   1

16   20 miles N. of Sp. F.   2

18   10 miles from Lamar South   1

19   Lamar   3

[6] This was a cowboy's tale. Moore later discovered the horse had accidentally been shot. Ms., "Biographical Notes," appended to "Diary."

23	From Chiv. to B. S. 5
25	Big Sandy 1
27	Head of Horse Creek 2
30	West of Republican 1
31	Bovina, froze 23
31	" left 2

June

5	Dug out 1
9	Bogged in Beaver 2
10	" " " 1
11	Bogged in Alkali Lake 2
19	Left on Horse Creek 1
29	Left one on bed ground with leg broke 1
	Total 60

April

19	J. E. Moore	$100.00
12	Sam Williamson, Cook	$ 40.00
13	Geo. Smith, Rider	$ 35.00
25	Charlie Tompkins, Rider	$ 35.00

April

25	Frank Times,	"	$ 35.00
25	R. G. Torrey,	"	$ 35.00
28	R. L. Glover,	"	$ 35.00
28	S. D. Holsel,	"	$ 35.00
28	Dill Shipley,	"	$ 35.00
28	Ed Green,	"	$ 35.00
28	A. L. Love,	"	$ 35.00

Bought of H. Humphrey 4–19–92   :   Channing, Texas

80 Oven @ 7	$5.60	1 Small "	.25
1 Stew Kettle	.75	1 Doz Cups	1.00
1 Camp Kettle	1.50	1 Doz Plates	1.00
1 Coffee Pot	1.50	2–3 Doz. Knives Forks	1.00
1 Spade	1.00	1 Doz Spoons	.40
2 Buckets	1.00	1 Bu. Steel	1.50
1 Fry Pan	.50	1 Bu. Knife	1.50
1 Dipper	.10	1 Large Spoon	.10
2 Dish Pans	1.20	1 Large Fork	.10
1 Wash Pan	.20		18.80

1	Ax & handle		$1.25	1 Oil Can	.50
100 lb.	Flour		2.65	1 Gal oil	.30
88 lb.	Bacon	9	7.92	1 Bot Lemon extract	.75
2 cans	B. Powder		2.50	1 Bot vanilla extract	1.00
25 lb.	Coffee		5.62	1 Doz Boxes matches	.25
20 lb.	Apples	10	2.00	3 Sks. Salt	.25
20 lb.	Beans	5½	1.10	10 lb. Lard	.95
2 lb.	Pepper	25	.50	12 Bars soap	.50
10 lb.	Grapes	7½	.75		64.07
25 lb.	Sugar	5½	1.38		64.07
90 lb.	Rope		13.50	1 Keg Pickles	2.75
6	Boxes ax grease		.60		$66.82
1	Lantern		1.00	Cash	$100.00

Bought of H. Humphrey : Channing, Tex. 4–20–92

1 coffee mill	$1.00	1 Keg	1.00
1 Shoeing Hammer	.75	50 lb. B. Bacon	5.50
1 Shoeing Pinchers	1.00	1 Monkey wrench	.75
1 Shoeing Rasp	.75	1 Sack	.20
4 Curry Combs	1.00	Wagon Bows	.75
8 lb. Hobble Rope	1.20	3 yds Crush	.40
5 gallon Molasses	3.00		$17.30

Bought of Jas. Mc. Masters : Channing Tex 4–19, 92

1 wagon sheet	$3.00
1 wagon whip	1.75
	$4.75

Bought of J. L. Vaughan : Farwell Park, Tex. 4–26, 92

120 lb. Gran. Sugar	5½	6.60	70 lb. B. Bacon	11¼		7.87
250 lb. Pat. Flour	3	7.50	9 lb. N. R. Soup			.50
25 lb. Oat Meal	8½	2.06	20 lb. Beans	5		1.00
40 Lard	9¾	3.90	6 lb. Table Salt			.15
25 lb. A. B. Coffee	22½	5.62	50 lb. Evap. Peaches		15	7.50
20 lb. Rice		1.65				44.35

Farwell Park April 28, 92

Sugar	$120	Coffee	25
Flour	250	B. B.	70
Oat Meal	25	Soap	9
Lard	40	Beans	20
Rice	20	Salt	6
		Peaches	50

Bought of F. M. Friend : 5–14 92 Springfield, Colo.

5 gal. Coal oil	1.15	40 lb. Bacon	4.00
50 lb. Beans	2.25	45 lb. Currents	3.00
200 lb. Flour	5.80	6 lb B. Powder	3.00

16½ lb. Flk. Hominy	.80
1 Lantern	1.25
484 lb. Corn 1.10	5.34
5 lb. Salt	.45

100 lb. Breakfast Bacon	14.40
2 gal. Sorghum	1.50
	43.24

Bought of Dwight Miser : 5–14 92 Springfield, Colo.

Potatoes 55 lb	.85
200 lb. Flour	5.80
40 lb. Bacon	4.00
Salt	
Corn	
984 Prunes	
Cinnamon	
Coffee Mill	

Lantern	1.25
5 gal. Coal oil	1.15
50 lb. Beans	2.50
45 lb. Currents	3.00
16 lb. Flk. Hominy	.80
1 Coffee Mill	.65
1 Horse Shoe Rasp	.85
2 gal Syrup	1.50

Bought of E. F. Martin : 5–14 92 Springfield, Colo.

1 Horse Rasp	.85
1 Coffee Mill	.65
	1.50
May 14 C. Bill	178.79

Bought of C. M. Lee : 5–19 92 Lamar Colo.

	$ Cts.
1 Keg Pickles	3.00
100 lb. Flour	3.00
100 lb. Spuds	1.25
50 lb. Gr. Sugar	3.00
12 lb. Coffee	3.00
170 lb. Corn	1.90
163 lb. Oats	2.45
50 lb. B. Bacon	6.25

1 Bell	.35
20 lb. Raisins	2.00
25 lb. Dr. Grapes	2.50
20 lb. Rice	2.00
40 lb. Lima Beans	2.75
1 Faucet	.15
Soap	.50
By cash	.85
	119.10

Lamar, Colo.
May 19, 92
Payed Eight Dollar to Powers Co Land Irrigation Co. for crossing 3 ditches.

Lamar, Colo.
May 20, 92
Payed to J. W. Galladge $5 Five Dollars for crossing canal eight miles from town.

May 19, 92
Lamar, Colo.
Payed to Geo. Smith $42.00 forty two Dollars for wages.

Lamar, Colo.
May 19, 92
Payed to D. N. Shepley $25.64 Twenty five dollars and sixty four cents for wages.

Bought of Ewing & Powell : Hugo Colo. June 2 92

100 lb. Flour	2.60
44 lb. Bacon	5.28
1 Soda	.10
1 Can B. Powder	.50
	8.48

Brush Colo.
June 10, 92
Payed to Sam Williamson $76 Seventy six Dollars for one month and twenty six days work at $40 per month.

Bought of Wm. Knearl : Brush Colo. June 10, 92

250 lb. Pat. Flour	7.50		Lard	2.40
175 Bacon	26.25		Rice	1.00
75 Sugar	4.50	20 lb. Currents		2.00
60 Coffee	15.00	5 lb. Prices B. Powder		2.25
3 Soda	.30		Cinnamon	.25
225 lb. Potatoes	2.25		Grapes	2.50
50 Prunes	5.00		Nut meg	.25
2 sax oats	2.25		Axle Grease	.50
Mustard	1.25		Matches	.30
Pickel	2.75		Keg Syrup	2.50
6 sacks salt	.60			82.10
Soap	.50		Dr. to Cash	130.00

Brush, Colo.
June 10, 92

Payed to Frank Stephens per M. S. $10 for crossing herd across South Platte.

Pine Bluffs, Wyo.
June 15, 92

Payed to A. J. Elliott $15 for watering herd and driving through pasture.

Bought of Baker Brothers : Lusk, Wyo. June 27, 92

300 lb. Flour	9.75	1 H. Stock		.35
200 lb. B. Bacon	28.00	6 pt. 6 Horse shoes		.72
30 lb. Arb. Coffee	7.50	½ Doz. Table Spoons		.20
40 lb. Lard	5.00	1 Stew pan		.35
25 lb. Oat Meal	1.25	1 Bunch Lamp Wicks		.10
10 lb. Baking Powder	4.50			75.60
2 lb. Soda	.20	Cash		100.00
2 gal. M. Syrup	2.50	6 lb. Durham		3.60
270 lb. Potatoes	2.70	1 Quire Paper		.25
269 lbs. Oats	3.70			179.45
255 lbs. Corn	2.78	July 22, Tongue River		
5 gal. oil	1.25	Bought of		
1 Cad. Matches	.50	70 lb. Potatoes		2.10
1 Case Corn 8	3.25	15 lb. Sugar		1.50
1 whip	1.00	1 lb. B. Powder		.50
		Onions		1.00
		Peas		.75
				5.85

Lusk, Wyo.
June 27, 92

Payed to R. L. Glover $70 Seventy Dollars for two months work, at $35 per month.

Expenses of 1892

Drew	$415.00	other expenses	27.23
Payed out	401.12	Total expenses	1,801.80
Chuck Bills	386.27	Private money	4.45
Watering Expenses	48.00	Company's money on hand	13.88
Wages paid out	1,340.30		
Wages taken up	825.89	total	18.33

General Rules of the XIT Ranch
January, 1888

No. 1

Whenever a person is engaged to work on the ranch, the person so engaging him will fill out and sign a blank, giving the name of the party employed, for what purpose employed, the amount of wages he is to receive, the date he will begin work, and deliver the same to the person employed, who must sign the counterpart of such contract, which must be forwarded to headquarters at the first opportunity ; and no one will be put upon the Company's pay roll, or receive any pay until this is complied with.

No. 2

Employees, when discharged, or on leaving the Company's service, are required to bring or send to the headquarter office, a statement from the person under whom they were at work, showing the day they quit the Company's service, and no settlement will be made with any employee, until such statement is furnished.

No. 3

Employees discharged from or leaving the service of the Company are expected to leave the ranch at once and will not be permitted to remain more than one night in any camp.

No. 4

The wages due any employee will not be paid to any other person without a written order from the employee to whom such wages are due.

No. 5

No person in charge of any pasture, or any work on the ranch, or any contractor on the ranch, will be permitted to hire any one who had been discharged from the Company's service; nor shall any one who leaves an outfit, of his own accord, with the intention of getting employment at some other place on the ranch, be so employed except by special agreement, made beforehand between the person in charge of the outfit he leaves and the one in charge of the outfit he wishes to work for.

No. 6

Private horses of employees must not be kept at any of the camps, nor will they be allowed to be fed grain belonging to the Company. No employee shall be permitted to keep more than two private horses on the ranch and all such horses must be kept in some pasture designated by the ranch manager.

No. 7

No employee shall be permitted to own any cattle or stock horses on the ranch.

No. 8

The killing of beef by any person on the ranch, except by the person in charge of the pasture, or under his instruction, is strictly forbidden. Nor is the person in charge of a pasture allowed to have beef killed, unless it can be distributed and consumed without loss. And all hides of beef killed must be taken care of and accounted for. It shall be the duty of each person having beef killed to keep a tally of the same and report the number, age and sex killed to headquarters every month.

No. 9

The abuse of horses, mules or cattle by any employee will not be tolerated; and any one who strikes his horse or mule over the head, or spurs it in the shoulder, or in any other manner abuses or neglects to care for it while in his charge, shall be dismissed from the Company's service.

No. 10

Employees are not allowed to run mustang, antelope or any kind of game on the Company's horses.

No. 11

No employee of the Company, or of any contractor doing work for the Company, is permitted to carry on or about his person or in his saddle bags, any pistol, dirk, dagger, sling shot, knuckles, bowie knife or any other similar instruments for the purpose of offense or defense. Guests of the Company, and persons not employees of the ranch temporarily staying at any of its camps, are expected to comply with this rule, which is also a State law.

No. 12

Card playing and gambling of every description, whether engaged in by employees, or by persons not in the service of the Company, is strictly forbidden on the ranch.

No. 13

In case of fire upon the ranch, or on lands bordering on the same, it shall be the duty of every employee to go to it at once and use his best endeavors to extinguish it, and any neglect to do so, without reasonable excuse, will be considered sufficient cause for dismissal.

No. 14

Each outfit of men that is furnished with a wagon and cook is required to make its own camping places, and not impose on the other camps on the ranch unnecessarily.

No. 15

Employees are strictly forbidden the use of vinous, malt, spirituous, or intoxicating liquors, during their time of service with the Company.

No. 16

It is the duty of every employee to protect the Company's interests to the best of his ability, and when he sees they are threatened in any direction to take every proper measure at his command to accomplish this end, and as soon as possible to inform his employers of the danger threatened.

No. 17

Employees of neighboring ranches on business are to be cared for at all camps, and their horses fed if desired (provided there is feed in the camp to spare) ; but such persons will not be expected to remain on the ranch longer than is necessary to transact their business, or continue their journey.

No. 18

Bona fide travelers may be sheltered if convenient, but they will be expected to pay for what grain and provisions they get, at prices to be fixed from time to time by the Company, and all such persons must not remain at any camp longer than one night.

No. 19

Persons not in the employment of the Company, but freighting for it, are not to be furnished with meals for themselves or feed for their teams at any of the camps on the ranch, but are expected to come on the ranch prepared to take care of themselves.

No. 20

Loafers, "sweaters," deadbeats, tramps, gamblers, or disreputable persons, must not be entertained at any camp, nor will employees be permitted to give, loan or sell such persons any grain, or provisions of any kind, nor shall such persons be permitted to remain on the Company's land anywhere under any pretext whatever.

No. 21

No person or persons, not in the employment of the Company, shall be permitted to hunt or kill game of any kind, inside of the ranch inclosure, under any pretext whatsoever, and all employees are instructed to see that this rule is enforced. Employees of the Company will also not be permitted to hunt or kill game except when necessary for use for food.

No. 22

It is the aim of the owners of this ranch to conduct it on the principle of right and justice to every one; and for it to be excelled by no other in the good behavior, sterling honesty and integrity, and general high character of its employees, and to this end it is necessary that the foregoing rules be adhered to, and the violation of any of them will be considered just charge for discharge.

No. 23

Every camp will be furnished with a printed copy of these rules, which must be nailed up in a conspicuous place in the camp; and each and every rule is hereby made and considered a condition and part of the engagement between the Company and its employees, and any employee who shall tear down or destroy such printed rules, or shall cause the same to be done, shall be discharged.

By Order of the Company,

ABNER TAYLOR,

Manager.

Bibliography

THE XIT PAPERS

The extensive files as kept by the XIT Ranch and the Chicago office constitute the great source of information upon this subject. They consist of thousands of letters, reports, and legal documents, and are in the Archives of the Panhandle-Plains Historical Society at Canyon, Texas. A guide to these records has been made by Seymour Connor, archivist for the Society, and issued in mimeographed form, 1953.

BOOKS, PAMPHLETS, REPORTS

Bolton, Herbert Eugene. *Texas in the Middle Eighteenth Century.* Berkeley, 1915.

Bulletin, U. S. Geological Survey, *No. 194*, Series F. Geography, 30. Washington, 1902.

The Capitol Freehold Land and Investment Company, Limited. Issue of 5 per cent Debentures, Prospectus. London, 1888.

Capitol Land Reservation in the Panhandle of Texas (Prospectus booklet, explaining the terms by which the lands were being placed on sale). Published 1901, reissued 1903.

Capitol Reservations Lands, Abstract of Title.

Cook, John R. *The Border and the Buffalo.* Topeka, Kansas, Crane & Co., 1907.

Dixon, Mrs. Olive K. *Life and Adventures of Billy Dixon.* Guthrie, Okla., n. d.

Dobie, J. Frank. *Texas and Southwestern Lore.* Austin, 1927.

Farwell, John V. *Report of the Managing Director, Year Ending October 31, 1886.* (Printed) London, 1886.

Gannett, Henry. *Boundaries of the United States* (third edition). *Bulletin No. 226*, Series F. Geography, 37. Washington, 1904.

Goodwin, Cardinal. *The Trans-Mississippi West.* New York, 1922.

Gregg, Josiah. *Commerce of the Prairies* (vols. XIX and XX of *Early Western Travels*, ed. by Reuben Gold Thwaites, *q.v.*).

Hammond, J. P. "The Founding of New Mexico," *New Mexico Historical Review*, Jan., 1926, Oct., 1926.

Hough, Emerson. *The Passing of the Frontier.* New Haven, 1918.

House Reports, Vol. I, Feb. 13, 1906.

House Reports No. 1883, 61 Cong., 3 sess.

Hunter, Marvin. *The Trail Drivers of Texas.* Bandera, 1924.

James, Edwin. *Account of Stephen H. Long's Expedition* (vols. XIV, XV, XVI of *Early Western Travels*, ed. by Reuben Gold Thwaites, *q.v.*).

Kendall, Geo. Wilkins. *Narrative of the Texan Santa Fe Expedition.* New York, 1844.

Land Booklet (printed by Capitol Freehold Land & Investment Co.).

Marcy, R. B. "Report of . . ." *Ex. Doc. No. 64*, 31 Cong., 1 sess.

———. *Exploration of the Red River of Louisiana in the Year 1852.* 33 Cong., 1 sess., *Ex. Doc.* Washington, 1854.

Pope, John. "Report to War Department on Route for Pacific Railway," 1854.

Prose and Poetry of the Live Stock Industry. Kansas City, 1905.

Prospectus, 3,000,000 Acres of Land in the Pan-Handle of Texas. (This prospectus was issued by Taylor Babcock Co. All references to it in the notes are to *Prospectus*), Chicago.

Reminiscences of John V. Farwell (by his elder daughter). Chicago, Ralph Fletcher Seymore, 1928.

Report, Bureau of Animal Industry, 1885.

Reports of the Capitol Building Commissioners to the Governor of Texas (1st, 2nd, 3rd, 4th, and "Final"). Austin, 1883–87.

Report No. 1186, 59 Cong., 1 sess. (Boundary).

"Report upon the Resurvey and Location of the Boundary Lines between the State of Texas and New Mexico" (Texas Land Office, 1911).

Southwestern Reporter, Vol. 65.

Thrall, Homer S. *A Pictorial History of Texas*, St. Louis, 1879.

Bibliography

Thwaites, Reuben Gold. *Early Western Travels, 1748–1846.* Cleveland, 1905.

Townshend, R. B. *Last Memories of a Tenderfoot,* New York, 1926.

United States Census Reports, 1880, III.

Wright, Robert M. *Dodge City, the Cowboy Capital.* Wichita, Kans., 1913.

LETTERS AND PERSONAL INTERVIEWS

Abbott, B. P. to J. E. H., June 24, 1927.

Aten, Ira to J. E. H., Feb. 26, 1928, March 1, 1928.

Austen, E. C. G. to J. E. H., July 7, 1927, Nov. 7, 1927.

Balfour, Wm. to J. E. H., June 29, 1926.

Baughn, H. K. to J. E. H., June 25, 1927.

Boykin, Sid to J. E. H., June 23, 1927.

Boyce, Wm. to J. E. H., June 28, 1927.

Bugbee, T. S. to J. E. H., July 17, 1925.

Bull, S. A. to J. E. H., Feb. 27, 1927.

Burns, R. C. to J. E. H., Feb. 22, 1927, Sept. 23, 1927.

Bussell, Dick to J. E. H., July 19, 1926.

Bynum, S. K. to J. E. H., Feb. 13, 1928, Nov. 5, 1927.

Cash, Harvey to J. E. H., June 20, 1927.

Cole, Mrs. Dan to J. E. H., July 7, 1927.

Connell, Ed. to J. E. H., Oct. 31, 1927.

Duke, R. L. to J. E. H., July 6, 1927, Nov. 8, 1927, March 21, 1928.

East, Jas. to J. E. H., Sept. 27, 1927, Oct. 8, 1927, Feb. 22, 1928.

Eubank, H. W. to J. E. H., July 1, 1926.

Farwell, John V. to Col. R. D. Bowen, July 7, 1926.

Farwell, John V. to W. S. Mabry, Jan. 25, 1927.

Farwell, John V. to Roberts, Samuel H., June 28, 1927.

Farwell, Walter to J. E. H., Sept. 22, 1927.

Findlay, George to Chas. Gray, May 20, 1910.

Findlay, George to *The Gazette* (Letter).

Findlay, George to J. E. H., Dec. 3, 1926.

Frye, R. J. to J. E. H., June 26, 1927.

Goodnight, C. to J. E. H., June 25, 1925, Jan. 26, 1926, Nov. 13, 1926, Jan. 12, 1927, Feb. 19, 1927, Feb. 25, 1927, April 8, 1927, Sept. 2, 1927, Sept. 16, 1927, June 1, 1928.

Hamlin, Jas. D. to J. E. H., Sept. 22, 1927, June 14, 1928.
Heissler, J. F. to Roberts, Samuel H., March 27, 1928.
Huffman, M. to J. E. H., Nov. 30, 1927.
Ingerton, Harry to J. E. H., April 13, 1927.
Irwin, Frank to J. E. H., Sept. 24, 1927.
Jones, Jas. to J. E. H., Jan. 13, 1927.
Jowell, G. N. to J. E. H., Jan. 17, 1927.
Le Fors, R. A. to J. E. H., Oct. 24, 1925.
Lloyd, Frank to J. E. H., Aug. 18, 1927.
Long, P. E. to J. E. H., July 15, 1928.
Mabry, W. S. to J. E. H., Dec. 27, 1927, April 27, 1928.
Matlock, A. L. to J. E. H., Dec. 1, 1927.
May, J. E. to J. E. H., June 29, 1926.
McAllister, J. E. to J. E. H., July 1, 1926.
McCanless, John to J. E. H., March 31, 1928.
McDermett, John D. to J. E. H., April 28, 1929.
McDonald, J. P. to J. E. H., June 25, 1927.
Mitchell, Frank to J. E. H., Dec. 1, 1926, June 10, 1927.
Mobley, J. B. to J. E. H., Sept. 23, 1927.
Moore, J. E. to J. E. H., Nov. 12, 1925, Feb. 26, 1927, Nov. 8, 1927.
Nelson, O. H. to J. E. H., Aug. 15, 1925, July 13, 1926, Feb. 26, 1927.
Owen, W. R. to J. E. H., Aug. 12, 1926.
Paul, J. C. to J. E. H., Sept. 12, 1927.
Roberts, Samuel H. to J. E. H., April 17, 1928, June 8, 1928.
Shannon, J. M. to J. E. H., Nov. 27, 1927.
Simpson, George to J. E. H., July 18, 1926.
Slaughter, W. B. to J. E. H., Oct. 9, 1926.
Smith, C. R. to J. E. H., Aug. 11, 1927, March 20, 1928.
Snyder, John to J. E. H., June 30, 1926.
Stagg, Allen to J. E. H., June 29, 1926.
Stevens, J. W. to J. E. H., Nov. 23, 1927.
Suezo, Pablo to J. E. H., Sept. 17, 1928.
Tasker, C. P. to Hank Smith (Letters). Panhandle-Plains Historical Society, Canyon.
Tate, W. A. to J. E. H., Oct. 31, 1927.
Taylor, Brent to J. E. H., Oct. 14, 1928.
Trujillo, Celedón to J. E. H., June 24, 1927.

Bibliography

Turner, A. L. to J. E. H., July 2, 1926.
Vincent, C. F. to J. E. H., June 26, 1927.
Wayland, J. H. to J. E. H., June 26, 1927.
Yearwood, J. Frank to J. E. H., Dec. 9, 1927.

MANUSCRIPTS

"The Capitol Syndicate or XIT Ranch," Chicago Office, Capitol Reservation Lands.

"Expenditures on the Texas Enterprise," Chicago Office (Transcript).

"Experiences of S. K. Bynum," Panhandle-Plains Historical Society, Canyon.

"General Rules of the XIT Ranch" (Chicago Office).

Gough, L. "Sketch of the XIT Ranch," Panhandle-Plains Historical Society, Canyon.

Haley, J. Evetts. "A Survey of Texas Cattle Drives to the North, 1866–1895," University of Texas.

Haley, J. Evetts. "Old Tascosa," Panhandle-Plains Historical Society, Canyon.

Harding, C. F. "The Receivership Fight" (Chicago Office).

Hatfield, Chas. P. "Account of the Mackenzie Battle," Panhandle-Plains Historical Society, Canyon.

"The Litigation of the State of Texas over the Capitol Grant in the Panhandle" (Chicago Office).

Mabry, W. S. "Recollections of the XIT Ranch" (Chicago Office).

McClure, J. G. K. "Among the Cowboys of Texas" (Chicago Office).

Maps of the XIT Lands (Dalhart Office).

J. E. Moore. "Diary of a Trail Trip to Montana, 1892." Transcript in the files of the Panhandle-Plains Historical Society, Canyon.

"Recollections of Charles Goodnight," Panhandle-Plains Historical Society, Canyon.

Records, Oldham County, Commissioners Court, Vega, Texas.

"Tombstone Camp Diary," Ira Aten Collection (copy in files of the author).

"Trujillo Camp Diary," Ira Aten Collection (copy in files of the author).

MAGAZINE ARTICLES

William Clinton. "The Largest Ranch in the World," *The Ladies Home Journal*, Feb. 1899.

Forest Crissey. "The Vanishing Range," *The Country Gentleman*, March 1, 1913.

Frank M. King. " 'Whiskey' was XIT Top Horse," *The Cattleman*, Vol. XIII (Feb., 1927).

Mrs. T. V. Reeves. "Cities Grow around Cow Camps," *The Cattleman*, Vol. XIII (May, 1927).

"Surveyed State Capitol Land," *Frontier Times*, Bandera, Texas, August, 1925.

NEWSPAPERS

Amarillo Northwest, Dec. 25, 1889.
Dallas Herald, Aug. 23, 1883.
Dallas Weekly Herald, Jan. 31, 1884.
Fort Worth Gazette, Sept. 25, 1892.
Galveston News, Oct. 22, 1874.
Midland (Texas) *Gazette*, March 18, 1904.
Southwest Plainsman (Amarillo), Feb. 20, 1926.
Sudan News, July, 1926.
Tascosa Pioneer (1886–89).

Index

Index

Index

Plemons, Judge W. B.: 208
Pope, John: reconnaissance of, 14
Powell, Wm.: herd, 189
Prairie Cattle Company: 60
Prairie fires: 80, 169; set maliciously, 171; moving cattle, 177; fighting of, 178 ff.; guards, 180

Quitaque: Indian trade, 27

Railroads: 204
Ranches: Frying Pan, 25; Diamond Tail, 43; F, 44; JA, 44; big companies, 48, 80, 101; Panhandle, 145; XIT rules, 242
Red River: 8 ff.
Resolution, Texas Legislature: 56
Reynolds, E. A. (ranchman): 41, 48, 81
Reynolds, G. T. and W. T.: located in Panhandle, 41
Rhea, J. E. and J. W.: buy land, 218
Riders, line: 166
Rito Blanco Division: 147
Roberts, Samuel H. (land commissioner): 222
Robinson, Sheriff Tobe: 117
Rock Island Railroad: 204
Rope corrals: 154
Roundup, general: 79
Rowe, Alfred and Vincent: on Salt Fork, 43
Rules, ranch: 116, 242

Salinas: Mexican settlement of, 34
Salt Lake Ranch: 46
Sanborn, Henry B.: Frying Pan Ranch, 25; founder of Amarillo, 201
Santa Fé traders: crossed Panhandle, 14
Santa Fé Trail: 9; methods of, 11
Saunders, Wood (Ranger): 111
Schnell, Mattheas (capitol contractor): 52
Settlement, growth of: 210
Shafter, Col. W. B. (scout): 29
Shannon, J. M.: builds fence, 87
Sheep: early on the plains, 31; methods of herders, 32
Shorthorns: 42; prize, 192
Singer, George W.: store of, 47 f.
Skelley, John: 20

Slaughter, John and W. B. (cattlemen): 44
Smith, Hank: in Blanco Canyon, 44, 172
Snowstorms on trail: 136
Snyder, D. H. and J. W.: deliver cattle, 82
Sotham, T. F. B. (cattle buyer): 189
Southern Kansas Railway: 204, 208
Sparks, Richard (early explorer of the West): 8
Sperling brothers: store of, 48
Spring Lake: first ranch, 46; Division, 147
Stagg, Allen ("wolfer"): 164
Staked Plains: 6; see also Llano Estacado
Steers: Old Blue, 183; Old Slate, 185
Stephens, J. Henry: land sales, 218
Stewart, W. H.: resolution on capitol, 49
Stock Association, Panhandle: 206
Stock farmers: need of, 209
Surveys: errors in, 63

T Anchor Ranch: 43
Taft, President William Howard: 66
Tanner, Ruck (wagon boss): 75, 79 f.
Tascosa: town started, 33; Pioneer, 167; beginning of, 194; Dodge City Trail, 230; Springer Trail, 230
Tasker, C. P.: locates ranch, 44
Taylor, Abner (member of XIT company): 52 f., 57, 64, 73, 81, 84 f., 216
Taylor, Dan: 42
Tefoya, José (guide): 28
Terrell, Senator A. W.: 205
Texas: public domain, 4; state house, 5, 49 ff.; Santa Fé Expedition, 9
Tierra Blanca Creek: 22
Tod, Wm. J.: 218
Tombstone Camp: 113
Tongue River: origin of name, 27
Towson, Fort: 9
Trail: outfits that drove, 126; wagons, 134; water troubles, 134; pranks, 135; northern, 136; wages, 138; song of, 139; life, 139; cowboys in North, 140; outfits, 140; cattle broken to, 141; advantage of, 142; close of, 143; cost of, 143; last herd, 143; logs of, 230–40